The Art of Life

The Art of Life

John Kekes

CORNELL UNIVERSITY PRESS

ITHACA AND LONDON

First published 2002 by Cornell University Press

Printed in the United States of America

Library of Congress Cataloging-in-Publication Data

Kekes, John.
  The art of life / John Kekes.
    p. cm.
  Includes bibliographical references and index.
  ISBN 0-8014-4006-8 (alk. paper)
  1. Ethics.   2. Life.   I. Title.
  BJ1012 .K38 2002
  170' .44—dc21

                                              2002002916

Cornell University Press strives to use environmentally responsible suppliers and materials to the fullest extent possible in the publishing of its books. Such materials include vegetable-based, low-VOC inks and acid-free papers that are recycled, to-tally chlorine-free, or partly composed of nonwood fibers. For further information, visit our website at www.cornellpress.cornell.edu.

Cloth printing   10 9 8 7 6 5 4 3 2 1

for J. Y. K.

Contents

PREFACE xi

INTRODUCTION
The Most Important of All Human Activities 1

PART ONE: SOME FORMS OF GOOD LIVES

CHAPTER 1
Self-Direction 13

1.1 The Challenge and the Response 13
1.2 Montaigne's Example 15
1.3 More's Example 19
1.4 Tradition and Individuality 25
1.5 What Self-Direction Is Not 30
1.6 The Conditions and Limits of Self-Direction 35

CHAPTER 2
Moral Authority 37

2.1 The *Sophron* 37
2.2 Authority 39
2.3 Moral Authority 45
2.4 Characteristics 48
2.5 Justification 56
2.6 Our Moral Authorities 59

CHAPTER 3
Decency 61

3.1 Decency as a Personal Excellence 61
3.2 Civic Friendship 63
3.3 Sympathy and Custom 67
3.4 A Pair of Exemplary Lives 72
3.5 The Core 79
3.6 Decency and Good Lives 83

CHAPTER 4
Depth 85

4.1 Hope or Hopelessness? 85
4.2 Understanding Depth 90
4.3 The Case of Oedipus 95
4.4 Inappropriate Reactions 99
4.5 True Hope 105

CHAPTER 5
Honor 107

5.1 Is Honor Obsolete? 107
5.2 Social and Personal Honor 108
5.3 The Honorable Life of Malesherbes 113
5.4 Self-Esteem 116
5.5 Honor and Some Contemporary Moral Mistakes 121
5.6 From the Particular toward the General 123

PART TWO: MAKING LIFE GOOD

CHAPTER 6
The Art of Life 129

6.1 The Moral versus the Aesthetic Approach 129
6.2 The Conflict 132
6.3 The Case for Practical Reason 135
6.4 Doubts about Practical Reason 138
6.5 The Case for Self-Creation 142
6.6 Doubts about Self-Creation 146
6.7 Morality and Personal Excellences 149

CHAPTER 7
Individual Ideals and Projects 158

7.1 Ideals and Projects 158
7.2 Personal Excellences and Virtues 164
7.3 Styles of Life 169
7.4 Moral Education 173
7.5 Personal Excellences 176

CHAPTER 8
Dominant Attitudes 177

8.1 The Integration of Life 177
8.2 Attitudes 180
8.3 Dominant Attitudes 189
8.4 Integration and Fragmentation 196
8.5 The Form and Content of Good Lives 199

CHAPTER 9
Aberrations 205

9.1 Going Wrong 205
9.2 Moralism 206
9.3 Sentimentalism 215
9.4 Romanticism 225
9.5 Getting It Right 232

CHAPTER 10
Good Lives 234

10.1 Good Lives and the Art of Life 234
10.2 Is Boredom a Problem? 239
10.3 Making Life Good 244

NOTES 253
INDEX 265

Preface

> What is at stake is far from insignificant: it is how one should
> live one's life.
>
> PLATO, *The Republic*

The art of life is the art of making a good life for oneself. It is an art
because it requires individuals to make a lifelong creative effort that
no one can make for them and for which no blueprint exists. For a
good life has to be constructed out of one's character, circumstances,
experiences, and ideals, which vary with individuals, societies, times,
and places. An essential element of this art involves reflecting on
admirable lives and adapting the ideals they represent to one's personal context. The first half of this book examines some admirable
lives. The second half concerns what we can learn from these fine
examples and what individuals can do to make their lives better.

Everyone wants to live a good life, but not everyone is prepared to
reflect on what it involves. Those who are, used to be the traditional
readers of philosophy. During the early decades of the twentieth century philosophy became a specialized subject, pursued by profession-
als and preoccupied with technical problems and method. This
change resulted in the elimination of much obscurity and dilettantism
and raised the standard of clarity and precision demanded of philosophical works. It also resulted in the alienation of those who tradi-
tionally turned to philosophy for help with their reflections but who
had no interest in technicalities. This book is addressed to them in the
conviction that serious philosophy can be accessible to reflective non-
specialists. It is written in the hope that there still are such readers and
that they may be interested in what it has to say about good lives.

The lives discussed in the first part have been central to my thinking about good lives for many years. I have gone back to them again

and again to consider them from different points of view and for different purposes. I do so once more here, and although the older material is much revised and put to new uses, I wish to acknowledge earlier uses. Chapter 1 draws on *The Examined Life* (University Park: Pennsylvania State University Press, 1988), Chapter 4; Chapter 2 uses portions of *The Case for Conservatism* (Ithaca: Cornell University Press, 1998), Chapter 7; Chapter 3 borrows from *Moral Tradition and Individuality* (Princeton: Princeton University Press, 1989), Chapters 3 and 4; Chapter 4 incorporates parts of *Moral Wisdom and Good Lives* (Ithaca: Cornell University Press, 1995), Chapter 8; and Chapter 6 is a revised version of *Pluralism in Philosophy: Changing the Subject* (Ithaca: Cornell University Press, 2000), Chapter 8. Permission to make use of this material is gratefully acknowledged.

Peter French, Eric Fried, and Joel Kupperman read and sympathetically commented on the entire manuscript. Their criticisms and help are gratefully acknowledged. My editor at Cornell University Press was, once again, Roger Haydon. It is a pleasure to express my gratitude for his good advice and judgment and for his helpfulness in all the phases of writing and revising the manuscript. The book is dedicated to my wife with love and gratitude for our many years together and for making a life of reflection possible.

Readers sometimes wish they could communicate their reactions to the author of a book they have found engaging. I invite such communications and will respond to them. They may be sent to johnkekes@aol.com.

JOHN KEKES

ITHAKA
Charlton, New York

The Art of Life

Introduction/

The Most Important of All Human Activities

> Moral philosophy is the examination of the most important of
> all human activities, and I think that two things are required of
> it. The examination should be realistic. Human nature has cer-
> tain discoverable attributes, and these should be suitably con-
> sidered in any discussion of morality. Secondly, since an ethical
> system cannot but commend an ideal, it should commend a
> worthy ideal. Ethics . . . should be a hypothesis about good
> conduct and about how this can be achieved.
>
> IRIS MURDOCH, *The Sovereignty of Good*

Most of human lives are spent in routine activities. We sleep, wash,
dress, eat; go to work, work, shop, relax; balance the checkbook, clean
house, do the laundry, have the car serviced; chat, pay bills, worry
about this or that, take small pleasure in small things. We do all this in
the intervals between familiar milestones: birth, maturation, aging,
and death; we have children and lose our parents; graduate, find a
job, get married, divorce, fall in and out of love, set up house; succeed
at some things, fail at others; make friends and have fights; move
house, change jobs, get fired or promoted, fall ill and recover, save for
retirement and retire. So life goes for just about everyone, allowing for
individual and cultural variations that affect the form but not the fact
of routine. These activities constitute everyday life. Everyday life is
what life mostly is. Keeping it going, however, involves constant
struggle. From a birth no one chooses to a death few desire, we have
to cope with endless problems. To fail is to suffer. And what is gained
from success? No more than some pleasure, a brief sense of triumph,
perhaps a little peace of mind. But these are only interludes of well-

1

being because the difficulties never cease. It is natural to ask, then, why one should continue on this treadmill. After all, it is possible to stop.

In the past, when there was a widely shared religious faith, if such questions were asked at all, they were readily answered in religious terms. This is no longer so. Many people are without religious faith; others who claim to have it live their lives unaffected by it; and those who are serious about it must contend with deep disagreements about how the faith should be interpreted. All the major faiths have fragmented into various sects that champion incompatible orthodoxies or, indeed, the repudiation of all orthodoxies. There is, therefore, no longer such a thing as *the* religious answer. There are many religious answers, and they all rest on faith that only a small minority of true believers accept without question. And, of course, the old answer that was given before secularization and schism changed religions did not tell the faithful how their lives can be good in the present world. It told them how they must live here and now in order to enjoy good lives in the hereafter. But the questions reflective people are asking now, in our present circumstances, are about what, if anything, could or would make their lives good in the sublunary world.

Maybe nothing would make them good. Maybe evolution has brought it about that we have a capacity to ask questions about our lives, and in civilized societies some even have the opportunity to employ their capacity. But it is folly to suppose that just because we can ask a question there is going to be an answer to it that we like. One may meet this realization with despair or cynicism. Both are injurious. They poison such goodness as life has by corrupting the innocent connection between a want and its satisfaction. There intrudes the gnawing question about the point of it all. Despair and cynicism cleave us into a natural self and a preying, harping, jeering, or self-pitying reflective self. We are thus turned against ourselves. Reflection sabotages our own projects. If this is the truth, then the human prospect is dim. Maybe a capacity has evolved in us, and it will undo us.

It is not surprising, therefore, that many people of sturdy common sense simply ignore the question. They go on with the business of living, do as well as they can, enjoy the comforts they may, and prudently keep out of deep waters. This evasion, however, is likely to be possible only for those who are succeeding in navigating life's treacherous waters. The young who are about to start tend to ask why they should follow their elders' mode of life. The old who look back may wonder about whether it was worth it. And the sick, poor, unlucky, and untalented may well ask, with various degrees of resentment, about the point of the enterprise in which they have not done well. It is not easy to ignore the question because it is persistently asked.

Nor is it reasonable to avoid putting the question to ourselves, quite independently of external challenges. It is demeaning to participate in all manner of activities, expending great effort, giving and getting hard knocks, obeying rules we have not made, chasing goals said by others to be rewarding, without asking why we should do all this. Is it not the very opposite of prudence and common sense to invest our lives in projects whose value we have not ascertained? Furthermore, there are exceptionally few lives uninterrupted by serious crises. Grief, ill health, social cataclysms, injustice, setbacks, lack of merited appreciation, being in the power of those who abuse it, and many similar adversities are likely to interfere with even the most prudently lived lives. The questions such adversities raise can be answered, if at all, only by having thought about life and about what would make it good. And that is what this book does.

Living a good life is the most important of all human activities because the importance of everything else derives from it. Everyone is trying—or wishes to be in a position of trying—to live a good life. But not everyone is good at it. Many lives are bad because the activity is difficult and there are formidable obstacles to doing it well. The aim of the art of life is to do it well. The material with which this art works is the life of its practitioner. And the happy result of its successful practice is a life that is personally satisfying and morally acceptable. Both are necessary, but neither is sufficient for a good life, because a personally satisfying life may be morally deplorable and a morally acceptable life may be filled with serious personal disappointments.

Personal satisfaction with one's life has two sources. The first involves aiming at a reasonable ideal and having good reasons to think that one has done tolerably well in approximating it. The ideal is to become one who exemplifies some particular personal excellence, such as altruism, creativity, justice, purity, sensitivity, wholeheartedness, wisdom, and so on. There are many different personal excellences, but they are alike in requiring the transformation of one's character from what it is at the end of adolescence to one that approximates more closely the personal excellence that is the ideal.

The possession of a personal excellence is shown by *how* activities are performed, not by what those activities are or by the state of mind that leads one to be engaged in them. To have a personal excellence is to *be* in a certain way, but being that way is to act in a manner that exemplifies the personal excellence. It is to do what one does altruistically, creatively, justly, purely, sensitively, wholeheartedly, wisely, and so on. One source of personal satisfaction with one's life is, then, the reasonable belief that one has done well at becoming the kind of person who habitually acts in the appropriate manner.

Another source of personal satisfaction has to do with one's projects. Each life involves countless different activities. Some of them are instrumental to the perpetuation of the life; others are chosen because they reflect a person's interests, aspirations, values, desires, or plans. Some of these latter endure and become a person's chief preoccupations throughout life. They may be athletic, commercial, familial, horticultural, literary, pedagogical, political, scientific, and so forth. These are a person's projects. They have goals and involve activities aimed at the achievement of the goals. In well-chosen projects, personal satisfaction is derived both from the achievement of the goals and from the performance of the activities. This has the important consequence that a life can be personally satisfying even if the goal of its project is not achieved. For a great deal of satisfaction may be derived from the activities themselves, regardless of whether they are successful. It may, then, be said that living a good life depends on engagement in personally satisfying projects in a manner that exemplifies one's ideal of personal excellence.

That, however, cannot be all on which it depends because if it were, good lives could be utterly immoral. It must be added, therefore, that good lives must also meet the universal, social, and individual requirements of morality. There are requirements to which all good lives must conform regardless of the characters, circumstances, ideals of personal excellence, and projects of their agents. Unless the basic needs of nutrition, shelter, rest, security, companionship, order, and so forth are satisfied, no life can be good. These requirements are universally human, and they hold for everyone, always, everywhere. Morality aims to formulate and enforce rules that protect the conditions in which basic needs can be satisfied. These conventions hold universally in the sense that their violation is normally morally wrong regardless of the identity of the violator or the violated. Yet these rules hold only normally, not absolutely, because their violation may be justified in exceptional circumstances, when the protection of even more important conditions of good lives depends on the violation of less important ones.

All good lives depend on the protection of these universal rules, but the rules take different forms in different societies. Good societies must provide adequate nutrition for their members, but there are perfectly justifiable variations in how this requirement is met. There is a wide range of morally acceptable social rules about what should and should not be eaten, how food should be prepared, at what times and with whom it should be consumed. Such rules regulate not only nutrition but also sexual practices, raising children, earning a living, treating illness, waging war, making agreements, punishing criminals, mourning the dead, and so forth. Social rules thus embody the local ways in which the universal requirements of good lives are met and in which characteristically human activities are customarily performed. The system of such social rules is a society's form of life. Its maintenance is necessary for the endurance and cohesion of a society, which, in turn, provides the framework in which people can live good lives. The identity of the particular rules that constitute that form of life is in constant flux, however. Following these rules in general is a necessary condition of sharing a form of life, but particular rules may be justifiably violated if they are incompatible with other rules that are more important for the maintenance of a society's form of life.

These universal and social rules protect conditions of good lives, but living a good life ultimately depends on what people do with their lives once these elementary requirements are met. In civilized societies the universal and social rules of morality provide a much wider range of possibilities than individuals can make their own. That is why they must make decisions about how to live, which of their desires to satisfy, what values to hold—decisions about their ideals and projects. Making these decisions involves trying to find a fit between the possibilities and limits that prevail in their context and their characters and circumstances. Good lives, then, combine personal satisfactions, derived from engagement in projects in a manner that reflects one's ideals of personal excellence, and moral acceptability, which depends on conformity to the universal, social, and individual requirements of morality.

It must be emphasized that this way of thinking about good lives is not supposed to be the only or the best way. There may be other reasonable forms that good lives may take. The claim is merely that the form that has just been outlined is a possible and a reasonable one. It is no more than one way in which lives can be good. But it is that. And having a reasonable answer to the question how to live a good life is not a small matter, not even if it is possible that there are other reasonable answers.

Expressing the claim in this way, however, may lead to misunderstanding. The form that has been outlined actually contains a wide plurality of forms that good lives may take. For there are many ideals of personal excellence, projects, universal and social rules, and ways of fitting them to one's character and circumstances. Living a good life depends on making reasonable decisions about which of the available alternatives one should adopt, and different people will make different decisions, each of which may be reasonable, because their decisions must reflect the differences in the characters and circumstances of the deciders. It is difficult to make these decisions, and the art of life is needed to make them well and to carry them out successfully.

There are good reasons for thinking of the art of life as an art. In order to make the necessary decisions reasonably, people must go beyond following rules; they must depend on their own resources. For the decisions they have to make require them to select from among the available ideals of personal excellence, projects, and universal and social rules those that best fit their characters and circumstances. The possibilities about which they have to make decisions may all be rule-governed, but their decisions about them cannot be, because their characters and circumstances are individual and different. The decisions they make must be based on their understanding of themselves and their circumstances, and of what it would be like for them, for the individuals that they are, to live according to some particular ideal of personal excellence and be engaged in some particular project. Such decisions require an imaginative effort, self-knowledge, and a realistic appraisal of the context of their lives. These decisions, therefore, must be individual and cannot be rule-governed because rules are, by their nature, general and these decisions are, by their nature, individual. Making them is something that individuals must do for themselves by using such resources as they bring to it. On the basis of their decisions they create their future lives by selecting and combining personal excellences, projects, prevailing rules, and aspects of themselves. The art of life, therefore, is an art because it is a creative, imaginative, individual endeavor to make something good. It is, of course, different from other arts because its product is a life, not a symphony, a poem, or a painting, and because artists of life cannot be separated from their works whereas in the other arts the artists are clearly distinct from their works, although dance may be an exception.

That the art of life is creative, imaginative, and individual does not mean, however, that it cannot be taught and learned or that individuals cannot improve their mastery of it. Teaching it proceeds by way of exemplary lives, and learning it consists in coming to appreciate what makes some lives exemplary. There is some scope here for rules that can be applied to other lives, but their scope is limited by individual differences, by the need to apply them to unavoidably different lives, and by there being no rules about how to do that.

For the same reason, imitation is doomed to failure. The learners cannot duplicate the activities that make a life exemplary because the nature of the activities changes with individual characters and circumstances. The learners must do what their exemplars did, while making the appropriate changes to take account of their necessarily different characters and circumstances. Nevertheless, that rules are of limited help does not mean they are of no help, and that imitation here is impossible does not mean one cannot learn from examples. The question is, How can that be done reasonably, how can decisions about how one should live escape being arbitrary, if they are left to individual creativity and imagination and are not governed by rules that apply to everyone living in a particular context? One aim of this book is to give a detailed answer to this question by showing how such decisions can be reasonable without being rule-governed.

As a preliminary indication of the form the answer will take, it should be noted that not being rule-governed does not mean that reasonable decisions cannot rely on rules up to a point. It means that beyond a certain point, particular reasons that *are* reasons, but only for a particular person in a particular context, must replace rules. This point is reached when people become committed to some ideal of personal excellence and project. Then they have to make decisions about how to pursue the ideal and engage in the project, given their particular characters and circumstances. This is the point at which individual creativity and imagination take the place of rules. And it is at this point that the nature of reasons involved in reasonable decisions changes. For the question is no longer about what reason there is *for* a particular decision. The considerations in favor of that decision are provided by the creativity and imagination of the decision makers. The question becomes rather whether there are reasons *against* following the promptings of creativity and imagination. The reasons are thus not a source of motivation that is a competing alternative to the motivation of creativity and imagination. The reasons take the form of evaluating the promptings of creativity and imagination. The aim of the evaluation is to find out whether their promptings are faulty, and if they are, to correct them. The role of reasons here is not to prescribe what should be done but to proscribe faulty courses of action.

In this context, however, the proscribed faults are the particular faults of particular people. For the faults have to do with giving a wrong answer to the question what they should do, given their particular characters and circumstances, in order to succeed at a particular project in a manner that reflects a particular personal excellence. If their answers are wrong, they are so because the people have made mistakes about themselves, or about their circumstances, or about the suitability of their projects and ideals of personal excellence to their characters and circumstances. Such mistakes are made by those who are deficient in understanding, or carried away by emotions, or motivated by illusion, self-deception, fear, or fantasy. The role of reason is to ascertain whether such mistakes have been made and to correct them if possible. Doing that, however, cannot but be an individual matter that varies from person to person, and that is why reasons here both are necessary and cannot be rule-governed. The art of life aims to cultivate one's creativity and imagination, reason well about overcoming their faults, and thus live a good life.

There are two ways of approaching the topic of good lives. One is to try to formulate the general conditions that make lives good and then decide whether particular lives are good on the basis of these conditions. This has been the dominant approach in the history of Western reflection on good lives. Plato, the Stoics, Christian theologians, Spinoza, Kant, Mill, Hegel, and numerous others, who disagreed with one another about many things, nevertheless agreed that there is an ideal, rule, value, or criterion that must be understood first, and that, and only that, makes it possible to identify particular lives as good.

Three quite general reasons count against this approach. First, those who have followed it have been unable to agree on what the standard they seek is. In fact, the nature of the standard is much more controversial than the goodness of the lives that the standard is supposed to determine. Second, it is assumed by the search for the standard that if it were found, it could be relied on to identify *the* form good lives must take. But there is no convincing reason for believing that good lives must take a particular form, and history, ethnography, and literature provide ample evidence for the view that good lives have many forms. Third, it is also assumed by those who follow this approach that good lives are fully identifiable on the basis of general characteristics that all good lives share rather than on the basis of particular characteristics that vary with individual lives. There is no persuasive argument for supposing that what makes one life good must be what makes other lives good, and there are very strong reasons for holding that the goodness of a life is inseparable from the individual character and circumstances of the person whose life it is. For these reasons, a different approach is followed here.

This second approach is not new. Examples of it may be found in some of the works of Aristotle, Plutarch, Montaigne, Hume, Mill, and Nietzsche; closer to our times, in Isaiah Berlin, Iris Murdoch, and Michael Oakeshott; and among contemporaries in Lawrence Blum, Harry Frankfurt, Peter French, Pierre Hadot, Joel Kupperman, Alexander Nehamas, Richard Shusterman, and Susan Wolf, among others.[1] The approach is to begin with fairly detailed examples of particular lives that are generally and uncontroversially recognized as good. Once these examples are available, it becomes possible to reflect on them and ask what it is that makes them good. This will allow the formulation of some general conditions of good lives, but these conditions cannot constitute anything like a full specification of good lives or anything close to the kind of standard that the alternative approach seeks. The assumption on which the present approach rests is that the unavailability of a full specification or a general standard is not a failure but a consequence of the variety and individuality of good lives. Lives are good if they are personally satisfying, morally acceptable, and free of cognitive, emotive, and motivational errors that vitiate the ideals of personal excellence and projects to which people have committed themselves. But since the ideals and projects that may give personal satisfaction, many of the moral rules that are to be followed, and the errors that are to be avoided are individually variable, no general account of good lives is possible. That, however, does not mean that the goodness of particular lives cannot be reasonably judged. Or so it will be argued.

The structure of the book follows from these considerations. The first part, Some Forms of Good Lives, contains five chapters. Each is a detailed examination of a life of personal excellence, namely, of a life of self-direction, decency, moral authority, depth, or honor. And each is a detailed and specific answer to the question what could or would make a life good. The second part, Making Life Good, contains four chapters, which provide an account of the art of life and of how it can be successfully practiced. This account relies on the lives described in the first part, lives that are made good by successful practice of the art of life. The chapters are on the art of life, on ideals of personal excellence, on the attitudes that make lives of personal excellence possible, and on some culturally prevalent forms of error that stand in the way of good lives. These chapters extract the lessons that can be learned by reflecting on the exemplary lives described earlier and show what individuals can do to learn from, but not to imitate, these admirable lives that combine personal satisfaction and moral acceptability. The final chapter summarizes one possible and reasonable approach to living a good life that emerges from the preceding argument.

PART ONE

Some Forms of Good Lives

1 /

Self-Direction

Let a man propose to himself a model of a character, which he approves: Let him be well acquainted with those particulars, in which his own character deviates from this model: Let him keep a constant watch over himself, and bend his mind, by a continual effort, from the vices, towards the virtues; and I doubt not, in time, he will find in his temper, an alteration for the better.

DAVID HUME, "The Sceptic"

1.1 The Challenge and the Response

In *The Republic* Glaucon tells the story of Gyges and his ring.[1] The magical ring permits Gyges to turn invisible and then back to visible at will. Gyges uses the ring to make himself powerful and rich. His invisibility frees him from having to worry about legal or moral sanctions, and he commits whatever crime suits his purpose. Glaucon asks, What would be the difference in the conduct of moral and immoral people if they had Gyges' ring? The answer he gives, as a challenge to Socrates, is that there would be no difference. If people could steal, kill, and take their pleasure with impunity, they would do so. The difference between moral and immoral people, Glaucon says, is that the former observe legal and moral rules whereas the latter do not. But what motivates the moral ones is that they care about their reputation and fear punishment. Gyges' ring removes these constraints, and in their absence the rules would have no hold on someone possessing the ring.

There are some people, however, whose conduct would not be changed by the possession of the ring. They would not act differently because what motivates them is their ideal of a good life and that would not be changed by Gyges' ring. The source of this motivation is the importance they attach in their lives to conscientiousness, or to altruism, or to justice, or to honesty. Hume's description fits them: by their "continual and earnest pursuit of character . . . [they bring their] conduct frequently in review. This constant habit of surveying [themselves] . . . as it were, in reflection, keeps alive all the sentiments of right and wrong and begets, in noble creatures, a certain reverence for themselves as well as others, which is the surest guardian of every virtue. . . . [Their] regard to a character with others seems to arise only from a care of possessing a character with [themselves]."[2] Such people are self-directed. It is clear that self-direction is a personal excellence, but it is not clear just what is involved in the "continual and earnest pursuit of character" and why a reflective survey of oneself would be "the surest guardian of every virtue."

A preliminary understanding of self-direction may be provided by the combination of a negative account of what it excludes and a positive account of what it includes. The negative account, as stated by Isaiah Berlin, captures one aspiration at the core of self-direction: "I wish my life and decisions to depend on myself, not on external forces of whatever kind. I wish to be an instrument of my own, not of other men's, acts of will. I wish to be . . . moved by reasons, by conscious purposes, which are my own, not by causes which affect me, as it were, from outside. I wish to be a doer . . . deciding, not being decided for, self-directed and not acted upon by external nature."[3] These are moving words, but they are unilluminating about what should shape one's decisions, will, purposes, and reasons. Even if they are one's own and not forced on one, that still leaves countless internal and unforced possibilities to choose from. Moreover, it is not obvious how anyone could escape the influence of external forces, causes, and nature. Clearly, much more needs to be said.

The positive account provides a basis for making decisions and efforts of will, choosing purposes, and weighing reasons: in Aristotle's words, "every one that has the power to live according to his own choice [should] . . . set up for himself some object for the good life to aim at . . . with reference to which he will then do all his acts, since not to have one's life organized in view of some end is the mark of great folly."[4] The positive account, then, is that one's ideal of a good life is the standard that should guide decisions, inform the will, and provide purposes and reasons. And the negative account specifies that the conception of a good life should be one's own rather than the result of influences over which one has no control.

The two accounts jointly circumscribe the general area within which self-direction may be found, but they do not distinguish between self-direction and authenticity, autonomy, and self-realization, to mention some possibilities that also fit the joint account. A satisfactory account must explain what self-direction is and how it differs from other things that may be confused with it. The first step toward such an account is a consideration of the exemplary self-directed lives of Michel de Montaigne and Sir Thomas More.

1.2 Montaigne's Example

Self-direction is a process of self-transformation that involves the gradual changing of one's character so that it will conform more closely to the requirements of one's ideal of a good life. Montaigne's life exemplifies a successful instance of it. But it also does more because Montaigne was conscious of what he was doing and articulate about what it involved. His *Essays*, a classic work on the subject of self-direction, simultaneously records his thoughts and imparts the significance for other lives of what he had learned about his own.[5] By concentrating on Montaigne's life, we can come to a better understanding of self-directed lives in general.

The salient facts of Montaigne's life are easily told.[6] He was born in 1533 into a Gascon Catholic family of lesser nobility, residing not far from the city of Bordeaux. He was educated first at home, where he learned Latin before French, and later at one of the best schools of France. He was trained in the law, and at the age of twenty-four he became a councillor in the Parlement of Bordeaux, where his duties required him to participate in legislation and to act as something like a magistrate. During this period he married; had six children, all but one of whom died in infancy; and formed the most significant relationship of his life: a friendship with Etienne de la Boétie, who died from a painful illness four years later. In 1570, after thirteen years of service, Montaigne retired to his estate "long weary of the servitude of the court and of public employments . . . where in . . . freedom, tranquillity, and leisure" (ix–x) he intended to read and reflect, and he began to record his thoughts in a form that eventually resulted in the *Essays*. But two years later he was called out of retirement to act as a mediator between the warring Catholics and Protestants of France. As a moderate Catholic and an experienced man of affairs, he was acceptable to both parties. He was intermittently engaged in this endeavor for four years. In 1580, when he was forty-seven, the first edition of the *Essays*, containing books 1 and 2, appeared. It was well received. Montaigne then traveled for almost two years, in Switzerland, Germany, and mainly in Italy. In his absence he was elected mayor of Bordeaux, a prestigious office he did not seek and was reluctant to accept. But he was prevailed upon, and when his two-year term came to an end, he was given the rare honor of a second term. After fulfilling this obligation he once again took up residence on his estate, finished book 3 of the *Essays*, and kept revising the first two books. The three books were first published together in 1588, when he was fifty-five years old. He continued revising them until the end. He died in 1592, a few months before his sixtieth birthday. He was generally regarded as a wise and learned man, an eminent scholar, and a distinguished public servant.

From the point of view of self-direction, one of the most interesting aspects of Montaigne's life is its relation to the *Essays*. Montaigne consciously intended his essays as the instruments of his self-transformation. They were meant as replacements of conversations with his dead friend; vehicles for articulating and reflecting on his attitudes; records of changes in his thought and sensibility; ventures in trying out arguments, thinking through various complicated matters, expressing scorn and admiration; they formed "a book consubstantial with its author" (504). As Montaigne says, "I have no more made my book than my book has made me. . . . [It is] concerned with my own self, an integral part of my life" (504). The *Essays* shaped Montaigne's life not merely because they reflected it but also because Montaigne reflected in them on his reflection and changed himself accordingly. "In modeling this figure upon myself, I have had to fashion and compose myself so often to bring myself out, that the model itself has to some extent grown firm and taken shape" (504). The *Essays* were thus both causes and effects, symptoms and diagnoses. They were efforts to take stock of how things were with himself, to firm up his resolve to change himself in certain ways, and to plan how to make the changes. Examining how Montaigne, and later More, coped in their lives with some of the tensions typical of many human lives will help us understand self-direction.

One of these tensions is between public and private life. In an essay written shortly after his retirement began, Montaigne wrote: "The wise man . . . if he has the choice . . . will choose solitude. . . . The aim of all solitude, I take it, is the same: to live more at leisure and at one's ease. . . . [But] by getting rid of the court and the market place we do not get rid of the principal worries of our life. . . . Ambition, avarice, irresolution, fear, and lust . . . often follow us even into the cloisters and the schools of philosophy" (175–76). The answer is to concentrate on the improvement of one's character, make it "withdraw into itself: that is real solitude, which may be enjoyed in the midst of cities and the courts of kings; but it is enjoyed more handily alone" (176). "We must reserve a back shop all our own, entirely free . . . our principal retreat and solitude. Here our ordinary conversation must be between us and ourselves. . . . We have a soul that can be turned upon itself; it can keep itself company; it has the means to attack and the means to defend, the means to receive and the means to give: let us not fear this solitude" (177).

About fifteen years later Montaigne added a comment to these passages: "Solitude seems to me more appropriate and reasonable for those who have given the world their most active and flourishing years" (178). So there is another strand in his thinking represented by what he did during his "most active and flourishing years." Public service was a traditional and expected part of the life of nobility, and as we have seen, Montaigne played his part with distinction as a councillor, a mayor of Bordeaux, and a mediator, even though these activities interrupted his solitude. His view was: "I do not want a man to refuse, to the charges he takes on, attention, steps, words, and sweat and blood if need be" (770). And Montaigne, we know, acted according to this view. But why did he do it? Because he saw himself living in the "sick age" of sixteenth-century France: "I perceive . . . the strife that is tearing France to pieces and dividing us into factions" (760), and he felt it was his duty to do what he could to make things better.

He found, however, that the laws he was administering were unjust, the system corrupt, and the religious wars, with their massacres and cruelty, disgusting (759). "Consider the form of this justice that governs us: it is a true testimony of human imbecility, so full it is of contradiction and error" (819). "How many condemnations I have seen more criminal than the crime" (820). "There is no hostility that excels Christian hostility. . . . Our religion is made to extirpate vices; it covers them, fosters them, incites them" (324). But how could Montaigne lend himself to what he knew was corruption? Not for gain: "I sometimes feel rising in my soul the fumes of certain temptations toward ambition; but I stiffen and hold firm against them" (759). He did it because although "the justest party is still a member of a worm-eaten and maggoty body . . . in such a body the least diseased member is called healthy; and quite rightly, since our qualities have no titles except by comparison. Civic innocence is measured according to the places and the times" (760).

Throughout his life Montaigne felt the tension between public and private life. His sense of duty, nurtured by the obligations of his social position, the admired examples of his father and La Boétie, and the expectations of the court and his fellow noblemen, impelled him toward public service. The attractions of personal happiness and tranquillity, the development of his thought and sensibility, and his fondness of reflection and rural life impelled him toward private life. His conception of a good life was connected with both. In some fortunate lives, spent in times less turbulent than those of sixteenth-century France, this tension calls for a judicious balance, and it may be achieved by experience and judgment. But Montaigne was not so fortunate; for him, public service conflicted with living a good life because the corruption of his age routinely required him to perform immoral acts. Montaigne saw this clearly, but he also saw the need for it: "In every government there are necessary offices which are . . . vicious. Vices find their place in it and are employed for sewing our society together. . . . The public welfare requires that a man betray and lie" (600). The tension Montaigne felt is known to us as the problem of dirty hands, from Sartre's play of the same name.

The obvious temptation is not to dirty our hands, but Montaigne did not give in to it because it would have meant abandoning his ideal of a good life and leaving public service to those who would corrupt it even further. It would have meant betraying his responsibility both to himself and to others. Instead, Montaigne struggled with the tension and articulated a way of coping with it that has enduring significance: "The mayor and Montaigne have always been two, with a very clear separation" (774). On the one hand, "an honest man is not accountable for the vice and stupidity of his trade, and should not therefore refuse to practice it: it is the custom of his country and there is profit in it. We must live in the world and make the most of it as we find it" (774). And again, "I once tried to employ in the service of public dealings ideas and rules . . . which I use . . . in private matters. . . . I found them inept and dangerous. . . . He who walks in the crowd must step aside, keep his elbows in, step back or advance, even leave the straight way, according to what he encounters. He must live not so much according to himself as according to others, not according to what he proposes to himself but according to what others propose to him, according to the time, according to the men, according to the business" (758). On the other hand, "I have been able to take part in public office without departing one nail's head from myself, and give myself to others without taking myself from myself" (770).

But how could he remain himself and engage in practices he regarded as vicious and stupid? Montaigne answered: by offering only "limited and conditional services. There is no remedy. I frankly tell them my limits" (603). He will dirty his hands only up to a point: "I do not . . . involve myself so deeply and so entirely" (774). The limits beyond which Montaigne will not go separate the deep commitments he will not allow his involvement to violate and the surface formed of his customs and habits, which he is prepared to adjust according to the time, the men, the business. His character is formed of a hard center and a soft periphery. He is willing to perform public service, to do his duty and participate in corrupt arrangements, so long as they affect only the periphery and do not compromise the center. But he does not depart one nail's head from himself because the center is reserved for his private life, his "back shop," his "principal retreat," the object of his reflection when he withdraws into himself, into "real solitude."

The general significance of the answer Montaigne found for himself is that since we live in a world that has not become appreciably purer since the sixteenth century, and since reason and morality require only our conditional services, we must learn to distinguish between the center of our character, where our deepest commitments lie, and the outer layers, which we can afford to compromise, if need be. One central task of self-direction is to draw and maintain this distinction, and this is just what More had done a century before Montaigne.

1.3 More's Example

Robert Bolt describes More as "a man with an adamantine sense of his own self. He knew where he began and left off, what area of himself he could yield to the encroachments of his enemies, and what to the encroachments of those he loved. It was a substantial area in both cases, for he had a proper sense of fear and was a busy lover. Since he was a clever man and a great lawyer, he was able to retire from these areas in wonderfully good order, but at length he was asked to retreat from that final area where he located his self. And there this supple, humorous, unassuming and sophisticated man set like metal, was overtaken by an absolutely primitive rigor, and could no more be budged than a cliff."[7]

More's years were 1478–1535. His main work—*Utopia*—was published in 1516. After many years of distinguished service to the throne, in 1529 he was appointed lord chancellor, a position from which he resigned in 1532. Two years later he was imprisoned in the Tower of London, and in 1535 he was indicted for high treason and executed. More went to his death because he would not obey his king, Henry VIII, who required More to confer legal and moral legitimacy on the king's wish to divorce his wife and marry Ann Boleyn, with whom the king was besotted.

The larger issues in the background were the struggle between religious and political authority for supremacy and between the Catholic Church and the Reformation as it played out in England. More, like Sophocles' Antigone, believed that the requirements of religion were fundamental. The king, like Sophocles' Creon, held that political considerations could override religious ones. After months of ingenious temporizing, More finally ran out of evasions and was forced to take a stand. He then refused to do what the king had demanded, and that was the reason for his imprisonment, indictment, and execution. More had unconditionally committed himself to the priority of his religious beliefs over everything else, and he was unwilling to take an action, not even to save his life, that would have violated this commitment. More had many other commitments as well, and from these he retreated, when pressed, in "wonderfully good order." Some of his commitments mattered more to him than others, but unconditional commitments were those that mattered most.

During his fifteen months of imprisonment More was engaged in two significant activities. One was the extensive writing of letters and shorter works in which he contemplates his plight, reflects on what he ought to do, and explains the reasons for the resolve he finally reached to go to his death rather than violate his unconditional commitment. The other was listening to a number of visitors—his daughter, various ecclesiastical authorities, and the king's representatives—who attempted to persuade him that his resolve was an act of inexpediency, stubbornness, pride, and disloyalty to his family, king, and country. His prison writings show him laying to rest his own doubts and answering his visitors.

To his visitors' pleas he replies that they constitute a temptation that "spreads gradually and imperceptibly while those persons who despise it at first, afterwards can stand to hear it and respond to it with less than full scorn, then come to tolerate wicked discussions, and afterwards are carried away in error, until like cancer . . . the creeping disease finally takes over" (CW 14:359).[8] He rejects "the soft speeches . . . [that] cajole him into leaving the way of truth" (CW 14:543). Yet he wonders about himself whether "will not weaklings who are . . . cowardly and afraid take heart so as not to yield under the stress of persecution even though they feel great sadness welling up within them, and fear and weariness and horror at the prospect of a ghastly death?" (CW 14:247). He tells his tempters: "I have ere I came here [the Tower] not left unbethought nor unconsidered the very worst and the uttermost that can by possibility fall. And albeit I know my frailty full well and the natural faintness of mine own heart, yet if I had not trusted that God should give me strength rather to endure all things, than offend him by swearing ungodly against mine own conscience, you may be very sure I would not have come here."[9]

The key word here is *conscience*, whose voice expresses More's unconditional commitment. More would not swear the oath his king demanded of him because "in my conscience this was one of the cases in which I was not bounden that I should obey my prince." And he will "stand still in this scruple of his conscience . . . [even if] all his friends that seem most able to do him good either shall finally forsake him, or peradventure not be able indeed to do him any good at all." Although "all the causes that I perceive move other men to the contrary, [they] seem not such unto me as in my conscience make any change."[10]

Unconditional commitments are the most serious convictions we have. They define our limits: what we feel we must not do no matter what, what we regard as outrageous and horrible. They are fundamental conditions of being ourselves. Unconditional commitments are not universal, for they vary with individuals. Nor are they categorical, for we may violate them. But if through fear, coercion, weakness, accident, or stupidity we do so, we inflict grave psychological damage on ourselves. This is what Oedipus and Conrad's Lord Jim have done to themselves.

More was a hero and a saint, and he died rather than violate his unconditional commitment. Most of us are made of softer stuff, but the violation of unconditional commitments is no less damaging to weaker people. There is a crisis, we do something that violates such a commitment, and we realize that we cannot come to terms with what we have done. If we were as we conceived ourselves to be, we would not have done that. So we are brought to the realization that we are not what we took ourselves to be. An abyss opens up at the center of our being: we disintegrate, go mad, or carry on in a desultory way looking in vain for a chance to undo the horrible thing we have done.

Many people have no unconditional commitments. Since having them renders one vulnerable, we may well wonder why we should be like More and create in ourselves the potential either to be driven to this state of "absolutely primitive rigor" or to fall apart. If we take nothing so terribly seriously, we are less open to lasting psychological damage. We cultivate greater suppleness and thus become better able to withstand the inevitable buffeting we suffer in navigating life's treacherous waters. A contrast between unconditional and defeasible commitments will show why this stratagem is inadvisable.

Defeasible commitments are the stuff of everyday life. They guide our intimate relationships, impersonal encounters with others in our society, and the various forms our personal projects may take. The way we raise our children, how we respond to our friends, our attitude to the work we do, the direction in which ambition takes us, the fears we fend off, and the hopes that sustain us are all guided by defeasible commitments. They are defeasible because they could be reasonably overridden if sufficiently strong considerations are found against them. The difference between them and unconditional commitments is that nothing we recognize as a good reason could override the latter because our judgments of what reasons are good and how strongly they weigh are dictated by unconditional commitments. They are the standards by which we measure, and unless we abandon the yardstick, there could be no rational consideration that would incline us to reject conclusions that have been properly derived from our unconditional commitments.

More loved his wife and children. Yet his commitment to marriage and parenthood was defeasible because his religious commitment was deeper. When it came to the point, More honored his religious commitment and went to his death, leaving his wife and children to fend for themselves as best they could. Others in More's position might have obeyed the king because they might not have had any unconditional commitments at all or because they had an unconditional commitment to marriage and parenthood, not to religion. Yet that could have been done only by other people because More was what he was because his religious commitment took precedence over his other commitments.

It is possible to live a good life just by living according to defeasible commitments. Lucky circumstances, phlegmatic temperament, much savvy, intellect not given to reflection and self-analysis, the absence of political upheavals and glaring injustice, the enjoyment of robust health, a busy life, a happy family, and many good friends may make it possible for a few fortunate people not to have to ask themselves the kind of fundamental questions that, if asked at all, lead to unconditional commitments. For most of us, however, these questions do arise because our defeasible commitments conflict, because our lives make it impossible or hard to live according to them, because we waver in our allegiance to them, and because we come to see the attractions of other ways of life. These typically unavoidable questions force most of us to ask ourselves what we most fundamentally care about. And that question leads directly to our unconditional commitments.

The cost of not having unconditional commitments is not being able to answer these questions about how we should live. This inability may handicap us in different ways. One is through the lack of a character in which beliefs, emotions, and motives form a coherent pattern. To have a coherent character is to have made unconditional commitments. The defeasibility of commitments means that there is a discrepancy among our beliefs, emotions, and motives and that we are pulled in different directions by the tensions inherent in our characters and circumstances. Unconditional commitments are constitutive of our moral identity whereas defeasible commitments leave us uncertain whenever situations become complex enough to raise the question whether these commitments should be honored. In the absence of a coherent character, we face complex situations with uncertainty and doubt. The psychological space left empty by the absence of unconditional commitments is thus filled with fantasy, fear, anxiety, and overcompensation, all of which color and mislead our responses.

The lack of unconditional commitments may also handicap us through the resulting incapacity to resolve conflicting interpretations of complex situations suggested by our various defeasible commitments. In the absence of unconditional commitments, we lack a standard for deciding what would count for or against honoring a defeasible commitment. And if honoring it is difficult, as it usually is in complex situations, then, human nature being what it is, we shall be tempted to count the difficulty itself as a reason against honoring the commitment. If we have only defeasible commitments, it becomes impossible to decide between good and bad and strong and weak reasons for violating them.

Loose commitments are on the periphery of our characters. Hume called them "a kind of lesser morality," and Jane Austen referred to them as "the civilities, the lesser duties of life."[11] Their objects are the manners and mores of one's society, the rules and customs of politeness, tact, and hygiene; the face one presents to the world; styles of clothing, furnishing, eating, socializing, and exercising; the rituals and ceremonies of everyday life; and so forth. More was a patriotic man who had a defeasible commitment to England. The form his patriotism took was fealty to his king. But for More this was a loose commitment. The author of *Utopia* understood that the forms of patriotism are historically and socially conditioned.

Loose commitments are comparable to aesthetic style: the way in which creative artists present their works and performing artists render their interpretations. If style is to be more than mannerism, it should be a vehicle suitable for the communication of substance. Analogously for people: their unconditional and defeasible commitments must be expressed in actions, so there must be loose commitments giving form to their expressions. But some forms are more suitable than others. When there were titles and honorifics, it was easier to express respect; before oaths and curses had become hackneyed vulgarities, they were reliable indicators of serious resolve and enmity; when kisses and embraces were not indiscriminately bestowed on pets, children, and casual acquaintances, they were meaningful signs of love.

Adherence to loose commitments is not a particularly praiseworthy moral achievement. Nevertheless, there need not be only a superficial connection between the forms loose commitments are and the substance that is constituted of unconditional and defeasible commitments. Ours is not a ceremonious age, and we are given to suspecting that attention to form is prompted by hypocritical attempts to disguise lack of substance. But in societies more homogeneous and less mobile than ours, there may be a seamless continuity from unconditional to defeasible to loose commitments. In such contexts, forms may have a natural affinity with substance. There is not much point in regretting that our society is not like that. But even the most earnest scourge of hypocrisy must recognize that it is easier to live good lives when there are generally recognized and available forms that they might take.

Reflection on Montaigne's life suggests that the resolution of the conflict between public service in a corrupt society and private life requires a sharp separation between the center and the periphery of our character; the corruption must not be allowed to affect the center. Further reflection on More's life suggests that the way to effect and maintain this separation is to distinguish among our unconditional, defeasible, and loose commitments. Unconditional commitments constitute the center, loose commitments belong to the periphery, and defeasible commitments range, according to their strength, on a continuum between the center and the periphery. One main task of self-direction is to discover what our commitments are and whether they are unconditional, defeasible, or loose. And another of its main tasks is to form a coherent pattern of our beliefs, emotions, and motives that reflects the structure of our commitments. The lives of Montaigne and More are admirable partly because they succeeded at both these tasks of self-direction in very difficult circumstances.

1.4 Tradition and Individuality

It is one thing, however to know *that* self-direction requires a coherent character and structured commitments and quite another to know *what* must be done to meet these requirements. It is tempting to think that meeting them depends on maintaining a sharp distinction between the traditions, which influence us, and our individuality, which gives content to our characters and commitments. If we think this way, self-direction becomes something like the moral analogue of economic protectionism. It keeps out foreign goods, the external traditional influences, and it invests in the development of native products, by nurturing individual internal resources. As a result, we see the development of our individuality in opposition to the surrounding traditions. The more traditions influence us, the less self-directed we are supposed to be; and the stronger our self-direction is, the more we are said to succeed in developing our individuality by freeing ourselves from traditional influences.

This way of thinking about self-direction has become widespread, but it is seriously mistaken. Traditions influence us not only by imposing requirements but also by strengthening the commitments we have; they provide not only limitations on the development of our individuality but also possibilities for growth; they are repositories not only of influences we should resist but also of examples, such as Montaigne and More, from which we can learn. If we were to succeed in excluding traditional influences, as this view of self-direction recommends, we would all have to begin anew. We would not know which of our many possibilities we should develop, we would not know how to judge their respective importance, we would not have examples to guide us, and we would deprive ourselves of the experiences of those who lived before us. In effect, this view of self-direction would oblige us to reject the possibility of developing our individuality in the light of history, literature, morality, and politics. It is a recipe for primitivism.

Nevertheless, it is not an accident that this way of thinking strikes a responsive chord in many people. For alongside the promise traditions hold out, there is the danger they threaten. If we concentrate on the promise, we risk becoming mindless conformists, apologists for the status quo, reactionary obstacles to reform. But the remedy is not to concentrate on the other extreme, the danger, and reject traditions altogether. The remedy is to strike a balance: to take what is good and say no to what is bad.

This suggests another way of thinking about self-direction: it consists in maintaining a balance between tradition and individuality. Its role is not to exclude traditional influences but to control the influences traditions have on the development of our individuality. One dominant aspiration of both Montaigne and More was to find this balance. Montaigne succeeded, More failed. So we turn, once again, to Montaigne's life to illustrate the general point. Montaigne was a conservative—not a reactionary, not a sentimentalist about tradition, not blind to how bad things were. "Our morals are extremely corrupt, and lean with a remarkable inclination toward the worse; of our laws and customs, many are barbarous and monstrous; however, because of the difficulty of improving our condition and the danger of everything crumbling into bits, if I could put a spoke in our wheel and stop it at this point, I would do so with all my heart" (497). There was a real danger in sixteenth-century France that, as Yeats wrote, reflecting on another time, "Things fall apart; the centre cannot hold; / Mere anarchy is loosed upon the world."[12] Order, even corrupt order, is better than anarchy. There must be laws and customs; otherwise, we can do nothing about what is barbarous and monstrous. "The worst thing I find in our state is instability.... It is very easy to accuse a government of imperfection, for all mortal things are full of it. It is very easy to engender in people contempt for their ancient observances.... But as for establishing a better state in place of the one they have ruined, many of those who have attempted it achieved nothing for their pains" (498). So what should we do? Should we acquiesce to corrupt order?

Of course not. To begin with, "it is the rule of rules, and the universal law of laws, that each man should observe those of the place he is in" (86). But what if the traditions are defective and conformity to them merely perpetuates their corruption? The answer, then, is to understand that "to compose our character is our duty ... to win, not battles and provinces, but order and tranquillity in our conduct. Our great and glorious masterpiece is to live appropriately" (850–51). If everyone aimed to do that, and if we but knew what living appropriately meant, then we would know how to accept what is good and reject what is bad in our traditions.

Yet there is an obstacle to following this advice, for "the laws of conscience, which we say are born of nature, are born of custom" (83). If the traditions are corrupt, they will corrupt the conscience from which we derive our understanding of what it means to live appropriately. Montaigne saw that, too: "The principal effect of the power of custom is to seize and ensnare us in such a way that it is hardly within our power to get ourselves back out of its grip and return ourselves to reflect and reason about its ordinances" (83). Notice, however, that crucial qualification, *hardly*. It is not beyond our power to step back and reflect, although it is difficult to do so. But nobody said, and it is naive to suppose, that living appropriately is easy. So we return to the question: How can we do *that*, if the very judgment of appropriateness is in danger of being poisoned by the corruption of the prevailing traditions?

The key is to recognize that "things in themselves may have their weights and measures and qualities; but once inside us, she [the soul] allots them their qualities as she sees fit.... Health, conscience, authority, knowledge, riches, beauty, and their opposites—all are stripped on entry and receive from the soul new clothing ... which each individual soul chooses.... Wherefore let us no longer make the external qualities of things our excuse; it is up to us to reckon them as we will" (220). There are two centrally important points to note here.

First, living appropriately begins with taking into ourselves traditional influences rather than pitting ourselves against them. Among these influences are the various possibilities, some of which Montaigne lists above, out of which we construct our ideals of good lives. Traditional possibilities, then, are part of the raw material with which self-direction begins. Consequently, traditions influence the development of our individuality by providing a stable and secure social context in which we can concentrate on making good lives for ourselves through self-direction and by providing a repertoire of possibilities from which self-directed agents can choose some to form their ideals of good lives.

So we must not think that when Montaigne says "I turn my gaze inward, I fix it there and keep it busy" (499), he is retreating from his traditions in order to nurture the home-grown products of his private, individual, inner life. What his gaze fixes on are the traditional possibilities. These for him were a rich mixture he derived from Catholicism, Stoicism, and Pyrrhonism; from the influential conversations with his friend, La Boétie; from the prevailing lifestyle of a country squire; from his extensive reading of Plutarch, Plato, and Herodotus; from his own travels and conversations with other travelers; from his experience as a public official; and so on. When he says "I have a soul all its own, accustomed to conducting itself in its own way" (487), what he has in mind is that he is accustomed to finding his way among the manifold possibilities open to him. The "liberty of judgment" of which he is so protective (500) means the liberty to weigh, to assess the appropriateness of various traditional possibilities open to him, given his character and circumstances.

The second point to note in the passage just quoted is that when we exercise our "liberty of judgment" to appraise the appropriateness of traditional possibilities, when we "reckon them as we will," we are engaged in self-direction. Self-direction essentially involves judgment, reckoning, returning into ourselves to reflect and reason, but the objects upon which we concentrate are traditional possibilities. And what we do in directing ourselves is adapt some traditional possibilities to fit our own cases.

A distinction between the creation and the acceptance of possibilities will help sharpen this point. We rarely create the possibilities we accept. Possibilities are normally created in some classic text, such as *The Republic*, *Nicomachean Ethics*, or the Bible; or they are exemplified in the life of a person, such as Socrates, Alexander, or Jesus; or they come attached to the traditional expectations of a public office, such as the justice of a magistrate, the courage of a soldier, the wisdom of a statesman, and so on. One of the benefits of belonging to a tradition is that we can find in it clearly formulated, well-tested possibilities that command general admiration and represent accepted standards of excellence. Self-direction assumes its importance in the context of our acceptance of traditional possibilities, not in their creation. It involves deciding whether we, ourselves, would wish to conduct some important aspect of our lives in accordance with a particular traditional possibility, and, assuming that we do, deciding what the acceptance of the possibility comes to in our lives shaped by our particular characters and circumstances.

Take, for instance, public life. It consists in participating in some tradition from which we derive many of the benefits that make good lives possible. Assume that many reasonable people accept this tradition and are prepared to act according to it. This is not the end but the beginning of self-direction, for we need to decide what form our participation should take, how important it is in comparison with our other possibilities, whether it should concentrate on criticizing the shortcomings of the tradition, contributing to its smooth functioning, defending it against detractors, or trying, creatively, to enrich it. Unless we answer these and similar questions, our acceptance of a traditional possibility may amount to nothing more than mindless conformity. The development of our individuality requires that we choose and adapt traditional possibilities, and this is one function of self-direction.

The importance of self-direction, however, does not mean that we are, each of us, the final judges of the reasons for or against particular possibilities. It means, rather, that we are the final judges of the reasons, and of how heavily they weigh, for or against *our acceptance* of a particular possibility. These two sets of reasons overlap for reasonable people, but not even for them do they coincide. For our reasons for accepting particular possibilities take into account *our* characters and circumstances whereas the reasons per se for particular possibilities are independent of personal considerations. Traditions carry a great deal of authority about reason per se, but self-direction ought to be authoritative about our reasons for accepting them. Of course, neither authority is infallible. It is just that they are more likely to be correct in their own context than other candidates.

If we go a little deeper, however, we find that not even the traditions responsible for the creation of possibilities are unconnected with self-direction. Traditions rest on the accumulated experiences of many individuals who also had to make the sorts of judgments we have to make now. Their judgments became subsumed into the traditions in which they participated because they have proved reliable. So there is nothing mysterious about traditions: they are repositories of good judgments tested by long experience, from which we can benefit, if we are reasonable. Traditions, therefore, are conditions of self-direction, not its enemies, because both the creation and the acceptance of possibilities of good lives essentially depend on them. The recognition of this dependence is not the surrender of individuality but the affirmation of one of its conditions. As Montaigne puts it in the closing words of the *Essays*, "There is no use our mounting on stilts, for on stilts we must still walk on our own legs. And on the loftiest throne in the world we are still sitting on our own rump" (857).

1.5 What Self-Direction Is Not
It will help to develop the emerging picture to contrast self-direction with authenticity, autonomy, and self-realization. It must be acknowledged, however, that none of these character traits lends itself to a definitive interpretation. They partially overlap, and they include a great variety of characteristics and activities whose interpretations are often equally unclear. The point of drawing the contrast is not to impose an interpretation but to reach a better understanding of self-direction by clarifying what it excludes and includes.

Authenticity is a central notion in existentialist thought. Its roots are in German romanticism and individualism.[13] The heroes of authenticity are creative artists who express their innermost selves in the works they create. They are, above all, original because they reject all that is inherited, conventional, customary, and commonplace. They free themselves of outside influences and thereby allow their unique individuality to shine forth. Most people are not creative artists, but they too can live authentically by making their lives into works of art. They succeed to the extent to which they become themselves, which means the extent to which they are motivated by deliberately chosen features of their characters as a suitable expression of their individuality. Being authentic entails finding out what one really is and then living accordingly. Those who are inauthentic live in bad faith. They

are alienated from themselves because they are motivated by considerations that are not truly their own. Morality, religion, politics, history, conventions, customs, and institutions are all obstacles that
stand between them and authentic existence. As Nietzsche puts it,
"The man who does not wish to belong to the mass needs only to
cease taking himself easily; let him follow his conscience, which calls
to him: 'Be yourself. All you are now doing, thinking, desiring, is not
yourself.' "[14]

Authenticity thus expresses in action what one is; self-direction
changes it. The first aims at self-assertion, the second at self-transformation. Growth in authenticity depends on reaching further back into
oneself. Growth in self-direction depends on reaching a balance between public and private life and between the cultivation of individuality and participation in traditions. Authenticity celebrates individuality; self-direction disciplines it.[15]

It may be thought that this contrast is too sharply drawn. Certainly,
the meaning of authenticity can be softened to allow that individuality may be expressed in traditional ways, provided these ways are
genuinely accepted by oneself. The softer the interpretation gets, the
less difference is left between authenticity and self-direction. What
matters is that self-direction includes the importance of traditional influences upon the development of individuality and excludes the cel-
ebration of unconstrained individuality as valuable in itself.

Autonomy is a key idea in Kantian morality. From there it has
passed on to become a cornerstone of egalitarian (as opposed to classical and communitarian) liberalism.[16] As Thomas Hill interprets it,

> autonomy . . . is a property of the wills of all adult human be-
> ings insofar as they are . . . prescribing general principles to
> themselves rationally, free from causal determination. . . . Two
> points in this conception are crucial. *First*, having autonomy
> means considering principles from a point of view that requires
> temporary detachment from the particular desires and aver-
> sions, loves and hates, that one happens to have; *second*, auton-
> omy is an ideal feature of a person . . . *reviewing* various moral
> principles and values, *reflecting* on how they may conflict and
> how they might be *reconciled*, and finally *deciding* which princi-
> ples are most acceptable.

And

> in this conception, one is most fully oneself, expressing one's
> true nature, when one 'rises above' the particular natural and
> conditional desires that distinguish one from others; and one
> does this by adopting principles from an impartial point of
> view and acting from respect for these principles.[17]

It is because all adults have the capacity for autonomy that they all
have equal moral worth and are entitled to equal respect, however
they may differ in their moral merits. And the capacity for autonomy
is the capacity to act according to rational principles that are universal
and impartial.

If autonomy is conceived of in this way, then it is clear that self-direction must be distinguished from it. For self-direction is an achievement, not a capacity, and it is an achievement in respect to which there
are great differences among people. Autonomy may be the basis of
equal worth and respect, but self-direction cannot be. Furthermore,
self-direction is always individual and particular, never universal and
impartial. It concerns what particular individuals need to do to transform the characters they happen to have, in the circumstances in
which they happen to find themselves, in order to live according to an
ideal of a good life that happens to appeal to them, among a plurality
of other available ideals. Rationality may require autonomous people
to act on universal and impartial principles, but the requirements of
rational self-direction are always individual and particular.

Autonomy need not be interpreted in this way. It may be thought of
as a disposition to evaluate desires and choices in the light of one's
ideal of a good life.[18] This way of understanding autonomy is much
closer to self-direction than the Kantian-liberal one. Whether or not the
differences disappear completely depends, first, on whether the liberal
case for equal worth and respect is based on autonomy and, second,
on the extent to which the balancing of private and public life and individuality and tradition are thought to be compatible with autonomy.
Differences are likely to remain because most egalitarian liberals appeal to the capacity for autonomy as a basis of equal worth and respect
and because the demands of public life and participation in traditions
are typically regarded as impediments to autonomous lives.

Self-direction may also be contrasted with self-realization. In the
Symposium Alcibiades compares Socrates to a sculpture by Silenus.[19] In-

side the sculpture, hidden from view, a golden figure is encased. The point of Alcibiades' comparison is that beneath the unprepossessing exterior of Socrates there is a precious interior, the true Socrates. The self-realizationist view is that what Alcibiades says of Socrates is true of everyone. The gold figure in each of us represents our potentialities. To realize oneself is to discover these potentialities and live according to them. Associated with self-realization is, in David Norton's words, the "ethical doctrine . . . that each man is obliged to know and live in truth to his [potentialities] . . . thereby progressively actualizing the excellence that is his innately and potentially."[20] The two fundamental requirements of self-realization were inscribed on the temple of Apollo at Delphi: "Know thyself" and "Accept your destiny." To know oneself is to know one's potentialities. And to accept one's destiny is to live so as to realize them. Self-realization, then, is the realization of one's potentialities. The supreme moral injunction of self-realization is that everyone should aim, as Norton puts it, "to become the person he potentially is."[21]

In German, self-realization is *Bildung*. Its cultivation by devotees of one prevalent form of Protestantism, pietism; by the authors and the readers of the vastly popular genre of bildungsroman; by philosophers such as Humboldt, Schleiermacher, and Nietzsche and the countless people they have influenced; and by poets such as Schiller and Hölderlin is one of the defining features of late-eighteenth- and nineteenth-century Germany.[22] Thomas Mann, reflecting in 1923 on what has gone wrong with German politics, calls attention to a feature of self-realization—a feature that also distinguishes self-realization and self-direction—that he thinks must bear a major share of the responsibility:

> The finest characteristic of the typical German . . . is his inwardness. . . . The inwardness, the culture of a German implies introspectiveness: an individualistic cultural conscience; consideration for the careful tending, the shaping, deepening and perfecting of one's personality or, in religious terms, for the salvation and justification of one's own life; subjectivism in the things of the mind, therefore, a type of culture that might be called pietistic, given to autobiographical confession and deeply personal, one in which the world of the objective, the political world, is felt to be profane and it is thrust aside with indifference.[23]

As Mann implies, self-realization has strong affinities with the Protestant tendency to search one's conscience and allow nothing—no institution, convention, or authority—to come between it and God. Its hero is Kierkegaard's Abraham, the man with a pure heart, who wills only one thing: to follow his conscience. If it prompts the transvaluation of what the world regards as values, as Nietzsche put it, then so be it. This may entail being prepared to do what is conventionally thought of as evil, as Abraham was prepared to kill Isaac, or recoiling from political involvement because it is seen as corrupting. Self-realization tends to yield extremes: heroes of conscience who stake their lives on what they think is right, such as Luther, and neurotic weaklings who are preoccupied with their inner lives and fail to notice the world around them, such as Werther. One great danger of self-realization is that it easily leads to political irresponsibility, to a detachment that *is* indifference, to a repulsive fastidiousness about the fine-tuning of one's soul.

Self-direction shares with self-realization the emphasis on living according to one's ideal of a good life, but because of a moderating element, self-direction does not easily succumb to the kind of extremes that plague self-realization. This element is the recognition that the public and private and the traditional and individualistic aspects of self-direction are inseparable. Self-direction is inspired by an ideal of a good life, but both the ideal itself and how it is pursued are products of the adaptation of traditional influences to one's character and circumstances. These traditions are repositories of the accumulated experiences of predecessors who, like oneself, have struggled to live good lives. Participation in a tradition provides a repertoire of options from which one can choose some as possibilities for oneself. Self-direction requires directing one's attention both inward, to understand one's individuality, and outward, to appreciate and learn from the examples of other real and imagined lives.

Self-realization breeds extremes because it directs the attention largely inward. It rightly emphasizes the importance of judging for oneself, but it wrongly supposes that participation in traditions is the abdication of that judgment. Self-direction, on the one hand, involves the contemplation of the riches of one's traditions and a willingness to enjoy them. There goes with a liberality of spirit—which is not the same as a liberal spirit—and a toleration born of understanding that others, no less reflective and well intentioned than oneself, may be guided by traditions whose historical roots one may recognize but not share. Self-realization, on the other hand, pits one against traditions, which are seen as obstacles to becoming oneself. "The political world," as Mann says, "is felt to be profane and it is thrust aside with indifference." For those committed to self-realization, there is always a battle between the private and the public, between the individual and traditional influences. The inner fortress of individuality is always besieged. To protect it, self-realizing people must retire into their private inner world, and the public world is seen as soiling. Participation in it tends to compromise "the careful tending, the shaping, deepening and perfecting of one's personality." Self-directed people, by contrast, have the resources of their traditions at their disposal, and their individuality is strengthened by them. As Michael Oakeshott puts it, such people "give us a sense that they have passed through an elaborate education which was designed to initiate them into the traditions and achievements of their civilization: the impression we have of them is . . . of the enjoyment of an inheritance."[24]

1.6 The Conditions and Limits of Self-Direction

The requirements of self-direction may, then, be summarized as follows. Self-direction is a conscious and deliberate process involving the transformation of one's character. Its aim is to enable oneself to live a good life by developing character traits and commitments that are conducive to it. Both the character traits and the commitments vary with lives and circumstances. But there are some requirements of self-direction that do not vary. First, one maintains a coherent pattern of beliefs, emotions, and motives. One's actions express one's motives, the motives are based on one's beliefs and emotions, and they concern what must be done to live a good life. Second, this pattern reflects a structure in which one's unconditional, defeasible, and loose commitments are distinguished. Third, these commitments are to possibilities, derived from various traditions, which are believed to be constitutive of good lives. Self-direction, therefore, requires participation in traditions, but the ultimate decision about the acceptance of some possibilities created by traditions is made by oneself. Self-direction thus does not involve withdrawal from the world; it involves conditional participation in it. It is conditional on living according to one's unconditional commitments and according to as many of one's defeasible and loose commitments as circumstances allow.

These are requirements of self-directed lives, but there are several reasons why meeting them does not guarantee good lives. One is that misfortune, injustice, scarcity, and other contingencies may pose insurmountable obstacles to living a good life that not even conspicuously successful self-direction can overcome. Another is that the goodness of lives depends not merely on self-direction but also on morality. The commitments that guide self-direction may be more or less immoral. Successful self-direction and surmounted obstacles make it possible to achieve what one wants but that may not be morally acceptable to want. Living the life one wants to live does not guarantee that it will be good. Part of the reason the lives of Montaigne and More are admirable is that they combined self-direction and moral acceptability, and did so under very difficult conditions. Lastly, even if a self-directed life achieves what one wants and is morally acceptable, it must be recognized that good lives can take forms in which self-direction has only negligible importance. The lives of soldiers, priests, nuns, reformers, civil servants, orthodox religious believers, and countless ordinary people living ordinary lives may be utterly conventional, unreflective, inarticulate, dictated by circumstances, dedicated to the subordination of the goodness of their lives to that of others, disciplined by rules that have been unquestioningly accepted, lacking a clear aim or focus, and still be personally satisfying and morally acceptable. Even at best, therefore, self-direction is only one among a plurality of ways in which lives can be made good.

These qualifications notwithstanding, self-direction is a personal excellence because it motivates one to exercise as much control over one's life as circumstances allow. It makes it possible to live in clear recognition of one's limits and possibilities. It provides a standard for choosing among the available possibilities. It resolves the tension both between private life and public involvement and between participation in various traditions and the development of individuality. It enables one to form an ideal of a good life and to maximize the chances of living so as to achieve it.

2/

Moral Authority

Yes, I've heard Pericles and all the other great orators . . . but they never affected me like that; they never turned my whole soul upside down and left me feeling as if . . . I simply couldn't go on living the way I did. . . . He makes me admit that while I'm spending my time on politics I am neglecting all the things that are crying out for attention in myself. . . . And there's one thing I've never felt with anybody else . . . and that is a sense of shame.

PLATO, *Symposium*

2.1 The *Sophron*

The village of Alona is in the highlands of Cyprus. It is inhabited by a closely knit Greek Orthodox community. The villagers marry one another, and it is exceptionally difficult for outsiders to become part of the community. For this reason, the Aloneftes, as the villagers are called, have been successful in maintaining their distinctive identity through many centuries up to the present time, even though they have endured great hardships. The leaders of the community are the priest, the schoolteacher, the heads of the richest families, and the *sophron*. The *sophron* has a centrally important part in the life of the village, and it is on him—always a male—that we shall concentrate.[1]

An essential part of the Aloneftes' identity is their tradition, which is a mixture of Hellenic, Byzantine, and Greek Orthodox elements. As J. G. Peristiany describes this tradition, the "Greek Cypriot highlander sees himself as the heir to classical Greece—and of Achilles and Nestor, of Pericles and Alexander, of the imprint of the Orthodox court of Byzantium whose ceremonial is re-enacted in his mountain church. Christ and the last Palaeologue [the rulers of Byzantium] were martyred to make him a man by instilling in him a faith that makes life worth living" (125). This tradition is a living presence to the Aloneftes. Quotations from Greek writers, from the New Testament, from hagiographies, and from the sayings of notable personages inform their lives, guide their conduct, and enliven their conversation (104–5). The tradition is an ideal pattern, a repository of principles "of a harmonious and perennial" order, but it is rich, complex, and full of "apparent contradictions" (104). If it is to be useful as an actual guide to conduct, it must be interpreted and applied; the ideal must be brought to bear on the reality that the Aloneftes encounter in their daily lives. This is the task of the *sophron*.

"As the *sophron*'s task is to mediate between ideals and reality, it is the flexibility of the ranking order of values and the casuistry explaining a choice that bestow exceptional importance on the *sophron*'s function within the community" (125). "The *sophron*'s wisdom consists in applying general principles to particular cases in such a manner that the general is not seen to bend so as to serve practical ends. . . . What distinguishes the wise from the merely knowledgeable is that the wise man knows not only the rules but also how to apply them for the common good. Mere knowledge pertains to 'professors,' a most derogatory term used for those who . . . 'talk wisdom as though it were a dead language.' Knowledge joined to the capacity to apply it is a constituent of wisdom. Pure knowledge is an ingredient of foolishness" (105).

Here is a villager speaking: "In Alona, the forces of good and evil are forever contending not only for the soul of man but also for the good name of the village. It is a wondrous thing that their extremes should cohabit here as husband and wife. We men of Alona spend our lives endeavoring to reconcile them. This is a hopeless but necessary task as the forces of goodness bestir themselves when evil threatens to overwhelm us. We assist them with the help of God and the advice of those to whom he has given sophrosyne [i.e., the *sophron*]" (111).

The *sophron* has the following characteristics: he "can neither order nor decide; he can only advise" (105); he is "reluctant" (107); "a man does not suddenly emerge as a *sophron*, neither is he groomed for, or appointed to, this dignity. *Sophrosyne* is gradually revealed in speech and action consistent with the image of a selfless and judicious man who applies these qualities to the welfare of his community" (114); "the *sophron* is a dedicated man who should allow no other aspiration, private or public, to distract him from his main duty" (114); he is of "old age—here [in Alona] situated in the early sixties" (116); he "could not be faulted in his behavior as a son, brother, husband, father, as schoolboy, farmer or elder. His everyday actions . . . are those of a sensible average man" (116). "It is only the undisputed recognition of these qualities by his fellow-villagers that warrants the use of the term *sophron*" (114). In short, the *sophron* is "a person who, without holding any office whatsoever, is endowed with sufficient moral authority both to reconcile conflicting values and, if asked to do so, to speak in the name of the best interest of the community" (106).

The Aloneftes are clearly fortunate in having *sophrons* who have well-deserved moral authority and to whom they can turn for advice with difficult moral problems. But what about us? Could we have moral authorities in our very different circumstances? Would we be fortunate to have them if we could? Might it be that we actually have them, although in a different form? To these questions there are no agreed-upon answers.

We live in a pluralistic society that contains many, often incompatible, traditions, and even if someone had moral authority in one of these traditions, how could that carry weight with those who belong to a different tradition? We are also suspicious of moral authorities because we think that to follow authority in moral matters is to abandon personal responsibility. We want moral agents to choose and decide for themselves. And we tend to attribute moral worth only to actions based on choice.

The argument that follows is intended to show that moral authority is a personal excellence that we have good reason to value, even in our pluralistic society, and that our suspicion of moral authority is a result of thinking about it in the wrong way. We first discuss authority in general, then focus on moral authority, then consider the qualifications that make those who possess them moral authorities, and finally offer a justification for relying on moral authorities by explaining why they are needed in a pluralistic society.

2.2 Authority
Discussions of authority tend to go wrong from the beginning. They start with considering authority and then, usually without notice or

excuse, switch to consideration of political authority. This tendency is shown equally by those who regret its loss and wish to shore it up,[2] by those who deny its legitimacy,[3] and by those who want to defend some suitably circumscribed and attenuated version of it.[4] They all assume that authority is a relation in which the authority makes those subject to it conduct themselves as the authority directs. The authority is thus thought to have a power, which it uses to get people to do things they would not do if it were not for the power the authority has over them. Opinions vary across the political spectrum as to the legitimacy of the power that authorities have and use, but they all respond to the supposed tension succinctly expressed by Robert Wolff as follows: "The defining mark of the state is authority, the right to rule. The primary obligation of man is autonomy, the refusal to be ruled. . . . Insofar as a man fulfills his obligation to make himself the author of his decisions, he will resist the state's claim to have authority over him."[5] The standard discussion thus begins with a suspicion of authority, and it goes on to consider how far the suspicion is justified.

The trouble with this approach to understanding authority is that it leaves no room for the thought that authorities are individuals, not states or other political units, and that what makes someone an authority—such as the *sophrons* are—is experience and good judgment rather than power. That this approach got it wrong is made obvious by the fact that the everyday lives of most people are permeated with various relations in which they seek out, willingly follow, and regard themselves as lost without authorities. These attitudes need not be unreasonable, craven, bamboozled, indoctrinated, or intellectually or morally slothful. That this is so becomes obvious if some of the prevalent forms of authority are recognized as more reasonable starting points than the exclusive concentration on political authority. Such forms are the relations between parents and children, teachers and students, physicians and patients, coaches and athletes, lawyers and clients, directors and actors, established practitioners in a field and beginners, clerics and the faithful, experienced old friends and inexperienced young ones, management consultants and floundering firms, superiors and subordinates in hierarchical organizations such as the army and religious orders, plumbers and homeowners, judges and juries, mentors and advisees, umpires and competitors, editors and authors, pilots and passengers, and so forth. Given these forms of authority, the idea that reason and morality dictate resistance to them must be seen as perverse. To be sure, people's authority may be phony rather than genuine, and then it would be folly to do as they say. But if they truly have authority and if others rely on it to help them do something they have difficulty doing on their own, then folly is to fail to do as they say.

The right question to ask, therefore, is how to tell real from spurious authorities rather than the politically inspired one of why reasonable people would subject themselves to authorities. The wrong question, however, has dominated discussions of authority, as Richard Flathman notes: "There has been a remarkable coalescence of opinion around the proposition that authority and authority relations involve some species of 'surrender of judgment' on the part of those who accept, submit or subscribe to the authority of persons or a set of rules or offices."[6]

The attempt to understand authority through the notion of surrender of judgment is highly misleading. It stresses submission, subordination, and the abandonment of responsibility. It implies that the recognition of authority is demeaning and detrimental to self-respect and that people with integrity and courage would reject it. And then one should ask how this fits people who accept the authority of their parents, teachers, older friends, physicians, mentors, or plumbers. The acceptance of authority may be unreasonable, but only if it is unnecessary or unhelpful. The possession of genuine authority, however, enables those who have it to respond to the needs of those who turn to them. Their acceptance in that case does not merit suspicion. The question is whether those who accept their authority are in need of it and whether the authority they accept is genuine. This is why the salient fact about authority relations is whether it is reasonable to accept the supposed authority as such, and not the fact that those who accept it have surrendered their own judgment. People often turn to authorities precisely because they cannot rely on their judgment: they do not know how to judge some complex situation, they distrust their own judgment, or they feel the need to reconcile the conflicting judgments of other people.

In trying to arrive at a better understanding of the nature of authority, we must start by distinguishing between a descriptive and a normative approach. The descriptive one is a historical, sociological, or anthropological inquiry about what is regarded as authoritative in some particular context and what reasons are given in that context for regarding it as such. The normative approach aims to discover whether these reasons are good. The normative approach presupposes the descriptive one, and the two often go together, but they are nevertheless different because they aim to answer different questions.

We shall concentrate on the normative question. Here it is useful to distinguish between de facto and de jure authority.[7] De facto authority is one that is actually accepted in a particular context, but it may or may not have official status. Authority that has official status is de jure. It derives its status from some formal procedure, training, rule, institution, or custom that legitimates the exercise of authority. De facto authority may or may not be de jure, and vice versa. A defrocked priest has lost his de jure authority, but he may retain considerable de facto authority if his congregation continues to regard him as a good priest.

Both de facto and de jure authority may be legitimate or not. De facto authority is legitimate if people have good reasons to accept it as such. Legitimate de facto authority not only has authority but also possesses the qualifications necessary for it. Similarly, the legitimacy of de jure authority derives not merely from the fact that the method by which the status is conferred has been followed in its case, but also from the additional fact that the method is successful in identifying the characteristics that those in a position of authority ought to have.

Many people with legitimate authority have no official standing because their status is not conferred on them by any formal method. Friends, mentors, teachers, and religious, financial, aesthetic, literary, or technical advisers may have legitimate de facto authority without any de jure authority. One reason thinking about authority in political terms leads to misunderstanding is that in politics legitimate authority is de jure. If political authority is thought to be the model for all authority, then, if an authority is de facto without being de jure, the suspicion naturally arises that it is illegitimate. If the suspicion could be allayed only by identifying and justifying the formal method by which the status has been conferred on it, then de facto authority could not be legitimate. The reasonable alternative, however, is to reject political authority as the model and to recognize that the legitimacy of de facto and de jure authority is established in different ways.

A further distinction between being *an* authority and being *in* authority will help clarify what is involved in an authority's being legitimate.[8] Being *in* authority is being in a position that carries authority with it. Those who are in that position are necessarily *in* authority. The position may be de jure, such as that of an elected official, or it may be de facto, like that of a mentor. To be *an* authority is to possess the characteristics that make the judgments of the authority better than the judgments of other people. But an authority may or may not be in authority because the comparative excellence of the authority's judgment may lack either de facto or de jure acknowledgment. A person thus may be an authority and not be recognized as such. The ideal case is when the person who is in authority has that position in virtue of being an authority. In that case, the authority is legitimate because the status and the qualifications required for it coincide.

The ideal case, of course, often fails to obtain. A person may be an authority but not be in authority; and the person in authority may not be an authority. If the suspicion of authority is based on thinking that the person in authority is not really an authority, then it deserves to be taken seriously. But if there is good reason to think that the two coincide, then suspicion is misplaced and the judgments of the person in authority should be accepted. It must be added, by way of caution, that even in the ideal case, authority holds only in a particular context and in some particular respect. It is an illegitimate use of authority to exercise it beyond its proper sphere. Once again, however, if the authority is exercised in the appropriate context and respect, then it is legitimate and it ought to be accepted as such.

The nature and legitimacy of different forms of authority vary with the context and the respect in which they are candidates for acceptance because their contexts determine who might accept them. The legitimate authority of an older friend, a music critic, and a president has different scopes. Authorities are authorities for a specifiable range of people who may accept them as such. Their nature also varies because the respects in which they are supposed to hold are determined by the different characteristics that make people an authority.

In trying to understand the required characteristics, we must bear in mind that the topic is considered normatively, not descriptively. The question is not what characteristics make people accept an authority as legitimate, but what characteristics make an authority legitimate. The descriptive question is answered if it is explained why people accept someone as an authority. The normative question is answered if it is explained why people ought to accept someone as an authority. The attempt to answer the descriptive question must begin with the distinction among three ideal types of authority: traditional, rational-legal, and charismatic.[9] Much has been written about this,[10] but it is irrelevant to the present question, which is the normative one.

When people accept an authority, they do not so much surrender their judgment as realize that they do not know how to judge or that their judgment is defective, and that the authority's judgment is better than what they could arrive at on their own. As it has been perspicuously put by Steven Lukes: "He who accepts authority accepts as a sufficient reason for acting or believing something the fact that he has been so instructed by someone whose claim to do so he acknowledges. . . . It is to act or believe not on the balance of reasons, but rather on the basis of a second-order reason that precisely requires that one disregard the balance of reasons as one sees it. Likewise, to exercise authority is precisely not to have to offer reasons, but to be obeyed or believed because one has a recognized claim to be."[11]

There are countless cases in which it is reasonable to accept authority in this sense and in which it would be unreasonable not to do so. In these cases, people need to form some belief and/or perform some action, but they are confused or uncertain about what the belief or action should be. They realize this about themselves, and they have good reason to follow the direction of someone else who knows better than they. In this manner, a student may accept a teacher's authority about how to understand a difficult work, a patient may accept a physician's authority about what medication to take, a novice may accept an experienced practitioner's authority about when routine operations have become so defective as to require not reform but drastic change, and a young person may accept an older friend's authority about the advisability of turning down a lucrative job offer because it would be corrupting. In all these cases, the authority has reasons for its judgment. These reasons can be stated, explained, and argued for. They are capable of what Carl Friedrich has aptly called "reasoned elaboration."[12] But the people who accept the authority's judgment are not in the position to appreciate the reasons or their elaborations. They are confused and uncertain because they lack the characteristics that the authority has. The reasons support the authority's judgment, but their significance, weight, and contestability are not available to the people.

The legitimacy of authority depends on its characteristics. People are reasonable in accepting an authority if they have good reasons to believe that it possesses the required characteristics. These reasons, of course, cannot be derived by people from a direct evaluation of the authority's characteristics, since for that they would already have to have the qualifications that they ex hypothesi lack. But the reasons can be derived indirectly by considering such matters as the authority's official status if it has one, its reputation, the success or failure of its past judgments, and so forth.

This way of thinking about the characteristics that make an authority legitimate is derived from the private realm, in which one individual accepts the authority of another. Not all authority relations, however, are like these. There are also public, especially political, authorities whose characteristics need not involve any particular personal excellence. Their qualifications derive simply from the procedure that is followed in placing them in a position of authority. The reason for having public authorities of this kind is to cope with what has been called the "coordination problem." That problem is to impose order and predictability on the otherwise chaotic actions of people living together in populous societies. Someone has to decide what forms contracts should take, when elections are to be held, what days are holidays, where public buildings should be built, and so on. If public authorities of this sort perform their tasks competently and if their status is conferred on them by the appropriate procedure, then they too are legitimate and it is reasonable to accept them as such.

In conclusion, it may be said that authorities in general may or may not be legitimate. Their legitimacy depends on their characteristics. If people lack the characteristics an authority has and if they need to make judgments about beliefs and actions to which the characteristics are relevant, then they are reasonable in accepting the authority's judgment in place of their own. If these conditions are met, there is nothing intellectually or morally questionable in accepting someone else's authority. If suspicion of authority is motivated simply by a desire to make sure that a putative authority has the characteristics that make it legitimate, it is a healthy attitude. But if the suspicion is based on the very nature of authority, then it is groundless.

2.3 Moral Authority

If authority is the genus, then moral authority is a species. There has not been much written on the latter.[13] The characteristics of moral authority vary with historical and social contexts, but our discussion will concentrate on moral authority in the context of a pluralistic society. The salient feature of such a society is that there neither is nor is it thought that there ought to be a single generally recognized moral authority in it. At other times and in other kinds of societies the pope, the king, the party leader, the oracle, the elder, the president, and so forth may have been publicly accepted as having moral authority, but times have changed. There still are people with moral authority, but they are many, not one, and they tend to be not public but private. Even if the moral authorities happen to have some official status, that is not what gives them authority.

Legitimate moral authorities are *in* authority because they are *an* authority. What makes them so is that they possess the required characteristics. In a pluralistic society moral authority relations tend to be private, and moral authorities tend to be de facto, not de jure. The latter requires some formal method to confer the status of authority, but in private relationships there is no such method. One individual may accept the moral authority of another, but the acceptance is a personal matter based on the belief that the authority possesses the required characteristics. This belief, of course, may or may not be justified. If it is justified, then the moral authority is legitimate and it is reasonable to accept it as such.

To understand what moral authorities do, consider an account of one occasion on which Confucius exercises moral authority: "We read of the Master teaching a return to the purity and sincerity of the ancient ceremonies. He deplores superstition and the mere outward observance of forms. Then Tzu-kung, one of the disciples, asks about the monthly ceremony at which the new moon is announced. . . . Would it not be better, he queries, if the practice of sacrificing sheep were done away with? Confucius reproves him gently. He calls him by his familiar name. 'Ssu,' he says, 'You care for the sheep. I care for the ceremony.' "[14]

This story reveals several significant features of moral authority. First, Confucius responds to a question that is put to him. He speaks because he was asked. He does not issue a command, impose his will, or tell Tzu-kung what he should do. He rather shows how he, Confucius, thinks about the matter. There is, to be sure, the clear suggestion that Confucius's way of thinking is better than Tzu-kung's, but let that go for the moment. Second, in thinking as he does, Confucius mediates between the moral tradition that both he and Tzu-kung recognize as their own and the moral problem that Tzu-kung raises. The problem is a problem for them only because their allegiance lies with the tradition. Confucius, then, thinks about the problem in the light of the shared tradition in the background. Third, in Confucius's opinion, the tradition is defective because the significance of ancient ceremonies has been lost and they have become empty forms. Tzu-kung's problem arises precisely because of this defect in the tradition. The ceremonies used to mark important occasions in the lives of people who belong to the tradition, but they no longer do that. An important part of their moral identity, therefore, has been lost. They are impoverished in the same way as Christians are who think of Christmas without religious sentiments or as Americans are who think of Fourth of July without patriotic feelings. It may be, of course, that the religiosity and patriotism would be misplaced, but there is no doubt that even if that were so, it would be a serious loss for those in whose lives they used to be significant values. Fourth, the question Tzu-kung is asking is difficult. There is no simple solution to the problem of how to cope with the defects that people recognize in their own moral tradition. Should they reaffirm the old values that are being violated or should they seek to replace them with new values that reflect changing circumstances? Answering that question requires understanding both the moral tradition and the new circumstances, judging the importance of the old values, and weighing whether the possible new values would be adequate substitutes for the old ones. It is not to be expected that most people, kept busy by the demands of their lives, would have the understanding, judgment, and sense of proportion, as well as the inclination, time, and seriousness, to ask and answer these questions. That is why they need a moral authority, as the Aloneftes need a *sophron*.

Consider now why and how moral authorities mediate between their moral tradition and some particular problematic case. The chief reason the mediation of moral authorities is needed is that the knowledge that most people in a moral tradition can be expected to have has become insufficient. As a result, they cannot rely on their moral intuitions. They encounter an increasing number of situations in which the simple connection between a hitherto morally acceptable convention and a particular case that clearly falls under it has been broken. The case is there and is pressing for evaluation and response, but it is unclear what they ought to be.

Is the sacrifice of sheep just an act of cruelty? Is it a waste of livestock? Is it a hypocritical show of piety? Is it a stalwart adherence to old values in a changing world? There is no intuitively persuasive answer because the old convention governing the sacrifice is no longer generally observed. So people do not know whether they should evaluate the sacrifice of sheep according to some other convention, or whether they should continue to stick to the old one that is falling into desuetude, or whether they should just do as they please because the case no longer falls under the jurisdiction of any convention. What is happening is that their moral identity has been changing. In a particular area of their lives their intuitions have become unreliable, and they feel uncertain in their moral outlook. Their situation is not unlike that of contemporary Americans in respect to marriage. It is called into question by secularization, countless people living together without marriage, the frequency of adultery and divorce, single-parent families, and homosexual unions. It is in just such cases that individuals need moral authorities to help them evaluate the situations they face in the no longer clear light of their moral tradition.

In order to answer the question how moral authorities provide the needed help, we must remember that they offer a judgment, not a command. They do not say: Do this rather than that; they say: If you look at the situation in this way, then it will become clear to you what you should do. Their judgment is not a decision, which they hand down, but an interpretation of a complex situation formed of a particular case, conventions of uncertain relevance, and the moral tradition itself. Do not think of the sheep, says Confucius, think of the ceremony. What really matters, he suggests, is the meaningfulness of human lives, not the life expectancy of sheep or the money a sacrifice takes. Or, as it might be said in response to current uncertainties about marriage, what matters is that people should form lasting intimate relationships with each other, that they should face the world together, that they should be united by love, appreciation, and delight in each other. To focus on whether they can or cannot have children, whether their relationship is sexual, whether their sexual relationship takes one form or another is to misjudge what is important. The judgments of moral authorities are based on a deeper appreciation of their moral tradition than what other people have, and on their ability to see through the complexities that bedevil others.

2.4 Characteristics

The judgments of moral authorities are better because they possess characteristics that people who solicit their judgments lack. The first of these characteristics is a thorough familiarity with the conventions of the moral tradition and considerable experience and skill in evaluating particular cases by subsuming them under the appropriate conventions. For the sake of brevity, this may be described as knowledge of the moral tradition. It should be understood, however, that the knowledge is both factual, involving knowledge of the conventions, and practical, having to do with the application of the conventions. It is, moreover, moral knowledge because its subject matter is living a good life, as it is understood in a particular moral tradition. If the tradition exists in a pluralistic society, then the moral knowledge will be of one or a few of a large number of morally acceptable ideals of a good life. The more pluralistic a society is, the less likely it is that there will be moral authorities whose knowledge ranges over all the moral traditions and ideals of a good life that are morally acceptable in that society. In a pluralistic society moral authority is likely to be confined to specific traditions, which may be aesthetic, academic, political, athletic, judicial, religious, scientific, charitable, journalistic, and so forth.

This knowledge is not particularly hard to acquire. Experience and continued participation in a moral tradition are normally sufficient for it. People who possess it know how to distinguish between simple and complex, routine and controversial, banal and surprising cases. They know what it is to treat someone in that context fairly or unfairly, harshly or indulgently, generously or meanly. They know what counts as negligence, scrupulousness, diligence, efficiency, or going beyond the call of duty. They know when they can trust their intuitions and when they have to stop and think. They are in general experienced practitioners who are skilled in applying the vocabulary of their moral tradition to evaluate relevant conduct. Anyone with sufficient motivation, moderate ability, and long enough practice will meet this elementary, but by no means sufficient, requirement of having moral authority.

That this kind of knowledge is not sufficient for having moral authority becomes obvious once it is seen that its possession is compatible with the rejection of or indifference to the moral tradition. Anthropologists studying the society, hypocrites living in it, and wicked people violating it whenever they can may all be familiar with the conventions and be skilled in mediating between the tradition and complex cases. They may know what the moral tradition prescribes, but they do not accept its prescriptions. They may act according to them, but only because expediency dictates it.

It is necessary, therefore, to add a second characteristic required for having moral authority: commitment to the moral tradition. People who are committed do not just know what the conventions are and how to apply them in complex situations; they also believe they ought to live and act according to them, and they endeavor so to live and act. Such people do not merely know what ideals of life are regarded as good in a moral tradition; they also think the ideals really are good. This, however, is still insufficient for moral authority because much depends on the manner in which the knowledge and commitment are acquired and acted upon. They may just reflect a rigorous moral education in the course of which people's minds and hearts are so thoroughly influenced as to make it impossible for them to regard any other moral tradition or basic dissension from their own as a live option for themselves. They know, of course, that other people at other places follow different conventions and have different commitments, but they know it only intellectually. There are cannibals, samurai, shamans, men with harems, and women with bordellos, but what has that got to do with them? They are immersed in their lives; they have no doubts about their moral tradition; what they can spare of their intellect and emotions for moral purposes is fully engaged in it; they see the world from its perspective; and insofar as they are morally motivated, their motivation has no contrary sources.

It is much easier to sustain this attitude in an absolutistic than in a pluralistic moral tradition. But even in an absolutistic one, the prevailing moral tradition, with its one or few approved ideals of a good life, is bound to be challenged by the failure of many people to follow the conventions. Evil is an unignorable feature of all moral traditions, and its existence and prevalence raise questions that cry out for an answer. If the countenanced ideals of life are good, then why do so many people live in violation of them? If they so live, how could it be that they often flourish? And why are good lives so difficult and chancy? Why is it that living decently and reasonably according to the conventions often fails to result in a good life?

To these questions, which will be asked in any moral tradition, others will be added if the tradition exists in a pluralistic society. For if pluralism prevails, competing ideals of a good life will be spatially and temporally contiguous and thus evident in everyone's life. People do not then have to go far afield to see others live in ways that cannot but appear as challenges to their own. It is therefore not only the prevalence of evil but also moral possibilities other than what they have adopted that will pose questions to most people. Moral authority depends also on the ability to give convincing answers to them. If, however, the knowledge and commitment required for having moral authority are formed without awareness of such questions, the means to give convincing answers will be lacking.

It is necessary, therefore, to add a third characteristic required for having moral authority: reflectiveness. This is a large topic that cannot be treated fully here.[15] In general, however, reflectiveness may be said to be directed toward a deeper understanding of the moral tradition and a broader comparison of the moral tradition with other moral traditions. The depth and breadth that result enhance the appreciation of the moral tradition if it is a morally acceptable one, or they lead to its criticism and possible improvement or abandonment if it has moral defects.

One object of reflectiveness is to understand the moral vision that is meant to be expressed by the conventions of a moral tradition. The vision is of human possibilities and limits and of how best to pursue the first and recognize the second. Reflectiveness aims to penetrate to the deepest level of a moral tradition and understand what motivates it. For Christians, it is the imitation of Christ; for Jews, it is the covenant with God; for egalitarian liberals, it is the autonomous life; for utilitarians, it is the happiness of humanity; for Plato, it is the transformation of the self as guided by knowledge of the Good; and so on for each of the major moral traditions. If the conventions of a moral tradition are seen as the forms in which the underlying vision is given concrete expression, then there will be a principled way of justifying, criticizing, or changing the conventions. For it will then be understood that it is not conformity to the conventions that is of the greatest importance but the translation of the vision into concrete forms. Conventions are the means by which this is done, and they can be more or less adequate to their purpose.

The conventions may change with times and circumstances, and they may become more or less faithful, practical, or realistic. Having understood the vision, however, a moral authority will have a ready way of evaluating actual changes or judging the advisability of future ones. Part of the authoritativeness, attraction, and persuasiveness of moral authority comes from the possession of a deeper understanding than most people have. It enables moral authorities to cut through the moral complexities caused by changing conventions. It involves judging the adequacy of conventions in the light of the underlying moral vision they were meant to express. The judgment may not be favorable, and so moral authorities may be critics of the moral status quo.

Reflectiveness is directed also toward understanding that the vision of one's own moral tradition is merely one among many. To have this kind of understanding is to see that here, as Peter Strawson puts it, "there are truths but no truth."[16] It is the essential feature of a pluralistic society that it is generally recognized in it that the morally acceptable visions of a good life are many. The fact remains, however, that of the many only one is one's own. One of the most difficult tasks of a moral authority in a pluralistic society is to combine the recognition of the plurality of morally acceptable traditions with allegiance to a particular one. If one knows that there are many truths, why live according to one of them?

The answer is that people's knowledge of the truths of other moral traditions is not like knowledge of their own. Moral traditions other than their own do not provide the perspective for evaluating the lives and conduct of themselves and others, they do not protect their ideals of a good life, they do not inspire and motivate them, and they do not engage their feelings and imagination, at least not to the same extent as their own. And if two ideals of a good life derived from two moral traditions were found to be equally attractive, it would still be necessary to opt for one of them, for one person can live and act reasonably only by trying to follow one of two incompatible moral visions. One task of a moral authority, therefore, is to remind people whose allegiance to a moral tradition is challenged by the possibilities of another that the evaluative dimension of their lives is defined by their own tradition, that its moral vision is theirs too, and that their ideal of a good life is intimately connected with the moral tradition whose framework makes living according to that conception possible.

This is not to deny, of course, that people may have reason to exchange their commitment to one morally acceptable tradition for another. Moral authority does not dictate what commitments people should have, but makes vivid to them the moral vision that lies behind the commitments they have made. The vision may fade; limited energy, lack of emotional agility, and the demands of everyday life often make it hard to concentrate on it; wickedness, weakness, and love of comfort frequently act as countervailing motivational forces; and the inevitable defects of the prevailing conventions further cloud the original vision. People often turn to moral authorities for help when they find themselves beset by such conflicts, doubts, and weakening commitments. Moral authorities can help people by reminding them of what they already know, but tend to forget under the pressure of their lives and circumstances: the moral vision that provides the rationale for living as they do.

Implicit in this account of reflectiveness is that being articulate is a further characteristic required for having moral authority. Those who have moral authority can make simple the situations others find complex because they have reflected more deeply and broadly on their moral tradition than those who turn to them for help. But they could not help if their reflectiveness merely enabled them to see clearly what appears to be obscure for others. They must also be able to communicate what they have seen, and to communicate it in a way that would make those who have not seen it see it too. Moral authorities must therefore be teachers, and as teachers they must know how to bring those who want to learn from the point of being lost in complexities to the point where their own efforts will suffice.

The plain statement of the plain truth will rarely accomplish this because what is plain to someone who has reflected sufficiently will not be plain to those who have not. This is why moral authorities in widely different contexts tend to communicate through stories, allegories, parables, myths, and striking images. The imaginative and emotive aura with which they surround the truth is not a sugar coating to make the truth easier to swallow, but a method of making its significance apparent. One of the greatest of these literary devices is Plato's allegory of the cave.[17] It is most apposite in the present context because it is not only a classic illustration of how moral authorities can communicate successfully, but also a depiction of the predicament of both moral authorities and those in need of moral authority. Plato writes, "The eyes can become confused in two different ways . . . it can happen in the transition from light to darkness and also in the transition from darkness to light."[18] Moral authorities must overcome the clouding of their vision as they proceed from light to darkness when they return to the cave; and they must do so in order to help those in the cave see better as they try to proceed from darkness toward light.

There are, however, two significant differences between Plato's and the present way of thinking about moral authority. The first is that Plato thinks that ultimately there can be only one authoritative moral vision, whereas in fact there are many. The second is that Plato thinks of moral authority in a far more intrusive way than it is warranted to do. For Plato, the vast majority live in circumstances that prevent them from seeing, and they must be made to see; otherwise, they will not be able to see by themselves. According to the present approach, their circumstances are less dire; most people can see, if only obscurely; they may come to realize this about themselves and then ask for help. It is only then that moral authorities should do what they can to show people how their own moral vision can illuminate the obscurities they face.

There is one further characteristic that moral authorities must possess in addition to the four already discussed. Its necessity emerges if it is borne in mind that people's acceptance of someone else's moral authority is always a matter of trust. It involves the belief that the judgment of the moral authority is better than their own. What is it about moral authorities that would make it reasonable for people to trust their judgment more than they trust their own? The answer cannot just be that the moral authorities possess the necessary knowledge, commitment, reflectiveness, and articulateness, for how could people know that they actually have these characteristics and not just claim to have them? Putative moral authorities, after all, can be pretended, phony, false, or deluded. There must, therefore, be something about the moral authorities themselves that would make it reasonable to trust them. It must not be hidden; it must be readily observable to anyone who cares to look. These requirements are met by the conduct of moral authorities, which is exemplary in the area of life where their authority holds.

The trust placed in moral authorities is warranted, therefore, by the way they live. They are placed in authority by others because they have shown how to live well according to a particular ideal of a good life. Their authority derives from the success of their lives. They show to those interested that their ideal of a good life is indeed good, that it is possible to live that way and succeed, and so they stand as examples to those who want to live that way. The requirement that the conduct of moral authorities must be exemplary bridges the gap between being a moral authority and being accepted as such. Articulateness alone is insufficient for this because it is unclear whether verbal facility is evidence of knowledge, commitment, and reflectiveness or merely of rhetorical talent. But if the life and conduct of putative moral authorities are of a piece with the moral vision they articulate, then they demonstrate in the most convincing way possible that they mean what they say, that it is reasonable to trust them, and that they are moral authorities indeed.

It is an implication of this way of understanding moral authorities that they do not set themselves up as such, but rather are discovered. They are found to be conspicuous successes at living according to their ideal of a good life, and that is why authority is attributed to them. The possession of moral authority, however, is only an unintended by-product of their conduct, not its goal. What primarily matters to them is living what they regard as a good life. That is and must continue to be the true center of their conduct. If others turn to them for help, decency and goodwill prompts them to try to give it. Their ability to help, however, is contingent on their lives remaining exemplary. It would undermine that very ability to use it in a way that would interfere with living as they have been. The exercise of moral authority, therefore, must always be a subordinate activity for those who genuinely possess it.

The point, of course, is not that moral authorities must be self-centered, but rather that they must be centered on living according to their ideal of a good life. If it is a reasonable one, it will include concern for the well-being of others. But the nature of that concern will not entail imparting a vision to them or teaching them how to resolve the complexities they face; it will not be didactic or pedagogical. It will involve interacting with them in the ways appropriate to the ideal of a good life. That there are other similarly engaged people who see their conspicuous success, and therefore recognize them as moral authorities, may often come to those so recognized as a surprising and unsought honor. It may also come as a burden because it may interfere with living the life they want and enjoy. This is probably part of the reason moral authorities seem often reluctant, distant, and somewhat removed to those who turn to them. In any case, it will perhaps be obvious why genuine moral authorities do not aim to impose their will on others and why they are likely to find their status an embarrassment of riches.

A further implication of the present account is that moral authorities are not exceptional figures who are hard to find, but familiar people often encountered in everyday life. If the knowledge, commitment, reflectiveness, articulateness, and exemplary conduct were thought of in absolutistic terms approaching perfection, then moral authorities would indeed be rare. But this is not how they should be regarded. Being a moral authority is a relation that holds between individuals. Moral authorities, therefore, are such for particular persons. Their authority derives from the possession of the required characteristics to an extent sufficient to enable them to judge better than others who turn to them for help and who distrust their own judgment about the complexities they face. Moral authority relations thus depend on the development of the respective characteristics of the people who participate in them. Moral authorities may themselves need moral authorities, and people who accept a moral authority may themselves be accepted as moral authorities by others. The essential feature of these relations is that a moral authority is regarded as having better judgment about complex situations than the people who turn to them. And having better judgment depends on and is demonstrated by the authorities' possession of the relevant characteristics to a high enough degree that they can help those who cannot help themselves. The possession of the characteristics, however, is always a matter of degree, and that is why a person who is a moral authority in one context may be in need of moral authority in another context. The determining factor is whether people possess the characteristics to a sufficient degree to resolve the complexities they face when the conventions of their moral tradition do not provide clear guidance.

One last implication of the account of moral authority remains to be made explicit. The possibility of being an accepted moral authority presupposes allegiance to a shared ideal of a good life and to a moral tradition upon which living according to that ideal depends. A moral authority excels at living in the way those who accept it want to live. Their shared allegiance provides participants in moral authority relations with an objective standard of evaluation: that set by the ideal of a good life. Moral authorities excel because they approximate it more closely than others. That is what makes them authorities, and not that they are charismatic, possess the trappings of status, command a large audience, or speak powerfully.

2.5 Justification

The preceding account was meant to provide two considerations that jointly require that moral authorities be recognized by all morally acceptable ideals of a good life. The first concerns the necessity of recognizing the possibility of moral authority. This is a logical requirement, and it follows from understanding the nature of good lives and of moral authority.[19] Those who commit themselves to living according to some ideal of a good life thereby commit themselves to recognizing that ideal as an objective standard with reference to which both their own conduct and that of others who share their commitment could be compared and evaluated. The standard is objective in the sense that how closely lives and conduct approximate it is a factual question whose answer is independent of what anyone thinks, feels, hopes, or fears. The standard is not objective in the sense that any reasonable person would have to accept it. There are many reasonable ideals of a good life, and people can accept or reject any of them without violating reason or objectivity. What cannot be done without the loss of reason and objectivity is to make a commitment to a particular ideal and then refuse to recognize it as a standard of moral evaluation that applies to all those who are similarly committed.

It follows from this that other people's lives and conduct may approximate the standard more closely than the agents' own. Others may have done better than they have done themselves at the most important endeavor of their lives, which is to make them good. If it is accepted further that at least some of those who have done better have done so deservedly, through their personal excellence and efforts, and not undeservedly, through injustice or luck, then reasonable people will see them as possible moral authorities from whom they may be able to learn how they themselves could do better.

The second consideration is that people's acceptance of moral authority is not just an abstract possibility, but a pressing practical need. For as a matter of moral psychology, no longer of logic, people are often confronted with complexities in trying to live according to their ideal of a good life, but they find themselves unable to resolve them. These complexities arise because the conventions of their moral tradition provide inadequate guidance about how they should respond in some particular situation. They recognize that their intuitive responses have become unreliable, but they do not know how to find a reliable response because they are wanting in knowledge, commitment, or reflectiveness. This is the situation in which people feel the need to rely on the judgment of others. If they are reasonable, they will rely on those whose lives and conduct are better than their own and who therefore can be supposed to have to a greater extent the characteristics they themselves lack. If they receive the help they need because the people to whom they turn have the characteristics that make it possible to provide it, then it is justified to accept them as moral authorities, with all that such acceptance entails.

This justification is in no way committed to the infallibility of moral authorities. Moral authorities are legitimate if they possess the required characteristics. It is reasonable to accept them as moral authorities if their characteristics enable them to make more reliable judgments about complex situations than the people for whom they count as authorities. This does not mean that their judgments could not be mistaken; it means only that they are less likely to be mistaken than the judgments of those who lack their characteristics. There are three different ways in which moral authorities may be mistaken.

The first is that they may be insufficiently informed about or attentive to the complex situations they are called upon to judge. These failings may or may not be culpable. They may lack the relevant information because they have been lied to or because they have not bothered to look. Similarly, their lack of attention may be the result of fatigue caused by the great demands placed on them, or it may be due to laziness and indifference. Assume, however, that they do not fail in these ways, that they are informed and attentive.

They may fail in a second way if their development of the required characteristics is unequal to the task at hand. Their knowledge, commitment, reflectiveness, conduct, articulateness, and the judgments based on them are, to be sure, better than those of the people who rely on them, but they are not sufficiently better to make their judgments reliable. They judge in good faith and as well as they can, but that is still not good enough. If they had developed the characteristics to a greater extent, they could make better judgments, but having developed them insufficiently, whether culpably or otherwise, they cannot. But even if their characteristics are adequate and they do not fail on their account, they may still fail for another reason.

The third kind of failure stems from the defects of the moral tradition within which they are accepted as legitimate authorities. Their judgments are good in mediating between the moral vision of their tradition and complex cases, but the tradition is morally defective. They judge well how complexities could be resolved in conformity with the tradition, but they end up making a mistaken moral judgment because in some respects their tradition is morally unacceptable. Confucius may be right that his tradition requires caring about the ceremony and not about the sheep, but he and his tradition may still be wrong to sacrifice sheep. And the same goes for the *sophrons* and their tradition.

Suppose, however, that there is no reason to think some moral authorities are defective in any of these ways, that their lives and conduct are exemplary, and that the judgments they have made seem to be reliable. There are then good reasons to recognize them as moral authorities and to rely on their judgments when the complexities of some situation make people distrust their own.

It needs to be added as a reminder that although legitimate moral authorities always judge from the point of view of their moral tradition, it is by no means the case that their judgments must always reflect the conventions of their tradition. Moral authorities are bound to be traditional because they bring the fundamental moral vision of their tradition to the judgment of complex situations. But they need not be conventional because they may think that some conventions prevailing in their tradition are defective expressions of the fundamental vision. Their judgments then serve the direct purpose of resolving the complexities they face as well as the more indirect purpose of criticizing and trying to remedy the defective conventions of their moral tradition.

2.6 Our Moral Authorities

If the foregoing account is correct, then we, in our pluralistic society, should also have moral authorities. But where are they? Who are our *sophrons*? Where is our Confucius? We do have moral authorities; they are easy to find if we look for them in the right place and with the right expectations; but we are reluctant to call them moral authorities. This reluctance stems from the failure to see that our moral authorities are cast in a different mold than they used to be. Our expectation is that moral authorities will conform to a model that held in the past. Our moral outlook, however, has undergone—is undergoing—deep changes, and the old model has so little attraction for us that even if we could find moral authorities that exemplify it, we would not be willing to accept them.

According to the old model, a moral authority may be a lawgiver, like Moses or Solon; or a charismatic moral teacher, like the Buddha or Jesus; or a prophet who rails against our evil ways, like Jeremiah, Savanarola, or Luther; or those willing to die for what they believe is right, like Socrates, many Christian saints, or Simone Weil. We distrust them one and all because we do not share their amazing certainty that they have privileged access to the truth. We respect and perhaps admire the strength of their convictions, but we believe, in our pluralistic age, that there are many moral truths, many fine moral traditions, and many reasonable ideals of a good life. As a result, we do not accept the pronouncements of moral authorities that aim to transcend time, place, and context and speak universal truths that hold good for everyone. We do not want to have the law laid down for us, we do not want to be sheep in a flock, we do not want to be shown The Way, we do not want to be railed at, and we have a healthy skepticism of martyrdom.

In holding these perfectly reasonable attitudes, however, we are repudiating not moral authority but the old model of it. We distrust moral authority because our expectation of what it is has been formed by the old model. But if the argument that has been given is right, we need moral authorities because the complexities of our lives and the infirmities of our judgments make it reasonable to turn to them for help, provided they indeed have the characteristics that make them legitimate.

If this is acknowledged, then the question where moral authorities may be found must be answered. Answering it is not hard if we are not handicapped by the wrong expectation shaped by the old model. Moral authorities are like you and me, except better enough to help us through our confusions. They are our influential teachers, close older friends, exemplary colleagues, dispassionate leaders of our field, comrades who have proved themselves in the struggles we now have, experienced practitioners of our craft—generally speaking, they are people who inhabit our context and whose knowledge, commitment, reflectiveness, articulateness, and exemplary conduct make it likely that they can help us if we turn to them for advice about the moral dimension of our shared activity. These are the moral authorities in our pluralistic society, our *sophrons*.

3/

Decency

Practice the civilities, the lesser duties of life.

JANE AUSTEN, *Sense and Sensibility*

3.1 Decency as a Personal Excellence

It is not obvious that decency is admirable. If understood in a narrow sense, it smacks of a puritanical attitude to sex. In a wider sense, it has to do with proper behavior. Propriety, however, seems to be only a superficial feature of conduct. In serious evaluations inner processes—reflection and motivation—count for much and appearances matter little. Decency thus tends to be assimilated either to politeness, which trivializes it, or to a silly view of sex that has been deservedly consigned to history. If this were all, it would be perverse to admire decency as a personal excellence. But this is not all. Decency can be a deep and serious attitude to life and conduct, and then it is an admirable achievement. Or so it will be argued.

The *OED* (1961) gives as the central current meaning of decency, "Propriety of behaviour or demeanour; due regard to what is becoming; conformity (in behaviour, speech, or action) to the standard of propriety or good taste." The unabridged *Random House Dictionary* (1987) virtually repeats this definition. Good taste inclines decency toward shallowness, but propriety leaves open the nature of the standard for which decency requires having due regard. If the standard is one of politeness, decency *is* shallow. But the standard may be of justice, honesty, or compassion, and that permits taking decency seriously. The decency of a judge toward someone accused of a crime, of a politician toward an embarrassing indiscretion in the past of an opponent, or of a donor toward the needy often involves important matters. Decency, therefore, need not be shallow.

The sense in which decency is a personal excellence is character-ized by a general attitude toward others in one's society. It concerns people with whom one has no close relationship. The attitude is formed of goodwill, fairness, helpfulness, and giving others the bene-fit of the doubt—a kind of low-level generalized benevolence. It is what people usually have in mind when they speak of common de-cency: a predisposition to wish well for others in one's impersonal en-counters with them. Decency, in this sense, obviously benefits others; equally obviously, a society is better off if decency in it is widespread. But it is perhaps less obvious that people benefit from their own de-cency because it is good to live in the kind of harmony with their soci-ety that decency fosters. If such harmony exists, people on the whole approve of the prevailing arrangements, and that is why they are fa-vorably predisposed toward their fellow citizens, with whom they join in sustaining these arrangements. Decency is thus the opposite of alienation. Naturally, decency can be misplaced. If it is unreasonable to regard the prevailing arrangements in one's society favorably, then decency is folly, not a personal excellence.

Consider, by way of contrast, a society from which decency has disappeared, as in this description of Stalinist Russia:

> Wherever you looked, in all our institutions, in all our homes, *skloka* was brewing. *Skloka* is a phenomenon born of our social order, an entirely new term and concept, not to be translated into any language of the civilized world. It is hard to define. It stands for base, trivial hostility, unconscionable spite breeding pretty intrigues, the vicious pitting of one clique against an-other. It thrives on calumny, informing, spying, scheming, slan-der, the igniting of base passions. Taut nerves and weakening morals allow one individual or group rabidly to hate another individual or group. *Skloka* is natural for people who have been incited to attack one another, who have been bestial by desper-ation, who have been driven to the wall.[1]

The value of decency is that it rules out *skloka* and it makes people feel at home in their society. Decency, however, may be deeper still than benevolence toward fellow citizens and allegiance to one's soci-ety. It may not be merely an outward manifestation, but also an in-ward trait constitutive of one's character and thus a dominant feature of one's moral identity. When it has this inward dimension, it becomes the personal excellence that is the subject of this chapter. That is the kind of decency (from now on simply decency) that is a deep and serious attitude to life and conduct.

3.2 Civic Friendship

Aristotle gives an account of an important aspect of decency that his translators call *civic friendship*.[2] Aristotle says, "Community depends on friendship; and when there is enmity instead of friendship, men will not even share the same path."[3] Aristotle understands by *philia*, which is translated as friendship, a much broader range of relationships than what we commonly include under the heading of friendship. He regards the relationships between parents and children, brothers and sisters, married couples, business partners, coreligionists, political allies, and so forth as possible forms of friendship.

> The central idea contained in *philia* is that of doing well by someone for his own sake, out of concern for *him* (and not, or not merely, out of concern for oneself). If this is right, then the different forms of *philia* . . . could be viewed as just different contexts and circumstances in which this kind of mutual well-doing can arise. . . . *Philia*, taken most generally, is any relationship characterized by mutual liking . . . that is, by mutual well-wishing and well-doing out of concern with one another.[4]

This well-wishing and well-doing is benevolently motivated, but it is important to be clear that benevolence need not be the sole motive of friends. The recognition that a friend wants something is a sufficient reason for trying to provide it. But friends may also be moved by their interest in sustaining the friendship. Friendship involves caring about friends for their own sake, but this is compatible with caring for one's own sake as well.

Aristotle distinguishes among character, pleasure, and advantage friendship. Character friendship is based on the mutual recognition of two friends that the other possesses some virtue. The more virtues the friends possess, the more perfect their friendship is. This kind of friendship is rare because few people possess the required virtues. Pleasure and advantage friendships are more frequent and less perfect because the pleasure or the advantage the friends derive from one another is produced not necessarily by their virtues, but by morally neutral qualities, such as physical attractiveness, complementary skills, or a talent for business.

Civic friendship is a form of advantage friendship. It is based on the advantage fellow members of a society derive from their association. As Aristotle says: "It is for the sake of advantage that the political community too seems both to have come together originally and to endure, for that is what legislators aim at, and they call just that which is to the common advantage. . . . The political community aims not at present advantage but at what is advantageous for life as a whole."[5] Civic friendship, then, is the relationship that members of a good or not-so-bad society have toward one another.

It is an advantageous relationship because it is essential to having a society in which citizens can live what they regard as good lives. The motivation for civic friendship is thus a mixture of benevolence and self-interest. Civic friends are genuinely benevolent: they habitually, spontaneously wish and do well for others. But self-interest also plays a role because they expect others to treat them similarly. In their society this expectation is reliably met, so that citizens are well disposed toward one another. The well-being of the society prompts these attitudes, and the attitudes, in turn, reinforce the society. But nobody plans that this should be so. That it happens is a consequence of political arrangements that suit the citizens because they can articulate and satisfy their desires in the prevailing framework.

Like all forms of friendship, civic friendship is reciprocal, but the reciprocity is unlike what exists in the other forms. In civic friendship it is not expected that the recipients of one's benevolence will immediately or even ever return the benefits conferred on them. Yet there is an expectation of return. Individual acts of civic friendship create a fund of goodwill from which the depositors can draw. Just as they are benevolent to strangers and passing acquaintances recognized to be fellow members, so they count on being benevolently treated by them.

Aristotle expresses this by contrasting two types of advantage friendships: "The *legal* type is on fixed terms; its purely commercial variety is on the basis of immediate payment; while the more liberal variety allows time but stipulates for a definite *quid pro quo*. In this variety the debt is clear and not ambiguous, but in the postponement it contains an element of friendliness. . . . The *moral* type is not on fixed terms; it makes a gift, or does whatever it does, as to a friend; but one expects to receive as much or more, as having not given but lent."[6] Civic friendship is this latter, moral type.

One reason for the difference in reciprocity between civic friendship and character or pleasure friendship is that the former is considerably more impersonal than the latter two. Civic friendship holds between fellow citizens, provided they have not disqualified themselves from it by *skloka*. So the personal qualities of civic friends are much less important than the personal qualities of character or pleasure friends. Part of the reason for this is that the encounters between civic friends are often casual and may not be repeated. They do not require the participants to know one another even superficially. Nor is it necessary that if they know the recipients of their benevolence, they should like them personally. The identity of the recipient is irrelevant; any citizen would normally qualify. This is why civic friendship is impersonal and why it is unimportant that the advantage it yields should be returned to the same person who has benefited the recipient.

Aristotle's distinction between legal and moral advantage friendship has the further significance that moral advantage friendship—civic friendship—goes beyond the claims of justice. In legal advantage friendships people trust one another because experience has convinced them of their mutual rectitude. They thus no longer exact a punctilious discharge of contractual obligations. They still expect advantage from their relationship, but the accounting is informal, the books need to be balanced only in the long run. In civic friendship, however, one "makes a gift, or does whatever [one] does, as to a friend." The conduct of civic friends is governed not by legal rules but by mutual benevolence. As Aristotle puts it, "Friendship seems to hold states together, and lawgivers to care more for it than for justice; ... when men are friends they have no need for justice, while when they are just they need friendship as well."[7] The reason behind this is that since people tend not to give others what they deserve when it conflicts with their own interests, it is necessary to have a legal system with explicit rules, judges, and enforcement. But the legal system is needed only because people do not always regard others in the spirit of friendship. If they did, they would be guided by benevolence to be generous in benefiting and compassionate in harming others, rather than by justice to give them no more or no less than they deserve. This is why if people were friends, they would have no need of justice.

Civic friendship is an important aspect of decency, but it is only an aspect. If we note the awkwardness of describing what Aristotle has in mind as a kind of friendship, it becomes apparent why decency requires more. Character and pleasure friendships are intimate relationships. Civic friendship requires the characterization of people as friends who do not, or barely, know one another and who have no lasting relationship. How could total strangers thrown together in casual encounters—in queues, airplanes, routine commercial dealings, waiting rooms—be described as friends? The difficulty is not that *philia* is imperfectly translated as friendship. Rather, the mutual benevolence that the fellow citizens of a society may feel is left unexplained. What is their mutual benevolence based on?

The Aristotelian answer is framed in terms of advantage. Civic friendship is based on the recognition of fellow citizens that by wishing and doing well for one another, they maintain the fabric of their society, and thus one condition of good lives for themselves and others is secured. But this attributes far too much calculation and reflection to ordinary people. It is implausible to suppose that the spontaneous goodwill, casual helpfulness, and trusting friendliness of people is the result of a ratiocinative process that yields the conclusion of a practical syllogism. People help each other because one needs it and the other can provide it without too much trouble. They are not thinking of the fabric of their society or of their own long-range goals. If they think at all, it is about how best to help. Nor is it that the lack of deeper thought at the time of action is dispensable because of past thought. It requires much greater theoretical interest than most people normally have to trace the implications of their conduct in their relatively narrow circumstances for their society as a whole. Who thinks this way when giving a ride to a stranded motorist, helping an old lady with her bags, or chatting about the weather with a bank teller? It is true that there is moral education in the background, but it consists in learning how to act, not the basis for acting that way. To say that benevolence is the basis is not enough because it leaves unexplained why benevolence, rather than justice, self-interest, ideology, or reputation, should motivate people. In other words, the Aristotelian account explains why the benevolence of civic friendship needs to be part of decency, but it does not explain what it is that predisposes people to treat their civic friends benevolently rather than in some other way. For that explanation, however, we can turn to Hume.

3.3 Sympathy and Custom

The details of Hume's general moral theory need not detain us. He believes that moral judgments are based on feelings of approval and disapproval. What is approved is good because it gives pleasure, and what is disapproved is bad because it causes pain. The objects of approval and disapproval are the virtues and vices, which manifest themselves in actions. Some virtues are natural because they are inborn. Others are artificial because they are habits that need to be instilled and cultivated. The paradigmatic natural virtue is benevolence. Being natural, it is possessed by all human beings. But all natural virtues have a common foundation in a deeper, more basic human characteristic: sympathy. Sympathy is thus the foundation of Hume's moral theory.[8]

Sympathy, according to Hume, involves the transference of a feeling from one person to another. We observe the behavior of others, infer what feelings motivate them, and come to have the feelings ourselves. "When any affection is infus'd by sympathy, it is first known only by its effects, and by those external signs of countenance and conversation, which convey an idea of it. This idea . . . acquires such a degree of force and vivacity, as to become the passion itself."[9] We see others crying, we infer that they are in distress, and we become to some extent distressed ourselves. The extent depends on the resemblance, contiguity, and causal nexus that holds between us. The more we resemble, the more contiguous we are, the closer is our causal nexus and the more we sympathize with them.

Sympathy is part of the natural workings of the mind, so it is involuntary: it consists in having to some extent the same feeling as the object of our sympathy has. Sympathy is thus neither pity nor identification that involves putting oneself in the place of another. It is actually having the feelings others have. Sympathy has moral force because we are not indifferent to the feelings of others. Some are agreeable and give pleasure, others are disagreeable and give pain. Moral judgments derive from the pleasure and pain sympathy causes us to experience.

It would be premature, however, to conclude that the benevolence of civic friendship is based on sympathy, because there are two conspicuous gaps in Hume's account as it stands. First, no reason has so far been given to suppose that sympathy motivates action. Why would the transferred feelings of others make us do anything about them? Say your marriage has fallen apart and you are sad; I observe the outward signs on your countenance and sympathize; I too become at least a little sad. But that is perfectly consistent with my doing nothing about your plight. If Hume had offered sympathy merely as an account of how we come to share the feelings of others, there would be no need to explain how it leads to action. But he means sympathy to be the basic motivation for cultivating and exercising the natural virtues, and that demands action. There is as yet no explanation of the link between sympathy and action.

The second gap in Hume's account is between sympathy and benevolence. Suppose it is true that in appropriate circumstances we naturally share to some extent the feelings of others. But why would that lead us to feel benevolent toward them? Other people may occasion some of our agreeable and disagreeable feelings, and we like the first and dislike the second. This, however, may lead us to shun them if they produce disagreeable feelings in us or if our envy of their agreeable feelings gives us more pain than the agreeable ones give us pleasure. Benevolence involves wishing others well and benefiting them, but sympathy, in Hume's sense, does not yet explain why we would wish and do that.

Both these gaps are closed by Hume's account of the role of reason in sympathy. His central idea is, first, that "human nature being compos'd of two principal parts, which are requisite in all its actions, the affections and understanding; 'tis certain, that the blind motions of the former, without the direction of the latter, incapacitate man for society," and second, that "reason alone can never produce any action, or give rise to volition."[10] Feelings and reason are thus both necessary for action: feelings motivate action, reason directs feelings and actions. Without feelings there would be no actions; without reason actions would not achieve their goal.

Feelings, however, lead to action only if they are accompanied by desires, and that may not happen. "Pride and humility are pure emotions in the soul, unattended with any desire, and not immediately exciting us to action. But love and hatred are not compleated within themselves . . . but carry the mind farther. Love is always followed by a desire . . . as hatred produces a desire."[11] When a feeling is accompanied by desire, it motivates action. Reason is needed in order to achieve both the immediate goal of the action, which is to satisfy the desire, and the more distant but no less important goal to coordinate the satisfaction of various desires over time. Reason directs feelings, desires, and actions by identifying objects that satisfy the desires, by finding the appropriate means of obtaining these objects, and by controlling the feelings and desires with a view of achieving the maximal satisfaction of various desires over time.

The gaps in Hume's account between sympathy, on the one hand, and actions and benevolence, on the other, are closed by his account of how reason controls feelings and desires. Feelings elicited by our own circumstances are called by Hume *original*; those elicited by sympathy with others are *sympathetic*. Some of these original and sympathetic feelings are accompanied by desires and lead to action. This is obviously the case with the original feelings of love and hatred. And it is also the case with sympathetic feelings *if* the people with whom we sympathize are intimately connected to us. The joy or sadness of someone we love will not only make us feel joy or sadness but also lead us to celebrate and congratulate or commiserate and console. But this affects only a very small circle of people. "Sympathy with persons remote from us [is] much fainter than with persons near and continuous," and "were we to remain constantly in that position and point of view, which is peculiar to ourselves," we would not respond to "persons who are in a situation different from us."[12] For we are so constituted that "our strongest attention is confin'd to ourselves; our next is extended to our relations and acquaintances; and it is only the weakest which reaches strangers and indifferent persons." As a result, "our natural uncultivated ideas of morality, instead of providing a remedy for the partiality of our affections do rather conform themselves to that partiality, and give it additional force and influence."[13] This is where "nature provides a remedy . . . for what is irregular and incommodious in the affections," through the correction of feelings and desires by reason.[14]

Reason corrects the partiality of our feelings and desires because we "from early education in society, have become sensible of the infinite advantages that result from it." The protection of these advantages "can be done after no other manner, than by a convention enter'd into by all members of the society. . . . By this means . . . the passions are restrained in their partial and contradictory motions. . . . Instead of departing from our interests, or from that of our nearest friends . . . we cannot better consult both these interests than by such a convention; because it is by that means we maintain society, which is so necessary to their well-being and subsistence, as well as to our own."[15]

We still need to know, however, *how* reason corrects feelings and desires and thus closes the gap between sympathy and benevolence and action. Hume's answer is that reason does this by means of custom, which is "a convention enter'd into by all members of the society."[16] It takes the form of generally approved and widely practiced patterns of action prevailing in a society. These customary patterns become conventional, and they are regarded as norms of action. They establish what kind of conduct is appropriate. Custom changes, but slowly. Rapid change is dangerous, for it undermines the many ways in which people treat others and expect others to treat them. If these expectations are not met, *skloka* may take the place of custom, or some charismatic figure may step in and impose its will in place of the conventional practices that have disintegrated. Custom is greatly preferable to either option because it is a civilizing and predictable force. "Custom," says Hume, "is the great guide of human life."[17] But how does custom guide reason in correcting feelings and desires and overcoming the partiality of sympathy?

Hume says, "The minds of all men are similar in their feelings and operations, nor can anyone be actuated by any affection, of which others are not, in some degree susceptible."[18] Part of this similarity is that we all start with limited sympathy. "It is wisely ordained by nature, that private connexions should commonly prevail over universal views and considerations; otherwise our affections and actions would be dissipated and lost, for want of a proper limited object."[19] The role of custom is to correct limited sympathy and make it extend beyond its natural sphere, which includes only oneself and a few others, and embrace all the people who live in one's society and are following the same conventions. The reason for doing so, as we have seen, is that "by this means . . . the passions are restrained in their partial and contradictory motions. . . . Instead of departing from our interests, or from that of our nearest friends . . . we cannot better consult these interests, than by such a convention; because it is by that means that we maintain society, which is so necessary to their well-being and subsistence, as well as to our own."[20]

These conventions establish a language of conduct. They enable those who share them to draw common distinctions between good and bad, right and wrong, blameworthy and excusable, supererogatory and dutiful, pleasing and offensive, and so forth. They provide a common way of evaluating people, institutions, and actions. Those who follow the same conventions come to live and act according to them and thus come to feel allegiance to one another and to the society in which the conventions, and thus their ways of life, are maintained. They see the conventions as guides to living a good life, not as rules that stand in the way. This is why it is reasonable to extend limited sympathy beyond sharing the feelings of casual acquaintances and strangers to feeling and acting benevolently toward them. But this extension is still limited, not universal, because its outer limits are set by customary, but socially variable, conventions.

By way of summing up the progress made toward understanding decency, we should note the distinction between its outward and inward aspects. Aristotle's account of civic friendship is of its outward aspect. It describes that happy state of a society in which fellow citizens wish and do well for one another in their casual, impersonal encounters. They share a benevolent disposition that is routinely expressed in action. This account, however, must be supplemented because it leaves unexplained the inner processes that lead fellow citizens to act benevolently toward one another. Hume's account of sympathy, reason, and custom provides that explanation by focusing on the inward aspect of decency. Benevolence is based on sympathy, which is part of the natural working of the human mind. We tend to feel to some extent what we observe others feeling. In our own case and in the cases of our intimates, original and sympathetic feelings naturally spur us to benevolent action. But our benevolence is limited because it extends only to a narrow circle. Reason corrects feelings and extends the limits of benevolence by bringing us to understand the great advantages of living in a society in which benevolence is sufficiently widespread to include most citizens. Reason works by way of the customary conventions of a society. The conventions define the forms that benevolence should take, unite a people by shared habits and judgments, provide an important part of their identity, and make life in that society predictable, secure, and pleasant. That is why custom is the great guide of human life.

These are the advantages Aristotle ascribes to civic friendship, Hume to benevolence based on sympathy and custom, and the present discussion to a conception of decency that combines Aristotle's account of its outward aspect and Hume's account of its inward aspect. Decency, thus understood, is of course an ideal, not a description of any person or society. Actual people and societies fall more or less short of it. But the ideal is worth pursuing because it makes life better.

We are, however, not yet in the position to redeem the earlier promise and show the depth and seriousness of decency as an attitude to life and conduct. For all that has been said, decency may still be no more than a superficial element in the lives of reasonable people. They may feel and act benevolently toward their fellow citizens, but their important concerns may lie elsewhere: in intimate relationships, personal projects, creative endeavors, political programs, religious commitments, and so forth. In order to make good on the promise, we need to show that decency can be just as important and reasonable a feature of people's lives as these other concerns. Reflection on Edith Wharton's great novel, *The Age of Innocence*, will make that possible.[21]

3.4 A Pair of Exemplary Lives

The milieu of the novel is upper-middle-class society in New York during the last decades of the nineteenth century. The chief characters are Newland Archer and Countess Olenska. Archer is a highly respected member of this society, a lawyer, engaged to May Welland, an equally respected young woman. Countess Olenska was born and raised in this setting, but marriage to a Polish count took her to Europe, where she and her husband lived for many years. At the beginning of the novel Countess Olenska returns to New York to seek the protection and comfort of her family and society, for she has left her corrupt husband and intends to divorce him. She is warmly received, but it is made clear to her that divorce is not countenanced by the prevailing conventions. The person who communicates this to her is Archer, who is acting both as a lawyer for her family and as a representative of their society. He explains to her in a succession of meetings that her intended divorce is contrary to the conventions of New York society, that it would weaken their society and hurt her family and friends. She ought, therefore, to give up the idea. She listens to him, upon reflection accepts the justification he offers, and abandons the idea of divorce.

As it happens, however, in the course of their several encounters, during which they discuss matters that are normally left unsaid, Archer and Countess Olenska fall in love. Having accepted the case against divorce, she is, of course, not free to marry him. He, being engaged to May Welland, is similarly constrained. This time, however, it is Archer who would go against the conventions of their society, and it is Countess Olenska who insists that the case he had made to her still holds. They give each other up, opt for a life of decency, and accept that their love is impossible. Countess Olenska returns to Europe, where she lives out her life in dignified and lonely separation from her corrupt husband. Archer remains in New York and grows old as an exemplary husband, father, lawyer, and pillar of society.

There are three increasingly adequate interpretations of this simple story. According to the first, decency forbids Countess Olenska's divorce. There is a conflict between decency and a good life, and opting for decency, as she does, calls for a sacrifice. The following conversation between Archer and Countess Olenska may be thought to support this interpretation. She says, "I want to cast off my old life, to become just like everybody else here." And again, "I want to be free, I want to wipe out all the past." She reminds Archer, "You know my husband—my life with him?" "In this country are such things tolerated? I'm a Protestant—our church does not forbid divorce in such cases." He replies, "New York society is a very small world . . . it's ruled by . . . rather old-fashioned ideas. . . . Our ideas about marriage and divorce are particularly old-fashioned. Our legislature favours divorce—our social customs don't." She asks, "But my freedom—is that nothing?" And he says, "The individual, in such cases, is nearly always sacrificed to what is supposed to be the collective interest: people cling to any convention that keeps the family together. . . . It is my business, you know . . . to help you see these things as people who are fondest of you see them . . . all your friends here and relations: if I didn't show you honestly how they judge such questions, it wouldn't be fair of me." She considers the case he put and after a time acquiesces: "Very well; I will do what you wish."[22]

Archer's case and Countess Olenska's submission strike our modern sensibility as outrageous. Here is an admittedly injured woman, wishing to free herself from an ugly marriage, and Archer, that plenipotentiary of decency, persuades her otherwise. We want to urge her to seize the day, be free, go after happiness, and sweep superficial conventions aside. Life is to be lived, not constrained by bloodless conventions. The recognition that this is a misguided response will point the way toward a better understanding of decency.

Well, then, why is it misguided to see this as an obviously mistaken choice of decency, dictated by conventions, over freedom, happiness, and a good life? A distinction between *rule-following* and *character-forming* decency will help with the answer. Rule-following decency is simply to conduct oneself according to the conventions of one's society. It is to do or not to do what the conventions prescribe or prohibit; to behave appropriately, respectably. Rule-following decency is akin to law-abidingness. Knowledge of the relevant prescriptions and actions that conform to them are required and sufficient. This knowledge is not hard to obtain for anyone familiar with the social context. Rule-following decency is all on the surface. What matters is what is done, not why it is done, so rule-following decency can be hypocritical.

Character-forming decency is essentially connected with motivation, with one's reasons for doing what the conventions prescribe. It is to have one's outlook informed by the prevailing conventions and to act according to them because one approves of them. People who are decent in this way accept the conventions, they are shaped by them, their ideals of a good life are inseparable from them, they are comfortable with them, and so they derive part of their identity from them. Character-forming decency, therefore, is deep: it is connected with what people are and want to be. It cannot be hypocritical.

The outrage provoked in modern sensibility by Countess Olenska's decision is misguided because it sees the conflict between decency and a good life as juxtaposing superficial propriety to the deep matter of trying to live a good life. It holds that she was wrong to allow herself to be persuaded by Archer's argument and he was wrong to lead her to it. They colluded in favoring superficiality over depth. The trouble with modern sensibility is that it fails to recognize the significance of the distinction between rule-following and character-forming decency.

Countess Olenska's decision was motivated by character-forming decency. She decided not to seek divorce because it would have violated the prevailing conventions of her society. The reason Archer could persuade her was that she was committed to those conventions, although she did not realize that they prohibited divorce even in cases in which the person seeking it was injured by the marriage. Archer explained to her that this was so. Once Countess Olenska understood that, her conflict was not between superficial propriety and the serious matter of trying to live a good life, but between alternative ideals of a good life. She felt deep allegiance to the society whose conventions prohibited divorce, and she felt similarly deeply that she wanted to be free of her ugly marriage. Her conflict was between what she saw as the good of her society and her own good, and she chose, with Archer's help, the good of her society. If her choice is seen in this light, we may still think it was mistaken, but it would be simpleminded to regard it as outrageous. We do, after all, celebrate people who sacrifice their personal good for social good, as Countess Olenska appears to have done. Modern sensibility prompts this simpleminded response, and that is why it is misguided. Of course, just because Countess Olenska and Archer are not obviously mistaken in favoring social over personal good does not mean that they are not mistaken. Their choice requires justification, and that is what we find when we consider the second interpretation, which is better than the first but still not right.

According to this interpretation, there is a conflict between decency and living a good life, but both Countess Olenska and Archer have strong reasons to opt for decency. If this is understood, the conflict becomes less important and its resolution in favor of decency involves a much smaller sacrifice than it seemed before. After she has made her choice, Countess Olenska and Archer discuss what made her accept his argument. She says, "I felt there was no one . . . who gave me reasons that I understood for doing what at first seemed so hard and—unnecessary. The very good people didn't convince me; I felt they'd never been tempted. But you knew; you understood; you have felt the outside tugging at one with all its golden hands—and yet you hated the things it asks of one; you hated happiness bought by disloyalty and cruelty and indifference. That was what I'd never known before—and it is better than anything I've known."[23]

The essential point that Archer made and Countess Olenska accepted was that since she regards New York society as better than anything she had known, it has a claim on her allegiance. Its conventions prohibit divorce; therefore, she ought not to seek it. Reason and many of her feelings favor this conclusion. She was born and raised in that society and imbibed its conventions from the cradle on. When she left and marriage took her to another society, she judged her husband and his society corrupt according to the conventions in which she was raised. These conventions define her limits, not consciously or intellectually, by making her feel that certain ways of living and acting are unthinkable. As an observer says of her, "If you are an American of *her* kind . . . things that are accepted in certain societies, or at least put up with as part of the general give-and-take—become unthinkable, simply unthinkable."[24] When she finds her husband following these ways as readily as she finds them unthinkable, she thinks he is corrupt, feels soiled, and leaves him. And she leaves him for her own people, her family and society, for the conventional milieu that has formed her. "New York simply meant peace and freedom to me: it was coming home. And I was so happy at being among my own people that everyone I met seemed kind and good, and glad to see me."[25] This is how many feelings prompt her decision. For how could she opt for divorce and show "disloyalty and cruelty and indifference" to her own people, whose conventions she shares and who have been so "kind and good" to her?

Yet the force of these feelings alone is not strong enough to make her give up divorce because she has feelings pulling also in the other direction. As strongly as she feels allegiance to New York society, so she feels revolted by her husband's society. One prohibits divorce, the other demands it. These conflicting feelings make her confused, indecisive, and in need of advice. Reason enters through Archer, who, at this stage, acts as her adviser. What qualifies Archer to be an adviser is the fact that his conduct up to this point, before he falters, is exemplary, and he is reflective and articulate about the system of conventions he accepts. He embodies character-forming decency. He has compared New York society with others and found it better. And he can not only make reliable judgments but also explain the reasons for his judgments. That is just what he does to Countess Olenska.

Seen in this light, the conflict between decency and a good life is softened. The society to which allegiance is supposed to be a duty can no longer be thought of as upholding a system of trivial and old-fashioned conventions that stand in the way of freedom, happiness, and good lives. Archer's justification shows that there is no sharp conflict between character-forming decency and living a good life. Countess Olenska's ideal of a good life is inseparably connected with living according to the conventions of the society that has formed her. These conventions define for her what a good life is. Divorce is at once contrary to it and something she wishes. What Archer shows her is that the conflict she faces is not between decency and a good life, but between a deeply and a superficially considered ideal of a good life. The superficial ideal is connected with getting what she wants now; the shoe pinches, and she wants to take it off. Wanting that, viewed in isolation from her whole life and its context, is reasonable and understandable. The deeper view, however, moves beyond immediate satisfaction and places the conflict in the perspective of her whole life. Of course, divorce would make her life better now, but it would also alienate her from her society, belonging to which is a condition of a good life for her. It would also involve a signal act of disloyalty to those who were good to her when she turned to them for help. It would, therefore, be impossible for her to have a good life if she were to divorce. So her choice is not between decency and a good life, but between the possibility of a short-term relief from her misfortune and the possibility of a good life in the long run. This is what Archer leads her to see, and this is why both reason and the balance of feelings prompt her to give up the idea of divorce.

We are, however, in the hands of a master, and Wharton's vision is too cool, too ironic, too understanding of human weakness to allow us to see Archer as the paragon he has so far appeared to be. In the course of all that advising and earnest conversation, he falls in love with Countess Olenska and she with him. But it is Archer now who is ready to go against the conventions in the name of their love. He wants her to divorce, and he is willing to break up his engagement, so that he and Countess Olenska could marry and, presumably, live happily ever after. Archer's feelings grew too strong, and they carried him away. The case he has made to Countess Olenska still holds, but he ignores it. If he were to reflect, he would realize that he is proposing to violate his own commitments, but in the grip of his feelings, he does not reflect. This time, however, Countess Olenska does for him what he previously did for her.

Archer tells her of his love, and she says, "Ah, my poor Newland— I suppose this had to be. But it doesn't in the least alter things." Archer replies, "It alters the whole world for me." Countess Olenska then says, "No, no—it mustn't, it can't. You are engaged to May Welland; and I am married." But he does not accept it. "He reddened under the retort, but kept his eyes on her. 'May is ready to give me up.' " "What!" she says, "Three days after you've entreated her on your knees to hasten your marriage?" But, he says, the lawyer coming to the fore, "she's refused; that gives me the right—." And to that, Countess Olenska has two highly significant rejoinders. The first is about Archer's appeal to his rights: "Ah, you've taught me what an ugly word that is."[26] Why is *right* an ugly word? Given their system of conventions, Countess Olenska has a right to divorce, and Archer explained to her why she should not exact that right. Archer has a right to break his engagement, and Countess Olenska explains to him why he should not take advantage of it. A right is a claim against others. This claim may or may not be cashed in. People may have a right to commit suicide, have an abortion, and see pornographic movies. But that is not an invitation to engage in these activities. There is a question of when rights should be acted on. What Countess Olenska is saying is that they should not act on theirs.

Well, why should they not? Because it would go against the spirit, although not the letter, of their conventions. It would be wrong of her to divorce and of him to break his engagement. It would make their lives better at the cost of "disloyalty and cruelty and indifference." It would not merely offend the sensibilities of "the very good people" who had "never been tempted," but also tear the fabric of their own, their family's, and their friends' lives. The victims of their disloyalty, cruelty, and indifference would not be just the untempted good people but also themselves and those they love and who love them. The goodness of their own and intimates' lives would be undermined if they acted on their rights. When Archer says: We have the right, he means: We would not violate rule-following decency if we did what was necessary to get married. Countess Olenska says, in effect: Exacting our rights would violate character-forming decency.

Character-forming decency is thus not merely customary conduct. It is also goodwill toward others in one's society, a sign of the frequently unarticulated belief that fellow members of a society share with one another a moral outlook that governs how they should conduct themselves and treat others. Character-forming decency translates this deep allegiance into practical terms. It is represented, on the surface, by rule-following decency and, more deeply, by not standing on one's rights if doing so is contrary to the spirit of the shared conventions.

The second of Countess Olenska's significant replies to Archer is, "I can't love you unless I give you up."[27] She means, they love each other for what they are, and that is partly defined by their shared conventions. If they violated the conventions, they would destroy part of what they found lovable in each other. Their love, therefore, requires that they should give each other up. But Archer protests, "What a life for you!" and she replies, "Oh—as long as it's part of yours." "And mine," asks Archer, "part of yours?" She nodded. "And that's to be all—for either of us?" "Well; it *is* all isn't it?"[28] The "all" is being part of the same society, sharing its conventions, having a moral outlook in common, and seeing each other as sharing a conception of a good life. That is why their lives will be part of each other's even though they will separated forever. She can truly say, "I shan't be lonely now. I *was* lonely; I *was* afraid. But the emptiness and darkness are gone; when I turn back into myself now I'm like a child going into a room where there's always light."[29] They give each other up, and that is a sacrifice. But they gain in return a sustained sense of worth and the disappearance of loneliness and fear. That makes their sacrifice much smaller than it seemed before.

3.5 The Core

This last remark of Countess Olenska leads to the third and best interpretation of their situation. According to the first interpretation, theirs is a conflict between character-forming decency and a good life, which Countess Olenska resolves by making the great sacrifice of choosing the former over the latter. According to the second interpretation, the first is superficial. The conflict is not between decency and a good life but between a naive and a reflective ideal of a good life. Divorce and breaking the engagement are serious possibilities only in the naive ideal. The reflective one excludes them because they violate their ideal of a good life. By excluding them, Archer and Countess Olenska make a small sacrifice. Betraying their society, friends, family, their love and self-esteem would be much worse. According to the third interpretation, their situation does not involve a conflict at all. This becomes apparent if we reflect on the questions that come naturally to contemporary readers of the novel: Why do they not leave? They are intelligent adults and they have money. Why do they not just move to France or Italy and enjoy each other and life?

The answer is suggested by a pair of lovers who did just that: Vronsky and Anna Karenina did pack up and go to Italy. And, of course, what happened to them was that their love faltered. They left behind the intrusive presence of their society and its conventions, but the anticipated joyful abandon did not occur. They soon became listless, distracted, irritable, and bored, even as they continued love each other. Their love, however, was as troubled in Italy as it had been at home in Russia, although for different reasons. The same thing would have happened to Countess Olenska and Archer, but perhaps not so soon, for they had greater resources than Tolstoy's pair.

But the question should be pressed: Why need anything bad happen? If the love between two people is true, they want each other's company, and the world is irrelevant. Flawed love will no doubt be quickly revealed as such if the lovers are left to their own resources. Presumably, however, the love between Countess Olenska and Archer was not flawed, and if it had been, they would still be better off having found that out. If it is fear of the truth that stops them from leaving New York, they are weak and they bring their separation upon themselves. If they are strong and really love each other, then they have nothing to fear. It is in this way that a contemporary reader may impatiently respond to all the nuances, fine discriminations, and interior struggles that Wharton presents. This, however, is another simpleminded response.

The mistaken supposition underlying it is that the relationship of Countess Olenska and Archer to their society and its conventions is contingent, changeable, and unimportant. It is supposed that they can abandon their allegiance with as little loss as they can change their clothes when the fashion changes. But this is not so. Countess Olenska and Archer have defined themselves partly in terms of their society and its conventions. They have derived from them some of their deepest convictions and their shared ideal of a good life. To abandon them would be to damage themselves both psychologically and morally since they have nothing to put in their place. It is not as if they would be converting from one ideal of a good life to another; they would merely abandon the only ideal they have. And that is not all: their love for each other also depends on sharing that ideal. For part of the reason they love each other is that they admire and respect each other's character and sensibility, and these, of course, have also been formed and sustained by the ideal of a good life that is sustained by the society and its conventions that they would be abandoning.

All this might be acknowledged by skeptical readers, but they could still ask why it is supposed that if they were to leave their society, they would be obliged to leave their character and sensibility behind. They would presumably carry their deep commitments and values, and they could continue to love each other partly because of them.

This is partly true and partly false. Their character and sensibility are not possessions of which customs officials could deprive Countess Olenska and Archer as they are leaving New York. But they are sustained by the conventional background that they would be leaving behind. Their characters are constituted of dispositions to conduct themselves in certain ways in certain situations. Leaving their society and its conventions for another involves a basic change in the situations to which they have to respond. The standards of appropriateness shift, their judgments and perceptions become unreliable, and what was natural and matter-of-course in the old setting is no longer fitting, or fitting in the same way, in the new setting. The conventions are different. It is not just that new ones are added and old ones are omitted, but also that the ones that hold in both contexts have different significance and importance. If they find themselves in a new society with its conventions, they have to learn what counts there as politeness and insult, forthrightness and forwardness, mockery and compliment, supererogation and duty, irony and humor, and so forth. They would not know the signs of guilt, shame, modesty, flirtation, or sarcasm. They would not know how exactly to express gratitude, appreciation, annoyance, friendliness, resentment, or generosity. They would lack the language of conduct. They would know what they want to say but not how to say it.

They could, of course, learn all this. But the more they learn, the more their character and sensibility will alter. The better they fit into their new society, the less remains of their previous identity. If they decide to stay aloof in order to maintain their old selves, they will fail. For the circumstances in which they could express their old selves will demand new responses, and they will alter their old selves. It is true that they can carry their character and sensibility into a new context, but it will change them in fundamental ways over time. If Countess Olenska and Archer love each other partly for their character and sensibility, then they are wise and show good judgment in rejecting the option of leaving behind the society and conventions that nourish their love. She is right in saying to Archer, "I can't love you unless I give you up." They cannot love and have each other in New York because their allegiance to its conventions makes that impossible; and they cannot love and have each other elsewhere because they would soon cease to be the people who fell in love.

Skeptical readers may still think this is making too much of changing societies. Many immigrants, exiles, and refugees changed societies and adjusted perfectly well to the necessary changes. But Countess Olenska and Archer are in a different situation. Immigrants, exiles, and refugees leave behind a bad way of life, which they exchange for something they believe to be better. And frequently they leave because they are driven to it. Nobody drives Countess Olenska and

Archer, and they both believe New York society is "better than anything I've known." Their judgment is not based on ignorance of other possibilities. Archer "had felt the outside tugging . . . with all its golden hands" and rejected it. And Countess Olenska fled in horror from the corruption "accepted in certain societies, or at least put up with as part of the general give-and-take." They are the kind of Americans for whom certain things are "unthinkable, simply unthinkable." And what that is is what their society and its conventions regard as such. That is what makes it psychologically and morally impossible for them to pack up and go.

It is a significant fact about Countess Olenska and Archer that they come to see this clearly. They realize that they are what they are partly because of their society and its conventions, that their identity and self-respect depend on living according to the conventions of their society and on conducting themselves with character-forming decency. These are conditions of a good life, as they conceive of it. When they fall in love and the conventions render their love indecent, their emotional dislocation is only temporary. Their reason and calmer feelings are powerfully there in the background awaiting the turbulence of their love to subside a little, and then they reassert themselves. They both understand and feel that their love is impossible. It is not social pressure, a sense of sin, or a hyperactive conscience that stands in the way. If it were any of these, there would be a conflict between decency and a good life. What really stands in the way is their realization that the good life they seek depends on their living according to character-forming decency. They recognize, therefore, as illusory the prospect of a good life that involves its violation. For the reflective people they are, there is only a flicker of a doubt before they understand that there is no real conflict facing them. As soon as they realize what is at stake, the supposed conflict disappears. For them, only the achievement of clarity involves a struggle.

It is a mistake, therefore, to think of Countess Olenska and Archer as making a big sacrifice to resolve a dramatic conflict, as the first interpretation suggests. Nor are they making a smaller sacrifice in a less dramatic conflict, as the second interpretation claims. They sacrifice nothing and face no conflict. They are momentarily tempted to betray what matters to them most, including themselves and their love, but their character-forming decency, aided by their sensibility, enables them to remain true. Of course, the degree of happiness they desire eludes them. They settle for a self-respecting life in which their love has no place. But they have no realistic alternative to that because acting on their love would deprive them of a good life, self-respect, and, therefore, also happiness.

3.6 Decency and Good Lives

As the just-completed account moves from the outward to the inward aspect of decency, so decency itself moves along parallel tracks from its superficial toward its deeper forms. Civic friendship is on the surface. Benevolence is just below, but when it is guided by sympathy, reason, and custom, it begins to deepen from the natural tendency to seek advantages to a disposition to conceive of a good life in terms of the conventions of one's society. As this disposition develops, so decency changes from mere rule-following to a dominant constituent of some people's characters. When it reaches this point, decency signifies the identification with the prevailing conventions. Those who have it cease to regard conventional conduct as instrumental to a good life. They see conventional conduct as living a good life. Their identification is so complete as to rule out a conflict between how they see the possibilities and limits of a good life and how their society sees them. Their society's moral outlook is their moral outlook. But decency goes further by placing the substantive demand on the moral outlook that it should require the mutual benevolence of those who share it. They ought to wish and do well for one another in both their personal and impersonal encounters. And what that comes to in concrete terms follows from the ideals of a good life that translate into individual terms the possibilities and limits defined by the prevailing conventions.

This account of decency is meant to make evident that when decency becomes a dominant constituent of character, it also becomes a deep and serious attitude to life and conduct. It goes far beyond superficial politeness and silliness about sex. It *may* represent an admirable achievement and it *may* be a personal excellence. But it is not bound to be one, and as the last step in the argument, it needs to be acknowledged that decency is not *the* key to a good life because it is neither necessary nor sufficient for it.

It is not sufficient because the moral outlook with which decency leads people to identify may be seriously defective. Living according to a defective moral outlook is not an admirable achievement, although it may be an achievement. A life of decency will be good, therefore, only if it consists in allegiance to a morally acceptable outlook. Decency is not necessary for a good life either, because good lives may take forms quite different from conduct according to the conventions of even a morally acceptable outlook. Decent lives may be good, but lives in which decency plays only a minor role may also be good. Artists, scientists, scholars, inventors, poets, religious believers, and social reformers may live good lives while paying very little attention to the prevailing conventions.

The acknowledgment that a decent and a good life need not coincide does not, however, change that fact that decency is one form that good lives may take and that living in harmony with a morally acceptable society is a great benefit for everyone, always, everywhere.

4/

Depth

Such is the disorder and confusion in human affairs, that no perfect or regular distribution of happiness and misery is ever, in this life, to be expected. Not only the goods of fortune, and the endowments of the body (both of which are important), not only these advantages, I say, are unequally divided between the virtuous and the vicious, but even the mind itself partakes, in some degree, of this disorder, and the most worthy character, by the very constitution of the passions, enjoys not the highest felicity.

DAVID HUME, "The Sceptic"

4.1 Hope or Hopelessness?

According to Kant, "All the interests of my reason, speculative as well as practical, combine in the three following questions: 1. What can I know? 2. What ought I to do? 3. What may I hope?"[1] Philosophical attention has largely concentrated on the first two questions. The third, however, is no less important because it leads to asking why knowledge should be sought and why actions should be moral. One of the most influential answers is almost as old as philosophy itself: the one that Plato expresses through Socrates. He regards the three questions as intimately connected. The knowledge that should be sought is primarily of the good. Morality consists in applying that knowledge to guide actions. The reason many lives are bad is either ignorance of the good or some character defect that allows appetites and passions, rather than knowledge of the good, to guide actions. If the good is known, and if actions reflect it, then the resulting lives will be good. That is why knowledge should be sought and why actions should be moral, and that is the object of true hope.

Doubts about the Socratic answer are as old as the answer itself. *Oedipus the King* is Sophocles' classic expression of it.[2] Before Oedipus was born, it was prophesied that he would kill his father and marry his mother. His parents, therefore, arranged to have the newly born Oedipus killed. But he survived and grew into adulthood, believing himself to be the son of the king and queen of Corinth, who had raised him. The prophecy was then repeated to Oedipus. To prevent it from becoming true, he exiled himself so as not to be in the proximity of his supposed parents. His effort to avoid the calamity, however, actually hastened its occurrence because it was to Thebes, the city ruled by his real father, that his wandering brought him. On the way to Thebes, Oedipus was provoked into a fight and killed several men, not unjustifiably given the prevalent mores, one among whom was his unknown father. Upon arriving in Thebes, Oedipus, at great risk to himself, solved the riddle of the Sphinx, thus succeeding where many others had failed in liberating the city from her oppression. As a reward, he was made king and was given as a wife the widowed queen, his unknown mother. As the play opens, all these events are in the past. The action concerns Oedipus's discovery that he is guilty of parricide and incest, crimes that he, in agreement with his society, finds deeply immoral. In the course of his discovery Oedipus realizes that he unknowingly and unintentionally caused the most serious and undeserved harm to Thebes; to his wife, who is his mother; to his children, who are his brothers and sisters; and to himself. Yet throughout his life Oedipus acted as well as can be expected from a reasonable and moral human being. He was guided by a reasonable conception of a good life, he took due account of such facts as he had, and his intentions were morally praiseworthy. Nevertheless, both he and others saw him as ruined by the harm he unknowingly and unintentionally caused.

The significant feature of Oedipus's situation for the present purposes is that he was a plaything of the gods. He had choices, and he busily made them. But the alternatives among which he could choose, the conditions in which he could do so, and his doom were all set by the gods. Oedipus was consequently only causally and not morally responsible for the harm he caused, and he did not deserve the harm he suffered. The fact is that through no fault of his own, Oedipus was manipulated by the gods for their own inscrutable purposes, and he was made to suffer a terrible fate by them. Sophocles' suggestion is that what befell Oedipus reflects the human condition. All human beings risk becoming the playthings of the gods, regardless of their knowledge of the good or of their motivation to act according to it.

The first reaction to this suggestion may well be that this cannot be the human condition because there are no such gods as Sophocles depicted. But this does not dispose of the matter because Sophocles' point can just as well be expressed in terms of the contingency of life, rather than the vocabulary of Greek polytheism. Contingency permeates human lives, including those that are guided by knowledge of the good and the motivation to pursue it. People may find themselves in wars, revolutions, tyrannies, natural disasters, epidemics, crimes, concentration camps, and emergencies. They may find as they act as politicians, physicians, firefighters, or officials of public health, criminal justice, or social welfare—as well as parents, friends, or lovers—that they have to make the weightiest decisions on the basis of imperfect knowledge among noxious alternatives that circumstances force on them. Such situations are not of their making, they have not sought to be in them, and they would gladly avoid them if they could. But they cannot, they must act, and the consequence may be that they cause undeserved suffering both to themselves and to others. Human life is full of such suffering, its victims may never be compensated, knowledge of the good and a corresponding motivation are often unavailing and go unrecognized and unrewarded, and people frequently do not get what they deserve.

What emerges, therefore, is the indifference of nature to human merit. The good may suffer and the wicked may flourish, and the books may not be balanced even in the long run. There is thus good reason to doubt that there is a moral order in nature. The order that exists does not seem to be evil or Manichean rather than good. It is more likely to be indifferent. Indifference is worse than neutrality because the latter at least implies the presence of some witnesses, even if they stand above the fray and remain uncommitted. That would permit hoping that they at least know about the human condition and that, perhaps, if things got really bad, their neutrality would be suspended. But there is no reason to suppose that this is so. There is no guarantee that what happens to people will be proportional to their merit. The attempt to answer Kant's third question should begin with the realization that this is so.

But if contingency permeates life, if the connection between what happens and what ought to happen is fortuitous, then the answer to Kant's question may well be that there is no reasonable hope. If the significance of this discouraging thought sinks in, it becomes very hard to justify the optimism assumed by the Socratic answer about the desirability of knowledge of the good and of the corresponding motivation. What may then follow is the state Wordsworth described:

> . . . inwardly oppressed
> With sorrow, disappointment, vexing thoughts,
> Confusion of judgment, zeal destroyed,
> And lastly, utter loss of hope itself
> And things to hope for![3]

Kant himself avoided this discouraging state. He relied instead on faith according to which "happiness stands in exact relation with morality, that is, with worthiness to be happy."[4] It seems that since reason would have led Kant to a subversive answer to his question about hope, he felt compelled to seek a tamer answer outside reason. Kant is not alone, of course, in succumbing to what is called here the transcendental temptation. A particularly clear expression of it is Hegel's:

> When we see . . . the evil, the vice, the ruin that has befallen the
> most flourishing kingdoms which the mind of man ever cre-
> ated, we can hardly avoid being filled with . . . a moral sadness,
> a revolt of good will—if indeed it has any place within us.
> Without rhetorical exaggeration, a simple truthful account of
> the miseries that have overwhelmed the noblest nations and
> polities and the finest exemplars of virtue forms a most fearful
> picture and excites emotions of the profoundest and most
> hopeless sadness, counter-balanced by no consoling results. . . .
> But in contemplating history as the slaughter-bench at which
> the happiness of peoples, the wisdom of states, and the virtue
> of individuals have been sacrificed, a question necessarily
> arises: To what principle, to what final purpose, have these
> monstrous sacrifices been offered?[5]

This is a clear-sighted diagnosis, and yet the assumption behind it is that there is a purpose that somehow redeems the suffering that human history so amply documents. But the assumption is merely another symptom of having succumbed to the transcendental tempta-tion. The hope it may give is false hope. There is no reason to think that a purpose exists, or for supposing that if it did, it would redeem the suffering concomitant with its realization. Do the pyramids compensate the slaves who built them? Would supernatural pyramids compensate human beings? Is it plausible to suppose that the new family God gave Job compensated him for the old one God took away?

It is an odd fact in the history of ideas that Kant himself articulated one of the most serious reasons for resisting the transcendental temptation. He argued in the first *Critique* that there can be no reason for postulating a purpose behind the known world because any reason that could be given must come from within the known world. The most that can reasonably be said about the world is that there is much in it that is presently not known and there is much in what is known that is beyond understanding, explanation, and control. There can be no rational warrant for going beyond this to claim knowledge of the unknown. If Kant had been consistent, he would not have done so. Be that as it may, an explanation can be derived from the first *Critique* of why hope is such a serious problem. If hope comes from the discernment of a purpose in the scheme of things, and if there is no reasonable way in which a purpose could be discerned, even if there were one, then there can be no reasonable hope.

If it is acknowledged that the contingency of life puts humanity in jeopardy, and if the false hope of a divinely ordained happy ending is rejected, then what can be reasonably hoped for? Perhaps there is nothing, and then ignoring the question may be the most reasonable course of action. A sturdy common sense may then lead people to carry on with their lives, do as well as they can, and avoid these unsettling thoughts. To do otherwise, by dwelling on the hopelessness produced by the acknowledgment of contingency, is to undermine the motivation for increasing control over their lives to the extent it is possible.

It would nevertheless be unreasonable to proceed in this way because the effects of contingency are not just freakish concatenations of unfavorable external circumstances, as a shallow reading of *Oedipus the King* may lead one to suppose. They are daily occurrences in all lives as a result of such internal conditions as the contingencies of genetic inheritance and the effects of upbringing and personal experiences. To foster a self-imposed blindness to them is to collude in weakening the possibility of control beyond the effects of contingency. There is, however, a much more promising strategy for alleviating a sense of hopelessness. The fact that humanity is subject to contingency cannot be changed, but a reasonable attitude can be cultivated toward it. This attitude is the result of depth, the personal excellence that is the subject of this chapter.

4.2 Understanding Depth

Depth in general is an admirable, highly desirable, and yet rare quality. One would expect that much has been written about it, but this is not so.[6] Perhaps the topic appears forbidding because the nature of depth is itself a deep and difficult question, since it forces those who ask it to decide what is ultimately worth caring about. The antonyms of depth are shallowness and superficiality, and its approximate cognate is profundity. The discussion will concentrate on depth primarily as it may be ascribed to individuals rather than to ideas, theories, or works. Individuals may be said to possess a deep understanding of some matter, or to feel deeply about a subject, or to offer a deep response to some question, problem, or situation. Of these complex psychological states, understanding must be ranked as having first importance for depth, for the depth of feelings and motives is questionable unless they are founded on understanding. If love or hate, for instance, involves self-deception, it may be regarded as strong or passionate, but it would be a mistake to ascribe depth to it. Similarly, the sorts of things people may be motivated to say or do in response to something may be deep or shallow, depending, in part, on the understanding that constitutes its background. Think of the contrast between Polonius in *Hamlet* mouthing the cliché, To thine own self be true, and Socrates repeating the Delphic injunction, Know thyself.

An additional reason for attributing to understanding a privileged role in depth emerges when we reflect on the distinction between the appearance and reality of depth. Portentousness, gravity, seriousness of tone and mien may disguise humbug rather than betoken depth.[7] The genuine article has a specific connection with truth which the counterfeit lacks. This connection is not that depth provides direct understanding of the truth. People lack depth if their minds are cluttered with accurate information about trivial facts, and someone may possess great depth on some subject and yet be mistaken about it. Kant was wrong on just about all the central issues he discussed, but who could reasonably deny him a place among the handful of the deepest philosophers?

Depth involves discerning an underlying unity among apparently complex and unrelated phenomena. To have depth is to see the same phenomena as many others also see, but to penetrate below their surface and construct a theory or a vision, depending on the subject matter, that leads to a possible understanding of the reality of which the appearances are manifestations. It is to possess a perspective, an organizing view that provides the foundation for understanding what was previously problematic, even if no one recognized its problems; like Plato on love, Aristotle on virtue, Einstein on relativity, Spinoza on freedom, Marx on history, Hume on causality, Freud on the unconscious, Nietzsche on morality, or Darwin on evolution. The essential feature of these perspectives is that they provide a *possible* way of understanding a very sizable segment of the world that is, in some respect, important.

The depth attributed to the authors of these perspectives is not destroyed, although it is diminished, if the proposed understanding does not survive the sustained critical attention it elicits. The world might have been like that, and if it had been, it would have been of great significance. Even false perspectives may move the understanding toward something important because, through the rejection of the possibilities they hold out, the truth is approximated.[8]

It is extremely unlikely, however, that depth would consist only in a purely theoretical understanding. Depth concerns important matters, and it is natural for the understanding it yields to influence emotions and motives. The more important these matters are, the more appropriate it is that understanding them should have a deep influence on emotions and motives. It is consequently better to think of depth as having cognitive, emotive, and motivational *aspects* than attempt to treat them, in isolation from one another, as different forms of depth. There *are* different forms of depth, but the differences among them are due to subject matter and not to the absence of some aspect of depth.

The form of depth that concerns us here has the human condition as its subject matter (from now on, this form is referred to simply as depth). The beginning of it is a deeper understanding of the human condition. Those who succumb to the transcendental temptation also seek this understanding, but their failure makes it reasonable to look for it in a different direction. They seek it beyond nature, in a supposed supernatural world. A more reasonable approach is to take very seriously the thought that human beings are part of the natural world. Depth may then come from a realistic view of the conditions of human lives that can be inferred from nature. If human beings are part of the natural world, then what they are, do, experience, and what happens to them are also part of it. And one of the things that happens is that the human aspiration to live a good life is jeopardized by contingency. No matter how reasonable and moral people are, their aspirations may be frustrated by circumstances over which they have no control. Facing this fact is the beginning of depth.

Depth begins, then, with descriptive knowledge of the human condition, but the knowledge does not remain merely descriptive. People are bound to care about the conditions of their lives, so they are forced to contend with the significance of contingency. The mere possession of this knowledge, therefore, carries with it an impetus toward its enlargement in the direction of incorporating emotive and motivational aspects. The emotive aspect includes desire for success, fear of failure, joy when things are going well, anger or frustration or sadness when they are not, and self-confidence or loss of nerve produced by understanding the odds against success.[9] The motivational aspect is responsible for the continued efforts to pursue ideals of a good life. These aspects, however, are separable only in thought. In actual life, reflection on human lives, projects, and the world forms an indissoluble amalgam of cognitive, emotive, and motivational aspects. Such reflection will lead to at least some depth because it is bound to yield some understanding of the human condition. But its possession may only be minimal or it may become a personal excellence that has a significant character-forming effect. If that happens, it provides some ground for reasonable hope.

Consider now why Oedipus's situation is so redolent with significance. It cannot merely be because he was manipulated into doing what he regarded as most seriously immoral. After all, sad as it is, people often inflict unwitting injury on those they love, and undeserved suffering and self-loathing are common enough. The source of its significance is that Sophocles depicts a conflict between an understanding of the human condition and something else. This something else is not just human aspirations, and it is not even human aspirations pursued reasonably and morally. It is rather the *expectation* that aspirations pursued reasonably and morally will be realized. Oedipus's situation forces those who understand it to reflect on the discrepancy between the human condition and this expectation, and therein lies its significance.

The expectation is that the contingency of life can be overcome by reason and morality. In Oedipus's situation this expectation is disappointed; that is why it is tragic. It shows the futility of human will and intellect, as Oedipus stumbles toward the discovery of his predicament. The dramatic reversal of his fortune moves those who behold it to pity and fear, as well as to a deeper understanding of the human condition. The result of the disappointed expectation is the realization that Oedipus's situation is emblematic of the human condition. Hopelessness then ensues. To see life as some tragedies suggest is to see that there is no consolation, no hope.

If the development toward depth continues, however, then it leads to abandoning this illusory expectation. Depth makes it possible to understand that the illusory expectation rests on the mistaken view that reason and morality are sufficient for the realization of human aspirations. The expectation will be seen then as a lingering remnant of a state of mind left behind by those who understand that contingency may frustrate even the noblest aspirations and that the aspiration may be one's own. The effect of depth, then, will be to wean its possessors from the expectation whose disappointment makes the human condition appear hopeless. That condition will remain the same regardless of whether the illusory expectation is held or abandoned. Depth, however, will change the attitude toward it by freeing those who have it from the hopelessness that the illusory expectation produces when it runs afoul of reality.

It may said against this that the possibility of developing depth is also subject to contingency and so it is pointless to recommend its development. But this is not so. The extent to which contingency affects lives varies with context and circumstance. In some cases, its effect is decisive, people are powerless to resist it, and then the recommendation *is* pointless. It would be misplaced, if not obscene, to urge people on the way to the gas chamber to develop depth. But not all situations are like this. In ordinary life it is often possible to cultivate depth. Oedipus could certainly have done so before calamity overtook him. The recommendation of depth has a point, therefore, for the vast majority of people whose lives are merely liable to but not ruined by contingency.

The question should be pressed, however, of what good depth is if it does not change the facts. Why is it more reasonable to try to realize aspirations with the understanding that the attempt may fail no matter how reasonable and moral it is than to acquire that understanding as a result of failure? There is a long and a short answer. The short one is that depth makes lives better. Those who have it will cope with adversity better than Oedipus did. Depth leads to the appreciation of why it is better to understand one's vulnerability to contingency and to live a life informed by that understanding than to be shocked into the recognition that the unrealistic expectation that life is otherwise may well be disappointed.

This short answer, however, is general, and it does not provide much guidance about how to answer the further question that will be asked: What can *I* do in the face of the contingency of *my* life to make it good or better, given *my* character and circumstances? All human beings live in concrete cultural, political, and social contexts, and they are all saddled with a genetic inheritance and personal experiences that decisively influence the kind of character they have and can develop. A longer answer is needed, therefore, to bring out the practical implications of this general account for concrete situations. How can this general account be applied to the daily experiences of good and evil that people cause, enjoy, and suffer?

It would be a mistake, however, in searching for an answer to ignore altogether the general in favor of the concrete. For that would lead to losing the benefits provided by the accumulated experiences of those countless people who have faced the same question in concrete situations that bear various degrees of similarity to one another. Why not benefit from their experiences if it would make lives better? The fact remains, nevertheless, that the more the general is emphasized, the less likely it is that it will be relevant to particular concerns. There is therefore a great need here for striking a balance between the general and the particular.

This balance depends on understanding the general conditions that affect all lives, the particular conditions that affect specific individuals in their concrete situations, and the bearing the first has on the second. Maintaining this balance is intimately connected with good lives, so it is an important matter. But its achievement is rare because it is extremely difficult. To understand this rare, difficult, and yet important achievement, we need a longer answer to explain how depth should guide particular responses to the general human condition. The explanation is that it should do so through controlling the reaction to the understanding that has so far been reached. It needs to be understood that the inappropriate reaction to understanding the contingency of life and to the illusoriness of the expectation that it should be otherwise is one reason human aspirations may fail.

4.3 The Case of Oedipus

In order to develop an understanding that balances the general and the concrete, consider again what Sophocles shows about Oedipus. One important theme running through both *Oedipus the King* and *Oedipus at Colonus* is Oedipus's development toward greater depth.[10] The first play concerns Oedipus's discovery that he has unintentionally and unknowingly committed acts he regards as horrible violations of his deepest moral convictions. The discovery shatters the foundation of his moral life, he loathes himself, he reacts with rage and desperation, and he blinds himself, notwithstanding the realization that he had not had the control over his actions that he supposed himself to have. He nevertheless cannot escape, either in his own or in the public's eyes, the sense that he is morally ruined by what he has done, even though he was not a willing and knowing agent of his own deeds. The second play shows Oedipus as an old man facing death after many years of wandering as a blind, homeless beggar. The Oedipus of this play is a transformed man who has reflected on his own rise and fall and formed a well-considered judgment of what happened to him. After a lifetime of struggle and calamity, he dies at peace, having come to terms with his life.

At the beginning of the first play Oedipus is the respected and un-questioned ruler of Thebes. His subjects tell him, "We do rate you first of men, / both in the common crises of our lives / and face-to-face encounters with the gods" (K. 42–44), because "you lifted up our lives" (K. 49). Oedipus lives the life he wants to live, and that is to be first among men. He believes that the key to this aspiration is control and that control depends on knowledge and power. He celebrates: "O power— / wealth and empire, skill outstripping skill / in the heady rivalries of life" (K. 432–34). He is winning in the rivalries because of what he takes to be his superior character: "That is my blood, my nature—I will never betray it, / never fail to search" (K. 1193–94), and the impetus behind the ceaseless search is a passionate desire: "I must know it all, / see the truth" (K. 1168–69). Then, as ominous cracks begin to appear in his life, as his control slips, Tiresias, who speaks for the gods, tells him: "You're blind to the corruption of your own life . . . All unknowing / you are the scourge of your own flesh and blood" (K. 471–74). As a result, "your power ends. / None of your power follows you through life" (K. 1676–77).

As the action progresses, the superficiality of Oedipus's control is revealed. It is not that he lacks the knowledge and power he believes himself to have. Rather, the knowledge and power he has are not what is required for the control he seeks. Control *is* important and knowledge and power *are* its constituents, but they are different types of knowledge and power from what Oedipus pursues. He thinks that the point of having knowledge and power is to control others, not himself. He thus fails to understand the true nature of control that is worth having. That understanding would not have saved Oedipus from the calamity that befalls him—that he cannot and could not help. But he could have responded to the calamity in less self-destructive ways than he did if he had had a deeper understanding of control.

As it is, his response to his misfortune makes matters even worse. When the feebleness of his control is revealed, Oedipus responds with a desperate act of reaffirmation of the same misguided commitment to it. He reasserts his control by directing it against himself, the only remaining subject: in a wanton gesture, he blinds himself. When asked why he did such a horrible thing on top of all that has already happened to him, he says: "Apollo, friends, Apollo— / he ordained my agonies—these, my pains on pains! / But the hand that struck my eyes was mine / mine alone—no one else—I did it all myself" (K. 1467–70). The chorus, beholding his misery, comments on his search for the wrong kind of control that shaped his self-destructive response: "Pitiful, you suffer so . . . / I wish you'd never known" (K. 1481–82).

Oedipus, however, is strong, and his misfortune does not break him. He resolves to bear it and carry on because he still has a proud sense of his self: "My troubles are mine / and I am the only man alive who can sustain them" (K. 1548–49), and "It's mine alone, my destiny—I am Oedipus!" (K. 1496). And so there he is at the end of the first play, having lost the misguided power he sought, having suffered because of the misdirected knowledge he worked so hard to acquire, and yet, for the first time, having some real control over what little is left of his previous mode of life.

The second play opens many years after the end of the first: "Oedipus is no more / the flesh and blood of old" (C. 134–35). He has been transformed because he has acquired a deeper understanding of knowledge and power than what he had before and because his new and better understanding allows him to control both what he does and what he does not do. As for the power that is worth having, he learns that it is not winning "in the heady rivalries of life" (K. 434); its beginning is in "acceptance—that is the great lesson suffering teaches" (C. 6) and in "no more fighting with necessity" (C. 210). His attitude to knowledge also changes. The proud claims of the first play, resting on a misunderstanding of himself, "That is my blood, my na-ture—I will never betray it, / never fail to search" (K. 1193–94) and "I must know it all, / see the truth" (K. 1168–69), are replaced by "No no! Don't ask me who I am /—no more probing, testing—stop—no more!" (C. 225–26). Instead of using his knowledge and power as in-struments for the futile effort of trying to control the world, an en-deavor that almost destroyed him, he now uses them to try to control himself by understanding what he did and what happened to him and by shaping his responses to it. He says, reflecting on his past, "as time wore on / and the smoldering fever broke and died at last / and I began to feel my rage has outrun my wrongs, / I'd lashed myself too much for what I'd done, once long ago" (C. 486–90).

Oedipus's acceptance of contingency, his abandonment of the rest-less search for some key to himself outside himself, and the beginning of his self-knowledge, however, do not incline him toward a narcissis-tic concentration on the fine-tuning of his soul. The depth he is ac-quiring gives him a measure of knowledge and power and, conse-quently, some control, and it guides his response to the world. His knowledge concerns "the final things of life" (C. 656), and his power is exercised both to say no to the evil that comes his way and to fur-ther the cause of the good insofar as he can. The evil he rejects—in-deed, excoriates—comes to him in the persons of Creon, who fraudu-lently attempts to enlist Oedipus's help to shore up his crumbling power (C. 865–910), and Polynices, Oedipus's son, who has aban-doned his father to a miserable old age when he could have eased his plight without much trouble (C. 1524–84). His reaction to Creon and Polynices is passionate, and they show that the transformed Oedipus is not a burnt-out wreck, but someone who controls his feelings and directs them toward appropriate expression. Oedipus also uses his power on the side of the good by bestowing on Athens "the power that age cannot destroy, / the heritage stored up for . . . Athens" (C. 1718–19), which "will always form a defense . . . / a bulwark stronger than many shields" (C. 1724–25).

Oedipus thus attains at the end of his life a considerable amount of control, a growing understanding of "the final things in life" (C. 656), and a passionate commitment to opposing the evil and supporting the good that he encounters. He resolves: "No more fighting" (C. 210); "acceptance—that is the great lesson suffering teaches" (C. 6), because resistance is futile, "there is no escape, ever" (C. 303). He was wrong to struggle against contingency, and yet he sees that what happened to him was undeserved: "Say my unwilling crimes against myself / and against my own were payments from the gods / for something criminal inside me . . . no, look hard, / you'll find no guilt to accuse me of—I'm innocent!" (C. 1101–5). That contingency impinged on his life, that it made him suffer, that his reason and will achieved the opposite of what he intended—that, he came to understand, is just one unfortunate outcome of the human condition.

If this interpretation is correct, Sophocles shows Oedipus's development of depth.[11] Oedipus understands that reason and morality may be unavailing against contingency, that his expectation that the human condition is otherwise is illusory; he learns to abandon it, to balance his general understanding of the human condition and his specific understanding of the conditions of his own life, and to control his inappropriate reactions to what he has thus understood and learned.

The relevance of Oedipus's life for others is not that they should suppose that what happened to Oedipus—the unknowing and unintentional violation of the foundation of his moral life—will happen to them too. They should understand rather that the very imperfect control they have over their lives makes them liable to the sort of calamity that befell Oedipus. The point is not that they are doomed but that they are at risk. Sophocles suggests in these two plays that coming to this understanding and holding it in the focus of attention is important for the realization of human aspirations.

It still needs to be understood, however, how this understanding is going to affect the control people may have over their lives. How can it extend the control people have and reduce the risks they face? There is a sense in which it can do neither. Nothing can alter the contingency of life. Depth involves understanding that this is the human condition. But there is another sense in which it can extend human control.

Trying to control what is beyond control is unreasonable. But if it is understood that conditions beyond human control endanger the aspirations to live good lives, then it is possible, to some extent, to control one's attitude to this regrettable fact. This will help us face the realization that everyone is at risk, that misfortune may actually happen to anyone, including oneself. It will work in the first way by not allowing the understanding of being at risk to be falsified by some form of denial, or to provoke an overreaction, or to undercut the motivation to do what is possible to live a good life. It will work in the second way by preventing the exacerbation of misfortune, if it befalls one, through inappropriate reaction to it.

4.4 Inappropriate Reactions

Sophocles of course is a poet, not a philosopher. His way of showing Oedipus's development toward greater depth is suggestive and evocative, and it requires the reader to make an imaginative effort to appreciate the complexities of the play. For a philosophical understanding of what Sophocles suggests about depth, it is necessary to be more explicit and analytical. To begin with, depth is an anthropocentric notion. It involves understanding the human significance of some general conditions prevailing in the world. In this respect, the form of depth that concerns us here is different from scientific or aesthetic depth. The difference is not that the latter forms of depth are unimportant from the human point of view—all forms of depth are important. The difference is rather where their respective importance lies. Depth about the human condition is important because it involves understanding the significance of contingency for the human aspiration to live good lives. Scientific and aesthetic depth may affect good lives, but unlike depth about the human condition, they do not have that as their primary object.

A further difference is that originality plays an important role in scientific and aesthetic depth, but not in depth about the human condition. To see deeply into nature is to see something *in* nature that others have not seen. And aesthetic depth usually involves the creation of new forms of sensibility, expression, or representation. Depth about the human condition, however, concerns contingency, whose effects are hidden from no one. The facts of the human condition are not discovered by those who possess this form of depth; rather, they come to appreciate the significance of these quite familiar facts. What separates this kind of depth from shallowness and superficiality is thus not the possession of a greater amount of factual knowledge, but the extent to which the significance of commonly possessed factual knowledge is understood.

The contingency of life may be described *sub specie aeternitatis*, from the point of view of the universe, as Henry Sidgwick put it,[12] and *sub specie humanitatis*, from the human point of view. The first is indifferent to human welfare, the second essentially concerned with it. From both perspectives, contingency will be seen as an impersonal, inexorable, and unavoidable condition that takes no account of the merits or demerits of those who are subject to it.

Sub specie aeternitatis, the significance of this condition is metaphysical: it influences constituents of the world that roughly resemble human beings in size, texture, and duration. That some of these constituents are human beings is a matter of indifference from this point of view. The condition affects beehives, snowmobiles, zebras, and paintings as well as human beings. What matters metaphysically is understanding the condition, not adopting the point of view of the particulars that are subject to it.

Sub specie humanitatis, the significance of this condition is precisely how it affects human beings. Its salient feature from the human point of view is the threat it constitutes to the aspiration to live a good life. If this threat is understood narrowly, as part of the condition of human lives, then it is beyond human control. But if it is understood more broadly, as that condition *and* the human attitude to it, then it is possible to have some control over it since it is possible to have some control over the attitude. The realization of this possibility depends on the further development of depth, which in turn depends on not forming an inappropriate attitude once the human significance of contingency has been understood. The variety of inappropriate attitudes to the human condition is great. Discussing them would take a very long—and depressing—book, and this is not that book. It will suffice instead to discuss briefly four frequent, perhaps most typical, kinds of inappropriate attitudes: disengagement, denial, exaggeration, and resignation.

Consider this wonderfully suggestive description of Thomas Nagel's:

One summer . . . a large spider appeared in the urinal of the men's room. . . . When the urinal wasn't in use, he would perch on the metal drain at its base, and when it was, he would try to scramble out of the way, sometimes managing to climb an inch or two up the porcelain wall to a point that wasn't too wet. But sometimes he was caught, tumbled and drenched by the flushing torrent. He didn't seem to like it, and always got out of the way if he could. . . . Somehow he survived, presumably feeding on tiny insects attracted to the site. . . . The urinal must have been used more than a hundred times a day, and always it was the same desperate scramble to get out of the way. His life seemed miserable and exhausting.[13]

If the human condition is viewed *sub specie aeternitatis*, human beings may appear as that spider. But if that perspective is truly metaphysical, it will influence emotions and motives as little as does the spider's lot. Human beings can cultivate the attitude of a cool, dispassionate, uncommitted observer who contemplates the spectacle while remaining disengaged from it.

The cultivation of this attitude widens the distance between human beings as participants and as observers of their own participation. No matter how successfully that attitude is developed, however, human beings cannot cease to be participants because that would put an end to human lives. What the distance produces, therefore, is not a life of passive contemplation, for human beings cannot live such a life, but a life in which a disengaged attitude to human participation is cultivated. Human beings cannot cease to do what their nature dictates, but they can reject the naiveté of wholehearted enthusiasm toward the miserable and exhausting existence in the human equivalent of the spider's urinal. The result is a frame of mind in which human beings react to contingency by teaching themselves disengagement from the life that is endangered by it. They endeavor to cope with the human condition by distancing themselves insofar as they can from their humanity. The better they succeed, the weaker will be their emotional and motivational reactions toward the human condition. "If *sub specie aeternitatis* there is no reason to believe that anything matters, then that does not matter either."[14]

All this, however, rests on viewing the human condition *sub specie aeternitatis*, and the time has come to ask why that is supposed to be desirable. If that point of view were adopted, then, of course, what matters *sub specie humanitatis* would not matter. But it would be destructive of human aspirations to live a good life to adopt an attitude of disengagement from it. It would worsen the human condition to respond to the realization that contingency puts lives at risk by abandoning efforts to make lives better. The success of those efforts *is* endangered by the risk human beings face. But what must be faced is only the *risk* of failure, not its certainty. Oedipus's situation *is* like the spider's. The human situation, however, is like Oedipus's only in the sense that everyone is as much at risk as Oedipus was before his life collapsed. Most lives, however, have not collapsed, although they may do so. Disengagement would make collapse more likely by weakening the will and desire to exercise such control over one's life as possible.

Behind the attitude of disengagement, there is, therefore, the misjudgment of taking the state of being at risk for the state of being doomed. Risk holds out the possibility of success, not just of failure. Excessive fear of failure may lead to a loss of nerve, and that to an attempt to extricate oneself from the risky situation. But when the risk is integral to the human condition, human beings cannot extricate themselves from it. They can only face the risk well or badly. Disengagement leads to facing it badly because it worsens whatever chances there are of succeeding.

The strategy of viewing the world *sub specie aeternitatis* has notable successes to its credit. The great achievements of the physical and biological sciences have been made possible precisely by that objective, dispassionate, nonanthropocentric quest for understanding that is also behind the attitude of disengagement. From this similarity, however, no support can be derived for disengagement. The nonanthropocentric view is appropriate to understanding nature but not the evaluative dimension of human lives. The physical and biological sciences are not ex officio concerned with the bearing of their discoveries on good lives. To be sure, scientists are no less interested in good lives than anyone else, but they are interested in their capacity as human beings, not as scientists. Disengagement, by contrast, is a deliberate turning away from the interests of humanity. It is not a phenomenological bracketing of the human condition for the purposes of inquiry, but a conscious effort to replace, insofar as that is possible, the anthropocentric perspective that is inevitable for human beings with an alien nonanthropocentric one. The resulting disengagement is unavoidably committed, therefore, to downgrading the importance of what matters *sub specie humanitatis*. The strategy of coping with the prospect of failure by minimizing its importance and diverting the efforts needed for success cannot help but be self-defeating.

A second possible attitude toward the realization that it is impossible to avoid being at risk entails erecting some barrier that prevents facing the full implications of that realization. The barrier may be conscious, involving a deliberate effort to ignore or to dismiss the disturbing truth. Or it may be unconscious, in which case it takes the form of self-deception. It involves persuading oneself that one is invulnerable to the risk other people face, or that, although the risk is there, it is so insignificant as to be negligible. This state of mind is depicted in Tolstoy's Ivan Ilych:

> In the depth of his heart he knew he was dying, but not only
> was he not accustomed to the thought, he simply did not and
> could not grasp it. The syllogism he had learnt . . . "Caius is a
> man, men are mortal, therefore Caius is mortal," has always
> seemed to him correct as applied to Caius, but certainly not as
> applied to himself. . . . Caius really was mortal, and it was right
> for him to die, but for me . . . with all my thoughts and emo-
> tions, it's altogether a different matter. It cannot be that I ought
> to die. That would be too terrible.[15]

The trouble with this attitude is that it misdirects the attention and thereby increases the liability to contingency that rightly focused attention might mitigate. If it is kept firmly in mind that contingency may destroy or damage anyone, including oneself and those one loves, it will prompt concentration on what is important and prevent the frittering away of whatever opportunities there are on trivial pursuits. The denial of risk increases the liability to it whereas its acknowledgment strengthens the defenses against it. Its acknowledgment, however, can also go wrong because it may elicit an overreaction. This can go in the direction of heroism or despair. Both involve exaggeration and thus the falsification of the facts that need to be faced. It may lead to an inflation of one's powers or to a pessimistic overestimation of the threat presented by contingency. The younger Oedipus is an instructive example of one who swings back and forth between these pitfalls. He vexes heroically: "My troubles are mine / and I am the only man alive who can sustain them" (K. 1548–49), and he exaggerates in despair, declaring that he is "the man the deathless gods hate most of all!" (K. 1480). Then the combination of these inflated passions causes him to erupt in the spectacular reaction of self-blinding, which, of course, makes matters even worse than they already were.

Realism is one of the most important resources in facing contingency. One's troubles are rarely so great and one's life rarely involves struggles so glorious and heroic against overwhelming odds as it may seem in the throes of passion. Human beings cannot stop having passions, especially not in the midst of crises that provoke them. But they can stop them from getting out of hand. If they know the emotional excesses to which they are prone, they can recognize them when they are about to occur and they can stop themselves from being led by them to inappropriate action, as the younger Oedipus was led to self-blinding. And then, like the old Oedipus, while they still have their passions, they may also learn to control their strength and expression: "My rage has outrun my wrongs, / I'd lashed myself too much" (C. 488–89). Without this control they are liable to the risks created by the uncontrolled parts of their character, risks that add their destructive potential to those that exist beyond their control.

Yet even if the temptation to deny or to exaggerate what the understanding of contingency reveals is resisted, there remains the lure of resignation. People may come to wonder about the point of wholehearted engagement in life, if the efforts they make cannot free them from contingency. Understanding this truth and achieving of control over their passions may just sap their will. Instinct, training, the need to earn a living, the pleasures of life, a mild curiosity about the future, and intermittent bemusement afforded by being a spectator may make them carry on, but their hearts will not be in it. They will lack enthusiasm, dedication, and seriousness of spirit, and their lives will become permeated by a languid insipidity in which nothing really matters, like Eliot's J. Alfred Prufrock or Chekhov's middle-aged characters, desultorily talking away their lives during endless barren afternoons. What results is the very misfortune whose prospect motivated resignation, for what initially disturbs them is the fear that they will not attain good lives despite their best efforts. If this leads to making only minimal efforts, they collude in causing what they fear. The reasonable alternative is to make the best efforts while understanding that they may be unavailing and disciplining oneself not to allow one's passions to get out of hand when one faces the possibility of failure. What makes this alternative reasonable is that it helps make lives good.

There may, of course, be people who do not want to have a good life. What should be said about them depends on why they do not want it. One possibility is that they live under barbaric conditions in which their main concern must be with staying alive, and they have no energy left to wonder about how good their lives are. That countless people have lived and are living under such conditions is a sad fact. But it does not remove the point of asking how life should be lived when conditions are civilized. Another possibility is that people are living in civilized conditions and yet do not want a good life because they fail to understand its nature. The appropriate response is to do what reasonably can be done to make them understand it. Yet there still remain many people who live in civilized conditions, have the requisite understanding, and still do not want to have a good life. Such people are unreasonable, and they are likely to harm both themselves and others. The former is regrettable, the latter requires whatever action is appropriate to immorality.

The upshot of this discussion of depth may be formulated either negatively or positively. Put negatively, depth makes it possible to avoid an inappropriate attitude to what is understood about the human condition. In particular, it allows us to avoid such common ways of going wrong as disengagement, denial, exaggeration, and resignation. Expressed positively, depth involves an attitude to the human condition that combines continued effort to live according to an ideal of a good life, acceptance that contingency endangers its success, a balanced emotional response that tilts neither toward undue pessimism nor toward foolhardy quixoticism, and an undiminished commitment to exercise fully such control as possible over one's character and circumstances.

4.5 True Hope

The argument has aimed to show that depth presents a way of contending with the contingency of life. The alternative to the stark choice between false hope and hopelessness is to understand that contingency may frustrate reasonable and moral efforts to live a good life, that the resulting sense of hopelessness is due to an unrealistic expectation that the human condition is other than it is, that abandoning the expectation is to remove the ground of hopelessness, that the general understanding of the human condition must be brought to bear on individual circumstances, and that the key is to form an appropriate attitude to what has thus been understood.

Depth brings greater realism. It leads to the acknowledgment of the pervasive influence of contingency, but it mitigates its destructive consequences. This greater realism is ground for true hope: a hope chastened, purified, and strengthened through having resisted the temptations of disengagement, denial of the facts, exaggerated self-aggrandizement or despair, and resignation. It is hope without expectation of cosmic justice and without bitterness that the world is not more hospitable to humanity.

What is left is enough to fend off hopelessness. Human beings are vulnerable to contingency, but they need not be ruined by it. And even if it damages lives, it need not destroy them. Depth permits true hope because it avoids the futility of hounding the unresponsive heavens to relieve human misfortune and because it prepares its possessors to pick up the damaged pieces, if they can be picked up, and go on. True hope does not come from a guarantee that ideals of a good life pursued reasonably and morally will be realized. It comes from the confidence that one has done what is possible to succeed and that if failure comes despite reasonable and moral efforts, destruction still need not result. Depth does not promise good lives; it promises to cope with contingency as well as the human condition permits. These dark thoughts are, in a currently unfashionable sense, philosophical. This sense is what Bertrand Russell may have had in mind when he wrote, "To teach how to live without certainty, and yet without being paralyzed by hesitation, is perhaps the chief thing that philosophy, in our age, can still do for those who study it."[16]

5/

Honor

If I lose mine honour, I lose myself.

WILLIAM SHAKESPEARE, *Antony and Cleopatra*

5.1 Is Honor Obsolete?

Shakespeare's Antony speaks for a tradition that has endured from Homer to our times. Numerous contemporary writers believe, however, that honor has lost the importance it once had. Peter Berger says, "Honor occupies about the same place in contemporary usage as chastity. An individual asserting it hardly invites admiration, and one who claims to have lost it is an object of amusement rather than sympathy." According to Frank Henderson Stewart, "Honor no longer plays much part in our thinking," and "honor has lost its importance in recent times." Nicholas Fotion and Gerard Elfstrom note, "In the late twentieth century, honor is almost never discussed. . . . The silence appears to indicate that honor is no longer deemed either socially or intellectually important." As Charles Taylor puts it, "The ethics of honor . . . is subjected to withering critique . . . the search for honor condemned as fractious and undisciplined self-indulgence, gratuitously endangering the really valuable things in life." Curtis Brown Watson points out, "It is important to remember that the pejorative connotations now attached to honor . . . are . . . the converse of the favorable connotations which the word possessed in Elizabethan times." And John Casey says, "It is striking that whereas today the notion of honour finds almost no place in the thought of moral philosophers, it was a central and indispensable idea of ancient and Renaissance ethics."[1]

Consider now some honorable and admirable actions in contemporary life. In the notorious Profumo case, a British cabinet minister lied to the Parliament about having frequented a prostitute whose favors were also enjoyed by a KGB agent. Profumo was disgraced, lost his office, gave up his seat in the Parliament, and became an object of scorn. It is less well known that although a rich man, he spent the subsequent decades of his life doing volunteer work ten to twelve hours every day in the worst slums of London. That was honorable. In the Second World War a German conscript was ordered to take part in the execution of innocent civilian hostages in retaliation for partisan activities against the Germans. He refused. He was told that unless he obeyed the order, he himself would be executed alongside the hostages. He did not, and he was. His refusal was honorable. When a clothing factory accidentally burned down shortly before Christmas, the owner continued for many months to pay the wages of the workers until their forced idleness came to an end and the factory was reopened. That too was honorable. Elliot Richardson, who was attorney general in Nixon's cabinet during Watergate, had immense pressure brought on him to fire the special prosecutor he had appointed to investigate the whole affair. He resisted the pressure, as well as the blandishments that were dangled before him. He finally had to choose between firing the special prosecutor or being himself fired. He then honorably resigned. The young assistant professor who withdraws the book manuscript upon whose publication his tenure depends when he finds a serious flaw in the case he is making in it is also acting honorably. All these actions are honorable and admirable. What could, then, lead thoughtful people to deny that honor is a personal excellence that continues to have an important place in contemporary life? The answer requires understanding an essential feature of honor.

5.2 Social and Personal Honor

The *OED* (1961) lists as the first two definitions of honor the following: "1. High respect, esteem, or reverence accorded to exalted worth or rank; deferential admiration or approbation. . . . 2. Personal title to high respect or esteem; honourableness; elevation of character; nobleness of mind, scorn of meanness, magnanimity; a fine sense of and strict allegiance to what is due or right." The first definition is of the social aspect of honor, the second of its personal aspect. The contrast may be said to be between honors and honor, between the various forms of respect that the world accords and that in people in virtue of which respect is accorded. The first has to do with public recognition, the second with personal characteristics. Julian Pitt-Rivers offers a succinct expression of the two aspects: "Honour is the value of a person in his own eyes, but also in the eyes of his society. It is his estimation of his own worth, his *claim* to pride, but it is also the acknowledgement of that claim, his excellence recognized by society.... Honour, therefore, provides a nexus between the ideals of a society and their reproduction in the individual through his aspiration to personify them."[2] Under ideal circumstances, personal excellence is socially recognized and social recognition depends on the personal excellence of its recipient. In such circumstances, the worth or rank for which honors are given is not only believed to be exalted but actually is so, and the honorable person's strict allegiance is to what is really due or right.

Circumstances, of course, are rarely if ever ideal. Consequently, mistakes may inform both aspects of honor. One kind of mistake is involved in giving honors to people who do not deserve them. They are falsely believed to possess the features that merit the honors. The other kind of mistake occurs when people act honorably in maintaining their allegiance to what they mistakenly believe is due or right. They honorably uphold what is in fact morally wrong. In both kinds of mistakes the false beliefs must have some plausibility, for if they were so obviously false that anyone with normal intelligence would have to see them as such, it would tend to undermine the ascription of honor. It stretches the meaning of "honor" too far to call the status and recognition known moral monsters receive honors or to suppose that the allegiance of torturers or death camp guards to their brand of evil can be honorable. The mistaken ascription of honor should be an understandable mistake, not a perverse one.

The social and personal aspects, with the qualifications just noted, may be said jointly to define honor. But honor takes many different forms for two reasons. The first is that there are great historical and cultural variations both in the personal excellences and in the social recognitions that constitute honor. The second is that there are great variations also in how the social and personal aspects of honor are related to each other. By concentrating on the second reason, we can understand the mistake of those who believe honor has lost its importance.

The historical relation between the social and personal aspects of honor in the Western world gradually shifts away from the dominance of the social toward the dominance of the personal. This shift is important because it has a formative influence on the prevailing moral identity, on how people conceive of good lives and of the goodness of their own lives. When the social dominated over the personal, honor depended on social standing. How honorable people were depended on how honorable they were thought to be. Their sense of honor derived from the honors they received. The personal was the social because the personal was understood in social terms. The moral identity of people was constituted of the social positions they occupied. The higher the position, the greater the honor. Honor was thus seen as essentially hierarchical. In contemporary Western life the personal dominates over the social. How honorable people are depends on how close they come to living according to ideals of personal excellence they have accepted. They may spurn the honors they receive or ignore honors altogether because what matters to them is their own estimate of themselves. Honor is thus seen now as essentially personal.

These two extremes and the shift from one to the other are idealizations. Historical shifts are rarely unambiguous. There have always been a large number of intermediate states in which the social and personal aspects of honor were intermingled in different proportions. The shift, however, is unmistakable, even if its realization in various contexts is gradual and uneven. The history of this shift has been well surveyed, and there is no need to repeat it here.[3] These surveys, however, are descriptive. Making a case for the continuing importance of honor requires supplementing them with the evaluative claim that this historical shift constitutes not merely a change but an improvement. There are good reasons for regarding the shift as moral progress because the shift away from the social and toward the personal moves from a superficial to a deeper conception of honor. The extent to which the deeper rather than the superficial conception prevails is the extent to which moral progress has been made in this particular respect. But why is the social aspect superficial and the personal deep?

Perhaps the best exemplification of a context in which the social dominates over the personal is the heroic life depicted in the Homeric epics.[4] The honorable man is the hero, and he has to prove his heroism again and again in battle against other heroes. Those who prevail are honored with status and riches. The more honors they have, the more honorable they are. But the Homeric hero is always at risk because he continually has to put his life on the line to defend his community from outside attacks and to attack other communities to enrich his own. Honor in this context is highly competitive. The more one person has, the less there is for others. It is certainly true that part of the motivation to gain honor is to gain honors. It cannot be true, however, that the honor is constituted of the honors. For the honors are given to winners in these competitions, and winning depends not on the possession of honors but on personal characteristics, such as courage, strength, martial skill, and cunning, which make winning possible. A hero is thus honored for his personal excellences. Consequently, even in the Homeric context the personal aspect is bound to be deeper than the social.

The relevant difference between the Homeric context and ours is not that in the Homeric context social standing was more important than personal characteristics but that now it is the other way around. Social standing could not have been more important because if it had been awarded in disregard of personal characteristics, the community would soon have been enslaved by those who tied social standing to heroic personal characteristics. The relevant differences are, first, that the personal characteristics they honored were public and had to be demonstrated in highly competitive contexts in which life and death were the stakes, whereas the personal characteristics we honor need not be displayed publicly and competitively.[5] And second, the ancient Greeks had to connect social standing to personal characteristics, whereas we do not.

It constitutes genuine moral progress to realize that the essential feature of honor is constituted of what people are and not of their social standing. In some contexts it is very important that the two should go together because the survival of the community depends on honoring certain people with certain characteristics. In other contexts, however, this is not so. Homeric communities had to give the best they had to those who ensured their survival, but we can afford the luxury of separating personal honor from social honors. The realization that they can be separated, that the deep aspect of honor is personal and its social aspect is superficial, and that the personal characteristics that deserve honor are much more varied than the Homeric Greeks supposed is moral progress.

There is yet another reason for thinking that the shift constitutes moral progress. The exigencies of their lives forced Homeric Greeks to maintain a very tight connection between social standing and personal characteristics. Their survival depended on honoring martial excellences. The conditions of our lives are more civilized, so we have loosened the connection between the social and personal aspects of honor. But with this loosening comes the increased risk of error. Honorable personal characteristics may not be honored, and honors may be awarded to people who do not deserve them. For us, it is an entirely contingent matter whether social standing reflects personal excellences. That this is so is just a fact about our lives and circumstances. It may well be thought, however, that this fact constitutes the opposite of moral progress, since the Homeric Greeks strove to give people what they deserved whereas we do not.

This line of thought, however, is overridden by another. We rightly congratulate ourselves for having achieved greater control over the conditions of our lives than was enjoyed ever before. We want to leave the goodness of our lives as little to the mercy of contingencies as possible. One contingency is the risk of error in the distribution of honors. We have become aware of that risk. We know that honors given may not be honors deserved and that honors deserved may not be given. We thus distrust social standing as a mark of honor. This makes us concentrate more than our predecessors did on the deep aspect of honor and less on the superficial one. We care more about what personal characteristics people have than about their social standing. And we do not think this way just about other people; we think about ourselves in the same way. It matters less to our moral identity what others think of us than used to be the case when one's social standing was an essential component of moral identity. This too is moral progress because it gives us greater control over our lives by reducing further the influence of the contingency that is a consequence of the all too familiar errors in the distribution of honors. If honor is not dependent on honors, then we can maintain our self-esteem even if we fail to get the honors to which we are entitled.

We have now reached the point where the question of what leads thoughtful people to deny that honor continues to have an important place in contemporary life can be answered. The answer is that these people are impressed by the discontinuity between the past and the present that our moral progress has brought about. Their mistake is that they fail to see that there is also continuity. They see that we denigrate social standing as a mark of honor, and they mistakenly conclude that we denigrate honor.[6] They fail to see that we continue to honor various personal excellences, that it is right to honor them, and that personal honor continues to make an important contribution to the self-esteem of many people in the contemporary Western world.

Skeptics about the contemporary importance of honor may respond by claiming that the shift from social to personal honor is so radical as to require new terminology. Instead of talking about personal honor, they talk about integrity. James Collins, for example, says, "Honor may mean the public respect that is due to a person because he has certain qualities of character or has accomplished certain things. But, when we say that a person is a man of honor, we usually mean that he has a specific character trait which can be described best as *personal integrity*." Or, as Stewart puts it, "it is the integrity of certain persons that *makes* them honorable." Or, in Cora Diamond's words, "integrity appears to be a moral virtue . . . because we think of it as having some essential connection with not acting dishonorably."[7] This, however, is merely a verbal point that gives no reason whatever to think that the referent of "personal honor" has lost its importance. Even if the dubious claim that the word *honor* is falling into disuse were true, it would no more follow that its referent is losing its importance than the infrequent use of the word *automobile* implies that cars are losing their importance. It does not matter what personal honor is called; what matters is that it is a personal excellence that has intimate connection with self-esteem, whose possession makes many lives better and whose lack makes many lives worse.

5.3   The Honorable Life of Malesherbes

We can understand better the connection between honor and self-esteem if we have an example of an honorable life before us. The examples introduced earlier (Profumo, the German conscript, the factory owner, Richardson, and the assistant professor) are of honorable acts. Whether these acts add up to honorable lives depends on what else has been going on in the lives of their agents, and that information is lacking. Consider, therefore, the life of an honorable man about which there is sufficient information.[8]

Lamoignon de Malesherbes was a French aristocrat, Tocqueville's great-grandfather and model in life. He was a remarkable man. He was loyal to the monarchy, but saw clearly the corruption and the abuse of power of the administration that ruled in the name of Louis XVI during the years preceding the Revolution. He was influenced by the philosophes, and he used his impeccable royalist credentials to criticize the prevailing administrative system and to suggest far-reaching reforms. He thought that the common people of France had legitimate grievances and that the way the country was administered violated the long-standing compact between the monarchy, the aristocracy, and the people. He had the ear of the king, who could change the prevailing state of affairs. He was also an influential and powerful figure whose opinions carried much weight with his fellow aristocrats. Nevertheless, his advice was not heeded. It is impossible to say whether the Revolution could have been avoided if his reforms had been enacted. The chances are, however, that the terror, the massacre of tens of thousands of innocent people, and the rule of the mob formed of the worst elements of French society would have lacked the widespread support or acquiescence they in fact had. Be that as it may, Malesherbes foresaw the calamity, warned against it, and did what he could to ameliorate its causes. When he failed, he left the court, dissociated himself from those in power, and retired to private life.

The Revolution, of course, came, and the king was eventually put on trial for his life. The monarchy was replaced by a reign of terror, fear among the remaining aristocrats was widespread and justified, but Malesherbes volunteered to defend the king against the charges. Once again, he did the best he could, this time to represent what he believed were the legitimate claims of the monarchy against lawless, benighted, moralistic fanatics. He was, as before, an eloquent, fearless spokesman for reason and decency, but, as before, he failed. The king was beheaded. Malesherbes was remembered by the perpetrators of the terror, and the consequences of his defense of the king were not long in catching up with him, as he retired, once again, to private life. He and most of his family were imprisoned, falsely charged, and executed. Malesherbes was an honorable man who lived and died honorably. His case calls for two comments.

First, skeptics see honor as quaint, quixotic grandstanding motivated by the slightly ridiculous desire to cut a fine public figure. They see it as embodying a confusion between pride and duty, vanity and obligation. These charges rest on the mistaken supposition that honor must involve the recognition of one's social standing by others, or that honor presupposes the code of a caste. As we have seen, however, honor need not be sought from others and it need not be conferred by them. Malesherbes's conduct illustrates the arguments already given against this mistaken view. His fellow aristocrats did not honor him for proposing reforms, and his defense of the king was spectacularly unpopular. Malesherbes acted as he saw fit and was indifferent to what others thought. And although he belonged to a caste and subscribed to its code, that was a historical accident. Honorable actions may be dictated by personal ideals, love or friendship, commitment to a cause, professional obligations, a sense of justice, decency, or benevolence, and not just by the code of a caste.

Second, Malesherbes's honorable actions formed a pattern, and that pattern was a dominant feature in his life. But he was not fanatical about his honor. He had a close and loving family life, he had a keen interest in agricultural innovations and experimented with them on his estate, he was a learned and very well read man who conducted a lively correspondence with the intellectual luminaries of his age, he was a highly respected botanist whose catalog of plants that flourished in his part of France is still admired, and he used his considerable fortune to help those whom he thought were deserving: one among them, incidentally, was Rousseau, who thought highly of Malesherbes. Malesherbes, therefore, lived a full life, filled with interests, emotional ties, and intellectual pursuits. Honor was dominant in his life because his most basic commitment was to it: when his other concerns and commitments came into conflict with what he regarded as the requirements of honor, honor prevailed. If he had not lived in turbulent times, he might have avoided the wrenching conflicts that were forced on him between honor and other things he valued. But the conflicts did occur, and he resolved them in favor of honor.

To describe people as honorable, therefore, means not just that they act honorably on the appropriate occasions, but also that honor is a dominant feature of their lives. They differ from those in whose lives honor plays a lesser role because honor for them is the highest standard to which they turn to resolve their conflicts. People less committed to honor may have some other standard as highest, or they may have several standards that weigh equally with them, or they may have no standards at all and act as prompted by their feelings, desires, or interests. Not to have honor as a dominant feature of one's life does not exclude commitment to morality.

Honor is one form that moral commitments may take, but there are others. And, of course, all moral commitments, to honor or to other things, may turn out to be mistaken and lead to immoral actions. It is as possible to be honorable and wicked as it is to be courageous, conscientious, honest, or temperate and wicked. Being honorable consequently is neither necessary nor sufficient for living a good life. It is not necessary because good lives may take forms in which honor has no dominant place. Nor is honor sufficient, for good lives require that the commitments that are honored be morally acceptable. Nevertheless, an honorable life is one form that good lives may take. All evidence indicates that Malesherbes's honorable life was good, partly because it conformed to the universal, social, and individual requirements of morality.

5.4 Self-Esteem

We still do not know, however, what an honorable life consists in. To know that honor is the highest standard in honorable lives is not to know what that standard requires and forbids. The first thing that honor requires is loyalty, that is, steadfast adherence, especially when hardship, temptation, danger, or challenge makes it difficult. But what is it to which honor requires loyalty? It is always some valued object, such as an ideal, an institution, a person, a country, a way of life, a cause, and so on. What characterizes honor, however, is not the identity of the particular valued object, but the nature of the attitude toward it. The objects of honor vary greatly, but the attitude toward them remains the same because commitment to the varied objects is an essential component of one's moral identity. One's conception of a good life is inseparably connected with valuing whatever the object happens to be. The object, however, may still be valued for different reasons. One is that it is necessary for living according to one's ideal of a good life. Financial security, leisure, physical or psychological comfort, social stability, and the like are valued because they enable one to live a good life, but they are not what make the life good. Call these *enabling goods*. They enable one to have goods that actually make a life good, such as participating in a great institution, having a reciprocally loving relationship, following a noble way of life, practicing a worthy profession, or belonging to a distinguished culture or community. Call these *constituent goods*. Honor, then, may be said to be tied to the attitude of loyalty toward the constituent goods of one's ideal of a good life. One's moral identity is thus inseparably connected with valuing them.

The reason for valuing them, however, is not that they are constituent goods, but that they are worth valuing because they are good, fine, noble, great, lovable, beneficial, or inspiring in some other way. Because of their intrinsic excellence, they make life good. Thus they are not valued because they are constituent goods; they are constituent goods because they are valuable. Valuing them, therefore, is the moral achievement of being the kind of person who appreciates their intrinsic excellence. To live an honorable life is to pursue these intrinsically excellent goods. An honorable life is thus a double moral achievement: it is to live according to a standard that one regards as the highest, and the standard involves loyalty to some good that one has recognized as intrinsically excellent.

The connection of honor with achievement does not make honor competitive. The achievement is not to do better than others in pursuit of some good, but to recognize its intrinsic excellence and to do as well as one can to live according to it. The greatest achievement is to do one's best, which may or may not be better than what other similarly committed people can do. An honorable life, therefore, need not lead to great success at some endeavor. Malesherbes's life was honorable even though he failed to bring about the reforms he thought were necessary and he failed in his defense of the king. It was honorable because the cause to which he was committed was the intrinsically excellent one of making France into a state where reason and decency prevailed and because he did his best to achieve it.

When the social aspect of honor dominated over the personal, honor was competitive. The more honors a person had, the fewer were left for others. Honors can have meaning only if they are scarce. But now, when the personal aspect of honor dominates over the social, everyone can have great honor because doing one's best to pursue an intrinsically excellent good is open to everyone in civilized circumstances.

Honorable people esteem themselves because they value the manner in which they live. They do not value it merely because the life is theirs, but also because the constitutive goods of the life are intrinsically excellent. It is the dedication to these goods that is the source of their self-esteem. They would hold other honorable lives that were dedicated to the same constitutive goods in the same esteem, and they would not esteem their own lives if they lacked the constitutive goods. Their self-esteem, therefore, derives from the value of the constituent goods to which they are committed. Their lives are made estimable through their recognition of the intrinsic excellence of those goods and through doing their best to pursue them. They esteem being a creative artist, an officer of the law, an upholder of a cultural tradition, a fighter against injustice, a seeker of scientific truth, or a writer who tries to distill the sensibility of an age. It is their commitment to these constitutive goods that defines their moral identity, gives them self-esteem, provides their fundamental commitments, and confers honor on them. This is why Antony had it right when he said, "If I lose mine honour, I lose myself," and this is also why skeptics about the contemporary importance of honor have it wrong.

The self-esteem that honorable people feel must be distinguished from self-respect. Neither term has a univocal meaning, and there is a tendency to use them interchangeably. But doing so obscures important moral differences and contributes to the prevailing misunderstanding of honor. Self-respect is a notion central to deontological morality, and we may as well accept the account that John Rawls has given of it: "First . . . it includes a person's sense of his own value, his conviction that his conception of his good, his plan of life, is worth carrying out. And second, self-respect implies a confidence in one's ability, so far as it is within one's power, to fulfill one's intentions. . . . It is clear then why self-respect is a primary good."[9] Primary goods, in Rawls's sense, are "things that every rational man is presumed to want."[10] In a just society, according to Rawls, everyone can enjoy the primary goods, including self-respect. Self-respect is thus an egalitarian notion because justice requires that everyone should have it.

It follows from this account that self-respect is independent of moral achievement. It is connected with people's potentialities, not with what they make of them. The correctness of people's secure conviction about the worth of their conception of a good life or life-plan and their confidence in their capacity to fulfill their intentions depends on what they actually make of their potentialities in the course of living their lives. The realization of their reasonable potentialities is a moral achievement that is higher than self-respect, and it is that achievement that warrants self-esteem. Self-respect is based on promise, self-esteem on promise redeemed. Since people's moral achievements vary greatly, self-esteem is an inegalitarian notion.

The difference may be put thus: self-respect is a good to which all people may be said to be entitled because their human worth is the same, whereas self-esteem is a good to which people are entitled depending on their moral merits. Self-respect is egalitarian, self-esteem is not because, as Gregory Vlastos says, "the human worth of all persons is equal, however unequal may be their merit."[11] The essential moral difference that is obscured by using *self-respect* and *self-esteem* interchangeably is that people's moral achievements may vary and those who have realized their reasonable potentialities are entitled to feel better about themselves than those who have failed.

Living an honorable life, as Malesherbes did, is a high moral achievement. That is why Malesherbes was entitled to much self-esteem. It is, however, essential to point out that an honorable life is just one kind of life that merits self-esteem, and there are others. Honorable lives typically involve great effort, trials, much hardship; endeavors, pursuits, and often quests. But lives can constitute moral achievements, and thus merit self-esteem, and be perfectly ordinary in which people conscientiously do their mundane jobs, raise their children, and have a good marriage; or be lives of service in which they aim to alleviate the misery of others, even if, the world being what it is, they meet with little success; or be the lives of teachers of young children in which nothing particularly notable happens in the routine that involves the imparting of elementary knowledge and skills to generation after generation. Moreover, not only can lives other than honorable ones merit self-esteem; lives can be good even if self-esteem plays only a negligible role in them. People who have not tried to realize their potentialities, who have tried and failed, who have made serious mistakes about the suitability of their ideals of a good life to their characters and circumstances can still be kind, generous, decent, and fair. So the case for honor is not a case for a personal excellence that is necessary either for self-esteem or for a good life. It is a case for one important way in which people in the past and in the present can achieve self-esteem and a good life.

The sense of honor, like so much else, can go wrong. It can be inflated, and it can be misdirected. If it is inflated, people suppose themselves to be more honorable than their achievements warrant. It is, of course, a widespread human failing to exaggerate one's achievements. It turns the inflated sense of honor into vanity. But the sense of honor can also be commensurate with one's achievements, and then it can be free of vanity. Honor can also be misdirected. It can be derived from the pursuit of an evil or worthless object that is falsely believed to be good. If the object is evil, its honorable pursuit compounds the agents' wickedness. An honorable terrorist is worse than a fickle one because the first is steadfast in pursuit of evil whereas the second is not. Honor, of course, is not the only personal excellence that can be put to immoral uses. The same can happen to courage, intelligence, imagination, piety, and so on. If honor is derived from a worthless object, it becomes ridiculous or pathetic. Don Quixote sometimes appears one, sometimes the other. In such cases, the people's view of the value of their own pursuits is grotesquely at odds with their real value. Not even the most complete collection of canceled streetcar tickets merits being thought of as fine, noble, great, lovable, beneficial, or morally good. Honor can also be misdirected if its objects are not intrinsically excellent goods but the self of the agent. Honor then is thought to be warranted by what the agents take themselves to be independently of the goods they may or may not pursue. Such people's high opinion of themselves is disconnected from whatever their achievements happen to be. Their honor turns into unwarranted pride. Their focus is on their selves, not on the goods in whose achievement it is legitimate to take pride. Rightly directed honor, however, can go hand in hand with modesty. For honorable people can see that their achievements are minor in comparison with those of others or with those that are possible.

One source of doubt about honor is that it can turn into the wrong sort of pride, or into vanity, or become an aid to immorality. This may happen, but the doubt would be warranted only if it were also true that honor is bound to go wrong in these ways. There is no reason to suppose, however, that honor is any more prone to turning into a vice than many other personal excellences. And there is good reason to suppose that many people live honorable lives whose moral merits are undeniable because they do their best to pursue intrinsically excellent goods.

The foregoing account is intended to make evident what is involved in honor, how it is connected with self-esteem, why people value it, and what makes it into a personal excellence. It follows from it that living honorably engages people's beliefs, emotions, and motives. They must have a good enough understanding of the constituent goods of their lives to recognize their intrinsic excellence; they must have strong feelings of attraction, admiration, and appreciation for these goods; and they must discipline themselves to make, and not to deviate from making, the constant efforts that are required for living a life whose dominant feature is commitment to these goods. This account is incomplete, however, because it concentrates on the positive features of honor and says nothing about the negative features that motivate people to avoid dishonor.

Dishonor threatens those who are committed to living an honorable life and fail. Dishonor is the worst thing that can happen to people whose highest standard is honor, for it destroys their moral identity and self-esteem and makes them contemptible in their own eyes. Dishonor is not the lack of assiduity in doing what honor requires. People may not be as honorable as they could be because they are lazy, inattentive, weak, or insensitive. They rank low on their own scale of honor, but they rank. Dishonor is to act contrary to honor. It is to opt for what they regard as evil when they are committed to the good. They are not lukewarm or handicapped in honoring their commitments; they act in violation of them. They join those who attack their ideals, they undermine the institution they hold in highest regard, they betray the person they love, they disgrace their valued profession, or they side with the enemies of the culture or community that commands their allegiance. Threats, bribes, resentment, manipulation, self-deception, and so on may lead them to act in these ways. When they realize what they have done, their self-esteem is shattered and their moral identity is destroyed. They took themselves to be the opposite of what they have turned out to be. This is what happened to Adam and Eve after they ate the apple from the Tree of Knowledge, to Oedipus when he discovered he was guilty of incest and parricide, and to Othello when he realized Desdemona's innocence.

The desire to avoid this kind of moral disintegration motivates people to avoid dishonor as much as the desire to enjoy intrinsically excellent goods motivates them to seek honor. The account of honor may be summarized, then, by saying that an honorable life requires doing one's personal best in pursuit of what one regards as intrinsically excellent goods and what it forbids is to act in ways that are destructive of these goods. The attraction of honor and the repulsion of dishonor jointly account for the motivation to live an honorable life.

5.5 Honor and Some Contemporary Moral Mistakes

Two observations will conclude the case for the continued importance of honor in contemporary life. Both concern influential tendencies to focus on some moral considerations at the expense of others. They have led to a bias against the moral considerations they relegate to the periphery, and skepticism about honor is one unfortunate consequence of this bias.

The first of these tendencies reflects the domination of moral thought by consequentialism and deontology. Defenders of these approaches disagree about many things, but they agree that moral requirements must be universal and impartial. If a particular action in a particular context is right or wrong, then it is right or wrong regardless of who the agent is. The requirements of the consequentialist common good or the deontological practical reason are the same for everyone, and morality consists in acting according to these requirements.

Many serious criticisms have been directed against these approaches, but our present concern is with pointing out that if moral requirements had to be universal and impartial, then there would be centrally important contexts in everyone's life where moral considerations had no relevance. These contexts are the ones in which the identity of the agents makes a crucial difference in what they should do. People's choice of professions, friends, lovers, marriages, and amusements; their preferences about having children and how to raise them; about how to spend their money; their attitudes to music, sport, literature, illness, politics, and death; how reflective, gregarious, educated, public-spirited, or polite they are; and so on and on are all contexts in which their identity matters greatly. Their choices and actions in these contexts often have an important bearing on the goodness of their lives. Morality ought to help make reasonable decisions about such matters, but if moral requirements must be universal and impartial, then morality can provide little help. There is no doubt that universality and impartiality are important moral requirements in many impersonal moral contexts, but since there are many moral contexts that are personal, it impoverishes morality to exclude from it choices and actions that cannot reasonably be dictated by universal and impartial requirements.

The reason for stressing this point here is that the choice of an ideal of a good life that aims at self-esteem through honor is one of those personal decisions to which universal and impartial requirements have only marginal relevance. Honorable lives can be, but need not be, morally acceptable, and morally acceptable lives can be, but need not be, honorable. It is the domination of moral thought by the consequentialist and deontological emphasis on universality and impartiality that lends plausibility to doubts about the moral importance of honor. If, however, one takes a less restricting view of morality, the importance of honor will be recognized.

The second tendency that dominates moral thought is egalitarianism. It is motivated by the belief that human beings have equal worth and they are entitled to equal resources that make living a good life possible. The existing distribution of resources is unequal, so egalitarians are preoccupied with the question how society should be changed to eliminate the prevailing inequality. This preoccupation is now central to moral thought. Much needs to be said both for and against egalitarianism, but this is not the place to say any of it. What matters for present purposes is that egalitarianism focuses on contexts in which human beings should be treated in the same way. There undoubtedly are such contexts. But there are also ones in which they should be treated differently. These are contexts in which their moral merits are unequal because their moral achievements are greater or lesser and in which they deserve different degrees of praise or blame, benefits or burdens, rewards or punishments. Egalitarianism directs moral attention away from unequal moral merit, achievement, and desert and toward equal human worth, need, and rights. Since honor belongs to the context in which moral differences matter crucially, egalitarianism leads to doubts about its importance. A reasonable view of morality, however, must recognize the centrality of moral merit, achievement, and desert, and with them the importance of honor.

5.6 From the Particular toward the General

The first part of the book is now complete. Its aim has been to show in concrete detail some ways in which good lives can be lived. Self-direction, moral authority, decency, depth, and honor are personal excellences that, if pursued in morally acceptable ways—in conformity to the universal, social, and individual requirements of morality—make lives good. Such were the lives of Montaigne, More, the *sophron*, Newland Archer, Countess Olenska, Oedipus, and Malesherbes. These people lived in ways that stand as admirable examples of some good lives. So if it is asked what could or would make a life good, it is possible to point at these lives and say, That is what would!

Being able to do this is important because having these examples—to which numerous others could be added—can inspire those who are floundering in the tedious and demanding routines of everyday life and wondering about what could redeem their Sisyphean existence. It is, therefore, good to have these possibilities, but it is not good enough. Possibilities become live options only if people know how to make them possibilities for themselves. All the admirable lives of personal excellence have been lived in contexts quite different from our own. The descriptions of these possibilities must be supplemented, therefore, with an account of how to adapt them to a different context. How could we, at our time and place, and how could I, given my character and circumstances, live a life of one of these, or other, personal excellences? The next part of the book is concerned with answering this question.

Before indicating the direction of the argument in that part, it may not be remiss to stress what has and has not been claimed in the just-completed part. The claim is not that a good life must be a life of personal excellence. Good lives may take many different forms, and lives of personal excellence are only one of them. The claim is, therefore, only that lives of personal excellence may be good. Nor is the claim that lives of personal excellence are bound to be morally acceptable. They may or may not be. The actual lives that have been discussed were morally acceptable, but it is not hard to imagine that self-direction, moral authority, decency, depth, and honor may take morally deplorable forms. All lives may be vitiated by immorality. So the claim is that good lives must be both personally satisfying and morally acceptable. It is not enough if lives of personal excellence are satisfying; they must also conform to the universal, social, and individual requirements of morality if they are to be good. Moreover, although lives of personal excellence are committed to some one ideal that dominates in that life, it has not been claimed that the possession of one personal excellence rules out the possession of the others. People may have more than one personal excellence. The claim is rather that in lives of personal excellence, the pursuit of some one ideal is more important than the pursuit of any other. If that ideal can be combined with others, fine and good. But if it cannot be, if ideals conflict, then one ideal must become dominant and the others can only be recessive; otherwise, the life will be inundated with conflicts whose resolutions are unclear.

The argument in the next part begins with the observation that what made the lives that have been discussed in the first part good was the success with which Montaigne, More, and the others practiced the art of life. What needs to be understood is what makes the successful practice of the art of life possible. This is the subject of Chapter 6. It emerges from that chapter that the art of life consists in three different but related activities.

The first is discussed in Chapter 7. It has to do with commitment to the pursuit of some ideal of personal excellence. This leads people to look outside themselves for worthy ideals they could make their own. But doing so is not a matter of pursuing these ideals directly. Rather, it calls for engagement in whatever projects people happen to have in a way that reflects their ideal of personal excellence. The ideal is not to engage in any particular project, but to engage in whatever project is at hand in a way that reflects an ideal of personal excellence.

The second activity, considered in Chapter 8, is concerned with forming one's character, with making oneself into the kind of person who could live a life of personal excellence. This directs people's attention inward, toward forming the appropriate attitude to the life they have committed themselves to living. The attitude must dominate their character, in the sense that it must be the most important of their many attitudes, because its object is the goodness of their own lives. This attitude has cognitive, emotive, and motivational components, and what is required of it is that these components should form a coherent pattern in which beliefs, emotions, and motives are mutually reinforcing rather than pulling in incompatible directions.

The third activity, the topic of Chapter 9, is to avoid the numerous mistakes that may vitiate reasonable engagement in the first two kinds of activity. The pursuit of an ideal of personal excellence can go wrong in many ways, and so can the formation of attitudes. It is impossible to catalog all the possible sources of error, but it is possible to discuss some prevalent types of aberration that are characteristic obstacles to good lives in the present age: moralism, sentimentalism, and romanticism.

The emerging view, then, is that the successful practice of the art of life depends on the adoption of a reasonable ideal of personal excellence, on the formation of a coherent attitude that dominates in one's character, and on the avoidance of aberrations and other errors that vitiate these endeavors. These jointly may make a life personally satisfying, but a good life requires also that these activities be morally acceptable, that is, that they should conform to the universal, social, and individual requirements of morality.

PART TWO
Making Life Good

6/

The Art of Life

The delicate and difficult art is to find, in each new turn of experience, the *via media* between two extremes: to be catholic without being characterless; to have and apply standards, and yet to be on guard against their desensitizing and stupefying influence, their tendency to blind us to the diversities of concrete situations and to previously unrecognized values; to know when to tolerate, when to embrace, and when to fight. And in that art, since no fixed and comprehensive rule can be laid down for it, we shall doubtless never acquire perfection.

ARTHUR O. LOVEJOY, *The Great Chain of Being*

6.1 The Moral versus the Aesthetic Approach

The question whether there is an art of life may be understood as the question whether there is some general prescription that, if followed, would enable people to make their lives good, even though it is acknowledged that there are great differences among people and contexts in which the prescription ought to apply. It is widely assumed that the answer to this question is in the affirmative. The great religions; the poetic visions of Homer, Lucretius, Virgil, Dante, Milton, and Goethe; the philosophies of life of the Stoics, Epicurians, Skeptics, of Kierkegaard, Schopenhauer, Nietzsche, of the romantics, psychoanalysts, and existentialists all prescribe a general form that the art of life must take. Salvation, rationality, authenticity, faith, self-realization, and good works, living without illusion, self-deception, neurosis, false consciousness, bad faith, slavish adherence to phony authorities or to one's own bad self are some of the names under which arts of life are on offer. The reason, therefore, why the art of life presents a

129

problem is not that there is much doubt about its existence, but that there are deep disagreements about its nature.

One main source of this problem is the conflict between the moral and aesthetic approaches to the art of life. According to the moral approach, the key to the art of life is morality. According to the aesthetic approach, the key is people's creative development of themselves. The moral approach regards the art of life as a primarily moral art in which creativity typically plays only a minor role. The aesthetic approach regards the art of life as an essentially creative art in which morality may have only negligible significance.

These two approaches to the art of life reflect the ambiguity of the meaning of *art*. Art always aims at some product, but producing it may depend either on skills or on creative efforts. This difference, of course, is not absolute because skills and creative efforts may go together, but they nevertheless pull in different directions. Skills are typically the possessions of technique learned from other practitioners. Those who have them are usually artisans, craftsmen, or performers. They need to be competent at some traditional practice, but they need not break new ground. Creative efforts, in contrast, aim to be in some way novel or original, to change the traditional way of doing or looking at things. It is typical of artists that they make such efforts. The moral approach interprets the art of life as a skill. The aesthetic approach interprets it as a creative effort.

The ideal for the moral approach is Aristotle's *phronimos*, the practically wise person. The skill involved in practical wisdom is the application of knowledge of good and evil in the often complex circumstances of everyday life. The products of this skill are lives and actions that, in the variousness of characters and circumstances, reflect the requirements of morality. These lives are exemplified by Homer's Hector, Livy's Cincinnatus, Shakespeare's Horatio, and Henry James's Isabel Archer.

The ideal for the aesthetic approach is the creative life. The effort it requires centers on making oneself into a certain kind of person. The medium of the art of life is the life of the artist. The aim of artists' creative efforts is to develop the potentialities implicit in their nature and thereby give their lives such form, direction, and value as their characters and circumstances make possible. This may lead to a life dedicated to art, power, conquest, or the making of a new world. The resulting lives may be like those of Wagner, Julius Caesar, Napoleon, or Nietzsche.

Both approaches require justification. The justification of the moral approach is in terms of practical reason. Practical reason is the aspect of reason that guides human lives and actions, and it is to be contrasted with the theoretical aspect of reason, which aims at knowledge independently of its effect on human lives and actions. The basic assumption underlying the moral approach is that it is by living in accordance with practical reason that people can make their lives good. The justification of the aesthetic approach is in terms of self-creation, which leads people to break out of the mold of everyday life; free themselves from custom, convention, tradition, and the shackles of history; and leave behind conventional wisdom about what is possible and impossible, aim high, and give their best to achieve it. The extent to which people succeed in living in this manner is the extent to which their lives will be good.

Much more will be said about both approaches and their justifications, but even the little that has been said is sufficient to make clear that there is a conflict between them. The motivational source of the moral approach is practical reason; of the aesthetic one it is the will. Since the requirements of practical reason apply to everyone impartially and impersonally, the moral approach is universalistic. Since the will is employed to develop the potentialities of individuals, to overcome their limitations, and since potentialities and limitations vary with individuals and circumstances, the aesthetic approach is essentially connected with individual differences, with different levels of achievement and merit; it is thus individualistic.

Being guided by either practical reason or the will does not, of course, exclude the other, but it does relegate it to a subordinate position. It is well if practical reason aids the creative effort of the will, but if it does not, then it is but another confining limitation that good lives must overcome. And the contrary is true as well: it is good if doing what practical reason dictates coincides with what people happen to will, but if it does not, then the will must be altered so as to follow the dictates of practical reason. In the first case, following the aesthetic approach, people do what they do, not because it is practically reasonable but because they will it. In the second case, following the moral approach, people do what they will, not because they will it but because practical reason dictates it.

The critical aim of this chapter is twofold. First, it seeks to show that the claims of universalistic practical reason lead to an indefensible absolutism that, among its many defects, makes an art of life impossible. Second, it aims to show that the claims of individualistic will lead to an equally indefensible relativism with its own multiple defects, one among which is that it endangers the conditions in which the art of life can be practiced. The constructive aim of the chapter is to show that this conflict about the art of life can be resolved by combining the salvageable components of the moral and aesthetic approaches. This will help situate personal excellences within morality and deepen our understanding of them by identifying their moral and aesthetic features.

6.2 The Conflict

The art of life and the problems involved in its interpretation are well illustrated by John Stuart Mill's work. The art of life, according to Mill, has "three departments, Morality, Prudence or Policy, and Aesthetics; the Right, the Expedient, and the Beautiful or Noble." "To this art," says Mill, "all other arts are subordinate; since its principles are those which must determine whether the special aim of any particular art is worthy and desirable, and what is its place in the scale of desirable things." The art of life, then, combines factual propositions derived from what Mill calls science and general principles that "enjoin or recommend that something should be." These general principles taken together may be called "the Doctrine of Ends; which, borrowing the language of the German metaphysicians, may also be termed, not improperly, the principles of Practical Reason."[1]

The art of life must have "a *Philosophia Prima*" peculiar to it, and it comprises "the first principles of Conduct," for "there must be some standard by which to determine the goodness or badness, absolute and comparative, of ends." But this is not all: "whatever that standard is, there can be but one: for if there were several ultimate principles of conduct, the same conduct might be approved by one of these principles and condemned by another; and there would be needed some more general principle as umpire between them."[2]

"If that principle be rightly chosen, it will be found, I apprehend," says Mill, "to serve quite as well for the ultimate principle of Morality, as for that of Prudence, Policy, or Taste." Mill then says that "the general principle to which all rules of practice ought to conform, and the test by which they should be tried, is that of conduciveness to the happiness of mankind, or rather, of all sentient beings: in other words . . .

the promotion of happiness is the ultimate principle." For the "discussion and vindication of this principle," Mill refers the reader to the "volume entitled *Utilitarianism*."[3] And in *Utilitarianism* Mill says that the "greatest happiness principle" is "the foundation of morals," "the standard of morality," and "the criterion of morality."[4]

If this were all, we could simply conclude that Mill follows the moral approach to the art of life. In doing so, he opts for moral absolutism, for universality over individuality, for reason over will. He recognizes that aesthetic and prudential considerations, two of the three "departments" of the art of life, may conflict with moral considerations, which form the third "department," but these conflicts are settled by "the ultimate principle of Morality," the greatest happiness principle. If self-creation conflicts with morality, morality should prevail. The art of life is a moral art, and its aim is the greatest happiness possible for all sentient beings.

Since the art of life is moral, Mill thinks, it means that people trying to live a good life are required "to be as strictly impartial [between their own happiness and that of others] as a disinterested and benevolent spectator," that each person should form "an indissoluble association between his own happiness and the good of the whole," that "their ends are identified with those of others," and that the "feeling of unity . . . be taught as a religion, and the whole force of education, of institutions, and of opinion [be] directed, as it once was in the case of religion, to make every person grow from infancy surrounded on all sides both by the profession and the practice of it."[5]

Even Mill's sympathizers must be embarrassed by the oppressive priggish moralizing that is expressed in these lamentable lines. Mill simply does not face the consequence of his position that the extent to which the right prevails is the extent to which people must act contrary to their ideals of a good life. There may be good reasons for acting in this way, but these reasons, if they exist, cannot alter the fact that the art of life, in Mill's interpretation, requires the denigration of elements whose necessity to good lives Mill himself recognizes. If the art of life is the kind of moral art Mill takes it to be, then its universal, impartial, and impersonal claims prescribe that people ought to subordinate the goodness of their own lives to the goodness of other people's lives. Since the art of life is the art that enables people to make good lives for themselves, Mill's moralistic interpretation dooms it to failure.

The moralizing voice, however, is not Mill's only one. A quite different voice is heard when he says, "That the cultivation of an ideal nobleness of will and conduct should be to individuals an end, to which the specific pursuit of either of their own happiness or of that of others . . . should, in any case of conflict, give way."[6] Mill thinks that "the free development of individuality is one of the leading essentials of well-being," and he paraphrases Humboldt with great approval: "The end of man . . . is the highest and most harmonious development of his powers . . . that for this there are two requisites, 'freedom, and variety of situations'; and . . . 'individual vigor and manifold diversity,' which combine themselves in 'originality.' "[7] And he says: "He who lets the world, or his own portion of it, choose his plan of life for him has no need of any other faculty than the ape-like one of imitation. . . . What will be his comparative worth as a human being? It really is of importance not only what men do, but also what manner of men they are that do it. Among the works of man which human life is rightly employed in perfecting and beautifying, the first importance surely is man himself."[8]

As these passages make obvious, there is a deep conflict in Mill's work about the nature of the art of life. Mill rightly sees that morality, prudence, and aesthetics must be part of the art of life and that they conflict. But he attempts to resolve their conflict in favor of the moral approach in *Utilitarianism* and in favor of the aesthetic approach in *On Liberty*. He is pulled one way by the universalistic claims of practical reason and another by the individualistic claims of the will. His case illustrates not only the problem about the art of life, but also the predicament of reflective people who appreciate the force of both the moral and the aesthetic approaches and thus face the problem of resolving their conflict.

It must be acknowledged, of course, that Mill was aware of the conflict between the claims of practical reason and morality on the one hand and individual will and personal excellence on the other. It is generally conceded that even if a utilitarian resolution can be found, Mill has not found it. So we shall leave him in his state of conflict and turn to what is perhaps the most powerful attempt to resolve the conflict in favor of the moral approach: the one proposed by the greatest of those "German metaphysicians" to whom Mill refers and who thinks that the art of life consists in living according to "the principles of Practical Reason."

6.3 The Case for Practical Reason

Perhaps the central idea of Kant's moral thought is that the claims of practical reason and individual will come to the same thing: "The will is nothing but practical reason."[9] Kant denies, therefore, that there is a conflict between them. He certainly does not deny that it often appears as if they did conflict, but that appearance, he thinks, comes from mistakes people make in reasoning and willing. He also thinks, for reasons central to his position, that these two sources of mistakes are really one.

Kant thinks practical reason must be understood as a command. It tells how reason requires that one should act. It is, therefore, a command whose force rational people, insofar as they are rational, cannot fail to recognize. As a result, what they are commanded to do is what they will to do. For rational people, there cannot be a conflict between practical reason and their will. Kant thinks that if it is understood what practical reason and the will consist in, then it becomes apparent why there can be no conflict between them, or between either of them and morality. Practical reason and the will coincide because of their nature. Their coincidence, therefore, is a necessary, not a contingent, matter. Practical reason and the will are but two aspects of rational agency. The cement, so to speak, that holds them together is the freedom of rational people. If people act freely, then they act according to practical reason, their actions reflect their will, they act autonomously, and their actions conform to the requirements of morality. In order to understand Kant's reason for thinking that these implications hold, it is necessary to understand the internal relations that supposedly connect practical reason, will, freedom, autonomy, and morality.

Kant says that "will is a kind of causality belonging to living beings so far as they are rational. *Freedom* would then be a property this causality has of being able to work independently of determination by alien causes."[10] The will is thus a power people have to produce changes in themselves and their environment. This power may be exercised heteronomously or autonomously. In the first case, its exercise depends on alien causes, that is, on causes not within, or fully within, people's control. The laws of nature, events in their environment, physiological and psychological needs, and so forth may determine or influence their will independently of their own choices. In the second case, the exercise of the will depends wholly on people's choices, and this is what makes their will free. The freedom of the will thus means, negatively, that it is not dependent on alien causes and, positively, that it is subject only to its own control, that, as Kant puts it, it is a law to itself. If the will is free in this sense, then it is autonomous. The "freedom of the will ... [is] autonomy—that is, the property which the will has of being a law to itself."[11]

Kant thinks autonomous people will give themselves the law that he calls the categorical imperative: "Act only on that maxim through which you can at the same time wish that it should become a universal law."[12] That is, act according to a principle that you would want all people to follow if they were in your position. The categorical imperative, Kant claims, expresses the requirements of autonomy, practical reason, and morality. It does so for autonomy because it is a law that people choose to be guided by. If they are guided by their needs, desires, feelings, or ideals of personal excellence, then they are not acting autonomously, they are not in full control of what motivates them, because causes independent of their will determine or influence what needs, desires, feelings, or ideals of personal excellence they have. Autonomous people, guided by the categorical imperative, thus *must* act in abstraction of all contingent features of their characters and circumstances; otherwise, they would stop being autonomous.

If people act autonomously, then they also act according to practical reason because they act in accordance with a law that anyone and everyone who abstracted from contingencies would also choose. For practical reason just is to act in accordance with a principle that one thinks all people ought to act on if they were in one's situation. The task of practical reason, therefore, is to find a principle that applies universally, impartially, and impersonally to everyone in a particular situation. The categorical imperative tells people how they must think in order to find that principle. They must ask themselves how they think anyone ought to act, and then act according to the answer they give themselves. Rational people *must* be guided by the categorical imperative because if they were not, they would act contrary to how they themselves think everyone ought to act. To act contrary to the categorical imperative, therefore, would be inconsistent and thus irrational.

In acting according to practical reason and the categorical imperative, however, people are also acting morally. For they act according to a universal, impartial, and impersonal principle that states how people ought to act in a particular situation. If people are guided by the categorical imperative, then they must have some reason for thinking that the way they have concluded everyone ought to act is right. For otherwise they would not think everyone ought to act that way. So that when it comes to their own actions, they would be inconsistent if they were to act contrary to the way they think everybody ought to act. If they were inconsistent in this way, they would also be immoral because they would be acting in violation of how they themselves think everyone ought to act.[13] Rational people, therefore, *must* act morally because if they did not, they would not be rational.

It is for these reasons Kant thinks that the categorical imperative embodies the requirements of autonomy, practical reason, and morality; that violating one involves violating the others; and that meeting the requirements of one involves meeting the requirements of the others. As he puts it: "An absolutely good will, whose principle must be the categorical imperative, will . . . contain only the *form of willing*, and that as autonomy. In other words, the fitness of the maxim of every good will to make itself a universal law is itself the sole law which the will of every rational being spontaneously imposes on itself without basing it on any impuls[e] or interest."[14] Kant, of course, does not think that everybody actually acts according to the categorical imperative. Those who do not, fail because they are wanting in autonomy, practical reason, or morality. If they were not wanting in these ways, then they would act as they themselves would realize that they ought to act, if they had not been prevented from reasoning well enough about it.

Kant's position has far-reaching moral, political, and educational implications. But the implication that is of immediate relevance to the art of life is that, like Mill, Kant supposes that it is a moral art, that if self-creation conflicts with morality, then practical reason requires that morality should prevail. Ranking the claims of self-creation higher than or equal to those of morality is unavoidably irrational and immoral because its claims express contingent aspirations, whereas morality expresses an aspiration that all rational people must have insofar as they are rational. The crucial difference, according to Kant, is that the aspirations of self-creation are to realize various ideals that rational people *may* aim at, but the aspiration of morality is to *be* a rational person. That is why morality is a precondition of self-creation, and why morality must always prevail if they conflict.

"The practically *good*," says Kant, "is that which determines the will by concepts of reason, and therefore not by subjective causes, but objectively—that is, on grounds valid for every rational being as such."[15] Such objective determination by practical reason is expressed by the categorical imperative. By contrast, hypothetical imperatives express subjective causes that are "concerned with art . . . [and] with well-being."[16] Hypothetical imperatives thus express what Kant calls counsels of prudence and of art, and he says that such counsels are only "subjective and contingent," having to do with whether "this or that man counts this or that as belonging to his happiness." And he goes on, "As against this, a categorical imperative is limited by no condition and can quite precisely be called a command, as being absolutely, although practically, necessary."[17]

The implication of Kant's view for the art of life is that when the counsels of prudence, art, happiness, and well-being—in other words, self-creation—conflict with the command of the categorical imperative, then rational agency requires obeying the command and disregarding the counsel. And the reason he gives for this is that obeying the command is necessary for rational agency, and hence for morality, whereas following the counsel is not. It thus follows from Kant's position that practical reason and morality often require people to act contrary to what they rightly hold as their ideals of a good life. If the art of life is informed by Kant's views, then its practitioners must resign themselves to the fact that practical reason and morality often conflict with and take precedence over their ideals of a good life.

6.4 Doubts about Practical Reason

There are numerous reasons for doubting Kant's position, but only two of them are discussed here. The first emerges if it is remembered why Kant supposes that morality often requires people to act contrary to their ideals of a good life. His reason is that these ideals are contingent aims, whereas the requirements of morality are necessarily binding on all rational people. They are, as Kant thought, the preconditions of pursuing any contingent aims. But why should this be so? Why can people not be moved by ideals of a good life and rank them higher than the requirements of morality? Kant accepts that this can be done, that it is often done, but what he claims cannot be done is to have the support of practical reason for such ranking. It is, he thinks, always contrary to practical reason to act contrary to morality. And the reason for that is that morality comes to people in the form of a universal, impartial, and impersonal command, namely, the categorical imperative. They could not consistently make it a universal law that everyone should be motivated by the same ideals of personal excellence because rational people need not be motivated by them at all and because those who are differ widely in what ideals motivate them. It must be asked, however, why moral commands must be universal, impartial, and impersonal. Why could there not be moral commands that are binding on some people but not on others? Kant's answer is that there could not be such *moral* commands because moral commands are requirements of practical reason, and reason must be universal, impartial, and impersonal; otherwise, it is not reason. And with this, we have reached the heart of the matter.

It is easy to see that if reason is theoretical, then the conclusions reached by its means will hold universally, impartially, and impersonally. Theoretical reason yields factual truths that do not depend on the subjective preferences of anyone. Kant, however, takes great pains to avoid basing morality on theoretical reason because that is his way of avoiding unjustifiable metaphysical claims. Practical reason, however, is not theoretical reason. Its conclusions are not factual truths but, as Kant says, commands. Why should it be supposed that it is reasonable for a particular person to act only on a command that it is reasonable for everyone to act on? That there are *some* such commands may be acknowledged. There may be situations in which all reasonable people ought to act in the same way. Kant's claim, however, is much stronger than this. It is that *all* commands, insofar as they are reasonable and moral, require *all* people to follow them, and that if they fail to do so, then they are irrational and immoral.

The force of Kant's claim depends on his assimilation of practical reason to theoretical reason. Kant, however, gives no reason to suppose that they are assimilable, and there is a good reason to suppose that they are not. This reason is that the factual truths that theoretical reason yields are not attached to any individual, but commands are. Commands always tell individuals what it is they ought to do. What they ought to do, however, often depends on their history, character, relationships, circumstances, on how they conceive of their self-interest, on what ideals they hold—and these considerations vary with individuals. So it is the exception, not the rule, for commands to apply universally, impartially, and impersonally.

It is useless to try to avoid this central difficulty in Kant's position by saying that if individuals reasonably decide what they ought to do, then they must make the universal, impartial, and impersonal claim that everyone in their situation ought to do the same thing. For in the first place, there is often no one else who could be in the individuals' situation because their history, character, and so forth are unique. In the second place, individuals may reasonably decide that when the very possibility of living according to their crucially important ideals of a good life is at stake, it is justifiable to violate some relatively unimportant moral command and fail to keep a lunch date, not return a borrowed book on time, tell a harmless lie, or not be as helpful to strangers as they might be. They may rightly think that anyone in their position ought to do the same, so that they do make a universal, impartial, and impersonal claim, but it is contrary to morality. So moral commands need not be universal, impartial, and impersonal; and universal, impartial, and impersonal commands need not be moral. In that case, however, the ground falls out from under Kant's argument that practical reason requires that if they conflict, morality must take precedence over ideals of a good life because moral claims are, and the claims of these ideals are not, universal, impartial, and impersonal.

The second reason for doubting Kant's position is also connected with the differences between theoretical reason and practical reason as a command. The factual truths that theoretical reason yields are expressible as propositions, and true propositions are consistent with each other. One true proposition cannot contradict another because if it did, then either it or the other proposition would have to be false, which true propositions cannot be. But it is otherwise with commands. There is no reason why one command of practical reason could not require people to do something that is incompatible with another command of practical reason. This is true of all commands of practical reason, even of universal, impartial, and impersonal ones. If Kant is right, practical reason commands universally, impartially, and impersonally that one should not lie, cheat, steal, or murder; that one should help others, be kind, save endangered innocent lives, keep promises, pay debts, and so forth. But it is a plain fact of everyday life that such commands often conflict and call for incompatible actions. Helping someone may involve telling a lie; saving an innocent life may involve breaking a promise.

The significance of such commonplace conflicts is that even if Kant's account of practical reason and morality were correct as far as it goes, it would remain incomplete because it does not go far enough.

It is not enough to know that one ought to be guided by the universal, impartial, and impersonal commands of the categorical imperative; one must also know how to resolve conflicts among such commands. On the one hand, if there is some principle that helps do that, then practical reason must include it. In that case, however, Kant's claim that the categorical imperative expresses the requirements of practical reason and morality is mistaken. On the other hand, if there is no such principle, then the categorical imperative is at best an incomplete guide to conduct.

Kant's position cannot be rescued by arguing that conflicts among the bona fide commands of practical reason show only that it is people's reasoning and not the categorical imperative that is at fault. For even if people conclude that it ought to be a universal law that one of the two conflicting commands ought to be acted on, the other command remains universal, impartial, and impersonal. In disobeying it, they violate an absolute moral requirement. If, to avoid this difficulty, commands are watered down to allow for not following them in case of conflicts, then their absoluteness is abandoned. Commands, then, become toothless prescriptions to the effect that one should not lie, steal, cheat, and so forth unless there is a good reason for it. Practical reason, then, must include an account of what makes particular reasons good or bad, but Kant gives no such account. And it is hard to see how such an account, if one were given, could deny that a good reason for overriding a relatively unimportant moral command is that a person's ideal of a good life requires it. If this is conceded, however, then everything Kant means to deny is conceded.

The problem that underlies both these objections is that Kant does not realize how far-reaching are the implications of his reinterpretation of practical reason. If practical reason is a command, and not the application of knowledge gained by theoretical reason, then it is illegitimate to suppose, as Kant does, that the commands of practical reason have the features that the knowledge gained by theoretical reason has. That knowledge is of factual truths, and the propositions that express them must hold universally, impartially, and impersonally and cannot conflict. But commands are addressed to people whose characters and circumstances differ and who have, therefore, very different reasons for obeying or disobeying them. And quite apart from these individual differences, commands, unlike propositions expressing factual truths, can and often do conflict and thus lack the absoluteness that Kant attributes to them. It must be concluded, then, that Kant's argument that the moral approach to the art of life ought to dominate over the aesthetic approach fails.

6.5 The Case for Self-Creation

Two distinctions will help us understand the aesthetic approach to the art of life.[18]The first is between the aesthetic attitude and its objects. The attitude involves the appreciation of some object for being what it is. The appreciation, therefore, is not instrumental. Its object is valued not because of some goal beyond itself that it helps achieve or constitute, but because the object is fine, admirable, or great in itself. The object may make people happier, societies more just, nations more civilized, and lives more uplifting. The aesthetic appreciation of it, however, is not on account of its contribution toward achieving valuable goals, but for its intrinsic excellence, which is unaffected by the good or bad uses it may have.

The object toward which the aesthetic attitude is directed may be found in nature: a landscape, a sunset, or a human body; or it may be a human achievement: a work of art, an imaginative discovery, the ingenious surmounting of a formidable obstacle, or the elegant solution of a recalcitrant problem. But since we are interested in the aesthetic approach to the art of life, the objects that concern us here are human lives that merit appreciation because of their intrinsic excellence. Such lives are outstanding human achievements. They may be lives of artists or scientists: creative, brilliant, original, penetrating, and imaginative; lives of heroes: magnificent, confident, impressive, daring, adventurous, and charismatic; lives of conscientious protesters: noble, constant, steadfast, and incorruptible; lives of connoisseurs: refined, discriminating, elegant, sensitive, and graceful; lives of athletes: disciplined, energetic, competitive, robust, and determined; or lives of sages: wise, deep, serene, judicious, and learned. All such lives involve significant human achievements, accomplished in the face of obstacles that daunt others, made possible by the people's outstanding qualities. Their achievements are rare because most people lack the required qualities and cannot overcome the obstacles. These lives, of course, include self-creation, which, according to Kant, ought to be subordinated to morality. And they include also the lives of personal excellence that have been discussed in the five preceding chapters.

The second distinction is between two perspectives from which lives of personal excellence may be viewed: the actor's and the specta-tor's.[19] Both appreciate such lives, regardless of their moral standing, but they appreciate them in different ways. The spectators do so from the outside for being admirable, fine, and great, but they are not moved to model their own lives on them. The actors are so moved. They adopt these lives as ideals of how they themselves want to live. Their attitude is not like that of knowledgeable amateurs visiting a museum, but like the attitude of artists toward the master from whom they want to learn. The actors are inspired by these ideals of personal excellence to become more like the people who lived the lives. In order to succeed, they have to make great efforts to transform them-selves from what they are in their more or less ordinary state to ap-proximate as closely as they can the extraordinary state represented by the personal excellences that inspire them.

The required creative efforts depend on their will, but it is their in-dividual will that takes an individual form and has an individual ob-ject, rather than Kant's abstract and formal will that is the same for all rational people. The object of the will is individual because it involves the transformation of people from what they happen to be, given their contingent characters and circumstances, into what their ideals of personal excellence inspire them to be. The form of the will is also in-dividual because it involves the development of the contingent indi-vidually variable potentialities of the people so that they could be-come what they want to be. According to the aesthetic approach, the art of life aims to effect this transformation. It is barely a metaphor to describe people who are thus engaged as artists who work in the medium of their own lives.

It seems clear that many lives are good because of the people's mastery of the art of life thus understood. What is not clear, however, is how successful engagement in the art of life is related to morality. Mill of *Utilitarianism* and Kant, representing the moral approach, think the art of life must be practiced in conformity to morality, and if they conflict, then morality must prevail.

There are two deep reasons that tell against this view. One is that there are great problems with Mill's and Kant's justifications of their incompatible conceptions of morality. Quite independently of the art of life, many reasonable people reasonably reject both the greatest happiness principle and the categorical imperative to which Mill and Kant respectively appeal in order to justify what they take to be the requirements of morality. The other reason is the grotesque indifference to human psychology that permeates both these views. They require reasonable people to act contrary to the ideals of personal excellence which inspire them and to which they have dedicated their lives; to go against the very dictates of their will that they have with much effort trained themselves to follow; and to violate their hard-won sense of what makes their lives good. If reasonable people even pause to ask why they should do such violence to their most cherished ideals, then the answer, that some universal, impartial, and impersonal principle requires it, will seem to them to carry no conviction unless it can be shown how it bears on living the lives they have reasonably decided they want to live. This is not to say, of course, that they will be indifferent to morality. Morality has an important place in many personal excellences, and some place in any reasonable one. The aesthetic approach, however, ranks moral claims lower than the claims of personal excellence if they come into conflict.

The conflict between these two approaches was old even when Plato took formal notice of it as the "ancient quarrel between philosophy and poetry."[20] Although the quarrel is ancient, in the eighteenth and nineteenth centuries in Germany it recurred in a new form, and this constitutes a momentous event in the history both of this conflict and of approaches to good lives. This "great turning-point—it seems to me the greatest yet," says Isaiah Berlin, "is well enough known under the name of 'romanticism.' "[21] It is the product of numerous artists, poets, playwrights, novelists, and philosophers. Perhaps the pivotal figure in the struggle with its implications is Nietzsche. Romanticism, in Nietzsche's hand, is an interpretation of the aesthetic approach to good lives. This interpretation has a critical and a constructive aspect.

Its critical aspect is encapsulated in Nietzsche's notorious claim: "God is dead. God remains dead. And we have killed him."[22] This is his typically perfervid way of saying that the idea that there is an objective truth about values is no longer tenable. Values do not exist independently of our will; values are what we make them. The question is what values we should make. In the critical aspect of his thought, Nietzsche accepts Kant's argument against the possibility of a metaphysical foundation for values, but rejects Kant's argument for the coincidence of practical reason and morality. One should seek a "new immoral, or at least unmoralistic . . . anti-Kantian . . . 'categorical imperative' . . . which will articulate this *new demand*: we need a critique of moral values, *the value of these values themselves must first be called in question.*"[23] Nietzsche thus sees human beings, or as he would put it, the human beings that matter, as possessing autonomy and having to decide what to do with it. They must make a decision about the values that should guide them without the illusion that theoretical or practical reason can help them. The constructive aspect of Nietzsche's romantic version of the aesthetic approach is concerned with how that decision should be made, how autonomous lives should be lived.

Nietzsche thinks, "This is at bottom a question of taste and aesthetics"[24] and not of morality. It is "precisely morality" that is "to blame if the highest power and splendor actually possible . . . was never in fact attained."[25] "The subtle tricks of old moralists and preachers of morals," the "stiff and decorous Tartuffery of the old Kant as he lures us on the dialectical bypaths that lead to his 'categorical imperative'— really lead astray and seduce,"[26] and all of it ought to be rejected. Its rejection, however, has the positive goal of "clearing the way for new ideals, for *more robust* ideals."[27] "We immoralists . . . make it a point to be *affirmers*."[28] But what ideals do immoralists affirm? Nietzsche answers: they affirm the "Ego . . . this creating, willing, evaluating Ego, which is the measure and value of things."[29] The "noble type of man experiences *itself* as determining values; it does not need approval; it judges 'what is harmful to me is harmful in itself'; it knows itself to be value-creating. . . . [It has] feeling of fullness, of power that seeks to overflow, the happiness of high tension, the consciousness of wealth that would give and bestow. . . . Noble and courageous human beings who think that way are furthest removed from that morality which finds the distinction of morality precisely in pity, or in acting for others, or in *desinteressement*."[30]

The question still remains, however, what these affirmers of the ego have to do to create their own values. Nietzsche thinks they should ask themselves, "What does your conscience say?" And they will hear the answer if they listen well and honestly: "You must become who you are."[31] People who follow their consciences become "human beings who are new, unique, incomparable, who give themselves laws, who create themselves."[32] The way to accomplish that is "To 'give style' to one's character—a great and rare art! It is practiced by those who survey all the strengths and weaknesses of their nature and then fit them into an artistic plan until every one of them appears as art and reason and even weaknesses delight the eye. . . . In the end, when the work is finished, it becomes evident how the constraints of a single taste governed and formed everything large and small. Whether this taste was good or bad is less important than one might suppose, if only it was a single taste!"[33] This is what people who have achieved personal excellence have accomplished. Those who want to become themselves ought not, of course, imitate them; they should learn from them to do for themselves what these "highest exemplars" of humanity have done for themselves.[34]

6.6 Doubts about Self-Creation

Any attempt to assess Nietzsche's views is fraught with danger. This is partly Nietzsche's doing because he writes to provoke his opponents and sympathizers alike, and he succeeds. He is a fervent hater and lover. Being the intellectual that he is, it is ideas that he hates and loves with the deep passions of his brilliant and unsteady mind. Everything is either profoundly base or profoundly noble. This makes measured response difficult. There is also the problem that it is practically irresistible not to read Nietzsche in the light of subsequent history. The Nazis honored him. Numerous mass murderers imagined themselves to be Nietzschean *Übermenschen* with the strength, vision, and determination to rid the world of vermin and thereby create the postmoral world Nietzsche prophesied. We know, as Nietzsche could not, about the terrible uses to which some of his ideas have been put. If these dangers are avoided, hard as that is, there is still the most serious one of all that his fertile mind produced an amazing array of unsystematic and unsupported aphoristic dicta, many of which contain important kernels of truths obscured by exaggeration and bombast. This having had to be said, let us now assess the implications of Nietzsche's views for the art of life.

Nietzsche rightly sees that if morality has no metaphysical foundation and if its principles are commands rather than propositions about values—if, that is, morality is what Kant thinks it is—then there is no convincing reason why autonomous people should subordinate their pursuit of personal excellence to universal, impartial, and impersonal moral commands. Nietzsche thinks autonomous people ought to exercise their autonomy in pursuit of personal excellence, and if morality stands in their way, then they should see through its sham imperatives. The art of life is to choose one's ideals of personal excellence well and to train one's will to pursue them uncompromisingly. Anything else is a weakness that jeopardizes the goodness of one's life.

One of the things Nietzsche does not see is that morality need not be understood either as a Kantian system of commands or as a Platonic system of knowledge of the good obtained by means of metaphysics. Morality may be seen as a system designed to protect some requirements that all good lives have, regardless of how their goodness is conceived. The basis of the system, understood in this third way, is the factual, but not metaphysical, claim that all human beings have some physiological, psychological, and social needs that must be satisfied if they are to live good lives. Their satisfaction is a minimum requirement of all good lives, and one purpose of morality is to create the conditions in which they can be satisfied. Reasonable people pursuing personal excellence have good reasons, therefore, to conform to these requirements, since doing so protects the conditions on which their own pursuits depend.

More will shortly be said about this conception of morality. What has already been said, however, is surely sufficient to cast doubt on Nietzsche's claim that a stark choice must be made between Kant's moral absolutism and Nietzsche's immoralism. Nietzsche is right to reject Kant's view of practical reason and morality, but he is wrong to take that to be the rejection of practical reason and morality. It is a consequence of Nietzsche's tendency to see things in terms of extremes that he takes the rejection of Kant's moral absolutism to lead to a form of relativism. He recognizes no constraints—moral, rational, or other—on the pursuit of personal excellence. Autonomous people create their own values, make their own laws, and that is what is important, rather than what their values and laws happen to be. This is how Nietzsche could come to regard as admirable such moral monsters as the treacherous murderer Cesare Borgia and Napoleon, who pursued his ideal of personal excellence by orchestrating the slaughter of hundreds of thousands of people. Nietzsche is so obsessed with saying an understandable no to "old moralists and preachers of morals" that he fails to see that personal excellence can be pursued only within the constraints of practical reason and morality that protect the conditions on which the pursuit rests.

Another blind spot of Nietzsche is that he is led by his romanticism to an unacceptably narrow view, first, of the ideals whose pursuit may make lives good and, second, of the motivational sources for pursuing them. Consider ideals of personal excellence. Let us agree

that the lives of creative artists and scientists, heroes, honorable protesters, refined connoisseurs, disciplined athletes, and wise sages indeed represent the "highest exemplars," that they are admirable, and
that their lives are good. These lives, in effect, exemplify one of the
"departments" of the art of life, namely, the aesthetic one, having to
do with the beautiful and the noble, which, we saw earlier, Mill dis-
cusses. But what about the other two: morality and prudence? Why
does Nietzsche not recognize that moral and prudent lives may also
be good? Why could not principled, conscientious, dutiful, loving
moral lives or moderate, judicious, cautious, industrious, well-
planned prudent lives be as good as noble and beautiful lives? Nietzsche regards them with contempt. But this is nothing but a romantic
prejudice in favor of Promethean lives of Sturm und Drang, full of
strife, passion, excess, ecstasy, risk, and suffering—lives amazingly
similar to Nietzsche's. If ideals of a good life are created, not discovered, and if the key to such lives is the law that autonomous people
make for themselves, then it ought to be possible for them to value
ideals other than the romantic ones Nietzsche is led by his predilec-
tion to advocate. Romantic absolutism is only a little less absolutistic
and no less arbitrary than moral absolutism.

There is also the problem created by the narrow view Nietzsche
takes of the motivation on which the successful practice of the art of
life depends. It is a truism that the sources of human motivation are
many: reason, ambition, imagination, love, duty, need, shame, and so
on, routinely move people to action. Of all the sources of motivation,
Nietzsche focuses on one, the will, and claims for it a controlling role
in the pursuit of personal excellence. Why should one accept this?

There is no doubt that the will is normally involved in actions because people must get from motive to action. The same, however, is
true of reason, emotion, and imagination. Normal people normally
need to reason about what they want and how to get it; they have various emotions on that subject; and they have to envisage what it
would be like to achieve what their reasons and emotions prompt
them to seek. Nor is there any doubt that the pursuit of personal excellence is difficult and that people must make efforts of will to succeed. But, as before, the same difficulties call for careful reasoning, authentic emotions, and lively and accurate imagination of the ends
they aim at. Nietzsche nevertheless insists on the overriding importance of the will and denigrates the rest. The explanation, but not the
justification, for this is, once again, the romantic prejudice that good

lives are lives of strife. In those lives the will *is* primary. But this romantic prejudice rests on the arbitrary identification of the preferences of some German writers and artists in the eighteenth and nineteenth centuries with good lives. It is to Nietzsche's credit that he rejects the absolutism of principles, but he has not left behind the absolutistic frame of mind: instead of being dogmatic about principles, he is dogmatic about motives and about the ends he thinks are worth pursuing.

6.7 Morality and Personal Excellences

It follows from Kant's identification of practical reason and morality that if the pursuit of good lives through personal excellences conflicts with morality, then reason requires that morality should prevail. Nietzsche's reaction is to accept Kant's understanding of practical reason and morality, but reject them as guides to good lives. An alternative to both is to reject Kant's understanding of practical reason and morality, but accept them as guides to good lives, provided they are rightly understood. Their right understanding must allow that many moral requirements are not universal, impartial, and impersonal and that many requirements of practical reason are not moral. There are moral requirements that vary with societies and individuals, and there are requirements of practical reason that concern the pursuit of personal excellence. The right understanding, therefore, rejects two of Kant's basic assumptions: that the requirements of practical reason and morality are universal, impartial, and impersonal and that their requirements are identical. It must be emphasized that this understanding allows that *some* requirements of practical reason and morality may be universal, impartial, and impersonal and that *some* of their requirements may be identical. It is only the absolutist claim that is rejected.

The alternative approach is similarly circumspect about Nietzsche's insistence on the central importance of personal excellences to good lives. Many good lives involve their pursuit, but their pursuit must be reasonable, and morality often aids rather than hinders their pursuit. The aim of the alternative approach to the art of life may be expressed, therefore, as that of making room for personal excellences in practical reason and morality.

This approach, of course, raises the question how to resolve conflicts between morality and personal excellences. If the general answers of both Kant and Nietzsche, namely, that one should always override the other, are rejected, then what is the answer? The answer is that there is a reasonable resolution of these conflicts, but it is not general. It depends on the varying importance of the conflicting particular moral requirements and particular personal excellences to the goodness of a particular person's life. In order to explain this answer, we must distinguish among three levels on which such conflicts may occur: the universal, the social, and the individual.

The universal level includes the satisfaction of basic physiological, psychological, and social needs that all normal human beings normally have simply because they are human. Such needs are for nutrition and rest, some pleasure and appreciation in one's life, security and order, and so forth. All societies must have and enforce rules that aid the satisfaction of basic human needs. These rules protect the minimum requirements of all good lives; they are the basic moral rules. They are, therefore, universal because human beings are alike in having these needs, benefiting from their satisfaction, and being harmed by their prolonged frustration. If these rules are systematically violated in a society, then it is on the way toward disintegration because it loses the allegiance of the people who are prevented from making good lives for themselves.

The social level is characterized by two kinds of rules. One is concerned with the application of the universal rules. For instance, all societies must protect the lives of the people living in them, so they must all have a rule prohibiting murder. But this prohibition leaves open both whether murder can ever be justified and how far its prohibition extends. Does it end at the borders or does it include outsiders? How inclusive is its prohibition in the society itself? What is the status of suicide, abortion, capital punishment, war, euthanasia, infanticide, revenge, feuds, and other forms of killing? What is recognized as a mitigation or an excuse for murder? These are difficult questions that must be answered by all societies, and not just about murder, but about the application of the whole range of universal rules that concern the satisfaction of basic needs. Different societies, of course, may answer them perfectly reasonably, but differently, as history and anthropology testify.

Another kind of social rule is concerned with the protection of some possibilities whose realization would contribute to good lives. These possibilities go beyond the minimum requirements in respect to which good lives are alike. That there be such possibilities is necessary for good lives, but there are great variations both within and among societies in what they are. Personal excellences are among these possibilities, but there are also others: desirable occupations; accepted modes of intimacy; recognized private pastimes; ways of participating in political affairs; conventional forms of competition, love affairs, social protest, child rearing, paying respect; and so forth.

Societies, then, must have social rules, in addition to the universal ones, that protect the local interpretations of universally required rules as well as locally recognized possibilities that good lives may aim to realize. These rules are general but not universal. They apply to everyone, but only within a particular society. Outsiders living in their own societies are not blamed for having different interpretations and valuing different possibilities. The violation of such social rules is still prohibited, but less strongly than the violation of universal rules, for the universal rules protect conditions necessary for good lives whereas the social rules protect only interpretations and possibilities to which recognized alternatives exist.

The individual level is the context in which people are engaged in trying to make a good life for themselves. They form various intimate relationships; opt for ways of earning a living; make choices about travel, education, finances, having and raising children, physical fitness, political involvement, recreation, religious and ethnic allegiances, sexual practices, and so forth. And it is also in this context that they pursue various personal excellences, understood broadly enough to include both those favored by romantics and those that are prudential or aesthetic without Promethean strife. One task that people have in this context is to try to coordinate their pursuit of personal excellences with the pursuits of others. They want minimal interference with their own pursuits and maximum protection of the conditions on which their pursuits depend. They have good reasons, therefore, to adopt ideals of personal excellence that are likely to avoid interference and secure protection. One of the purposes of universal and social moral rules is to coordinate in this manner individual pursuits. People have good reasons, therefore, to conform to the moral rules because they aid rather than hinder their pursuits. Thus there are also going to be rules for individuals that regulate their own pursuits by adjusting their ideals of personal excellence to the universal and social rules. These individual rules, of course, vary from person to person since the kind of adjustment they call for depends on what forms the universal and social rules take and on what their ideals of personal excellence happen to be.

On all three of these levels the moral rules provide possibilities that may make lives good and set limits that protect these possibilities. On each level the rules establish rights, obligations, and responsibilities. They prescribe what people owe to their society, to the institutions and traditions to which they belong, to their friends, families, lovers, colleagues, and neighbors, as well as what they can reasonably expect for themselves. These rules create the conditions in which people can pursue their ideals of personal excellence and thus make good lives for themselves. The ideal case is when these rules are generally observed. In real life, however, the ideal case rarely holds because public and private reasons often diverge. Universal, social, and individual moral rules frequently conflict with ideals of personal excellence. These conflicts are conflicts for individuals, and they raise for them the question how they should live. If they follow the moral approach, they will resolve them one way. If they follow the aesthetic approach, they will resolve them in another. But since both embody considerations that they have good reasons to value, whichever resolution they opt for, they will lose something that their ideals of a good life require. The art of life is to resolve such conflicts in non-ideal cases in a way that minimizes the unavoidable loss.

The essential claim on behalf of the art of life is that these conflicts have a reasonable resolution, but what it is depends on the details of the conflicting public and private reasons. Their details vary, and so, therefore, reasonable resolutions vary from case to case. These variations, however, do not exclude the possibility of reasonable resolutions. To begin with, it needs to be borne in mind, contra Kant, that unlike theoretical reason, practical reason is always reason for particular people to act in particular ways in particular circumstances.

There are two types of practical reason that could guide actions in this particular manner: private and public. Private reasons lead people to perform an action because it makes their particular lives better. Public reasons lead people to perform an action because it strengthens the particular conditions in which everyone in a particular society could live good lives. Private reasons, of course, may include people's concern with good lives for others because reasonable ideals of personal excellence are not exclusively self-centered. Similarly, public reasons take into account good lives for particular individuals because they are among those who benefit from strengthening the conditions that make good lives possible for everyone in that context. By and large, public reasons are endorsed by the moral approach and private reasons by the aesthetic approach.

As we have seen, in the ideal case public and private reasons coincide because the conditions of good lives that are supported by public reasons are also conditions of good lives that people have private reasons to want. Among the conditions that people have private reasons to want are those that are endorsed by public reasons and make good lives for themselves possible. In non-ideal situations public and private reasons conflict. Their conflict may be described from the point of view of public reasons as being caused by ideals of personal excellence that violate reasonable conditions of all good lives. And they may be described from the point of view of private reasons as being caused by unreasonable conditions that prevent the pursuit of reasonable ideals of personal excellence. However described, these are the conflicts that concern us. Their resolution depends on the recognition that resolutions take different forms depending on whether the conflicts occur on the universal, social, or individual levels.

On the universal level the question is whether the universal rules that public reason endorses indeed protect the conditions of all good lives, regardless of what form they may take. This is a plain factual question that has a factual answer. For the question is whether the satisfaction of some particular physiological, psychological, or social need is basic to good lives. People in a society may believe that it is and be mistaken, or they may believe that it is not and be mistaken about that. If the conflict between private and public reasons occurs because people are correct in thinking that the public reasons are mistaken in these ways, then the conflict should be resolved in favor of private reasons. In all other cases, however, public reasons ought to prevail against private ones on the universal level. For the conditions public reasons protect are also the conditions of the good lives of the people whose private reasons lead them to oppose the conditions; consequently, their opposition cannot be reasonable since they want to live good lives. If the universal rules they oppose really protect the conditions of all good lives, then their private reasons for opposing them must be mistaken.

On the social level the question is whether it is right to exclude ideals of personal excellence that conflict with the social rules that govern both the application of the universal rules in the context of a particular society and the possibilities of good lives that go beyond the satisfaction of basic needs. These excluded ideals of personal excellence conform to the universal rules, but conflict with some of the social rules. The public reason in favor of these social rules is that the universal rules must be interpreted in one way or another and some possibilities of good lives must be provided beyond the satisfaction of basic needs, and the social rules embody conventional ways in which a particular society has provided these necessities. The private reason for opposing these social rules is that they exclude ideals of personal excellence simply because they are unconventional, and that is a poor reason for interfering with people's pursuit of them.

The reasonable resolution of the conflict on the social level depends on whether the conventions that prevail in a society indeed offer justifiable interpretations of the universal rules and a sufficient variety of possibilities among which people may choose to make some their own. The mere fact that there are interpretations and possibilities other than conventional ones is not a sufficient reason for opposing the conventional ones. A sufficient reason would be that the other interpretations and possibilities do not interfere with the pursuit of personal excellences that are already recognized on the social level and that they make possible hitherto unrecognized ideals of personal excellence that some people in the society wish to pursue. Since both public and private reasons aim to secure the conditions of good lives, if unconventional ideals of personal excellence are opposed by public reason on the ground that they interfere with these conditions, then the burden of proof rests on advocates of public reason. They need to make a case justifying the interference. If the case is made, private reason ought to give way. If the case is not made, private reason ought to prevail. Making and contesting such cases is, of course, difficult. But this results from the uncertainties of the details of particular cases, not from doubts about what would count, on the social level, for and against public and private reasons.

On the individual level the question is whether there could be public reasons for excluding ideals of personal excellence that conform to the universal and social rules and that individuals have private reasons to pursue. Here the presumption is overwhelmingly in favor of private reasons and against public ones. For if an ideal of personal excellence does not interfere with the satisfaction of basic needs, conforms to the local interpretations of universal rules, and does not endanger the pursuit of conventionally recognized ideals of personal excellence, then it is difficult to see what public reason there could be against pursuing it.

Ideals of personal excellence may be imprudent because they carry great risks for those who pursue them. Or they may be aesthetically displeasing because they violate the sense of decorum, beauty, or hygiene of others. Or they may be morally condemned from the point of view of some other ideal of personal excellence for violating moral rules other than the universal and social ones, such as those of religious, ethnic, or aristocratic codes. But the cost, if there is one, of imprudence, bad taste, and moral failure will be borne by those who pursue personal excellences that are open to such objections. They have private reasons to run these risks, and for reasons Mill gives in *On Liberty*, it is better to let them act on their private reasons, even if they seem weak, than to interfere to save them from their own folly, if it is that. On the individual level, therefore, if private and public reasons conflict, the presumption is in favor of resolving the conflicts by letting private reasons prevail. The presumption can be defeated, but only by adducing public reasons to show why an ideal of personal excellence that conforms to universal and social rules ought nevertheless to be excluded.

This approach to the art of life resolves the problem resulting from the conflict between the public reasons that follow from the moral approach and the private reasons that follow from the aesthetic approach by distinguishing three levels on which the conflict may occur. On the universal level the presumption is in favor of morality and public reasons. On the individual level the presumption is in favor of ideals of personal excellence and private reasons. On the social level there is no clear presumption in either direction because everything depends on the adequacy of the local interpretations of universal rules and on the richness of available possibilities. Which way the presumption falls depends on the details, and these vary from context to context. On all three levels, however, the resolution of the conflict is particular, not general. For the resolutions always depend on the nature of the private reasons that derive from a variety of ideals of personal excellence, as well as on the public reasons that derive from a variety of social rules that differ, change, and are constantly revised in all particular contexts.

It must be acknowledged, however, that this approach to resolving the conflicts may not succeed in all cases because there may be people whose commitments to their ideals of personal excellence are so strong as to give them private reasons that defeat any public reason that may conflict with them. Devout religious believers, uncompromising revolutionaries, dedicated artists, and others may just want to pursue their ideals even if they violate universal and social rules. Such people are not irrational because they act on private reasons; they are aware of the public reasons they reject, so they know what they are doing and why. They are not indifferent to the moral considerations that the universal and social rules embody, but it is their sincere conviction that their private reasons are weightier than the public reasons. If, however, these people are reasonable, then they realize that those who do not share their ideals of personal excellence do not think as they do about the respective weights of public and those particular private reasons. These other people have strong public reasons to prohibit the violations of universal and social rules by those who pursue ideals of personal excellences they themselves do not share. Both sides, therefore, will persist in their incompatible rankings of public versus private reasons.

When such conflicts occur, defenders of public reason have good reasons to prohibit the pursuit of personal excellences that violate universal and social rules. And those who are committed to their pursuit must take this into account as part of what their commitments entail. If they are reasonable, they know their commitments make them liable to moral sanctions and to their consequences. They cannot, therefore, reasonably protest if these consequences catch up with them. Such people may be described as conscientious objectors to morality who are willing to pay the price of their commitments.

It is in everybody's interest in a society that conflicts of this kind be avoided. It is better in general not to have people who pursue personal excellences that interfere with the pursuit of other personal excellences. And it is better individually not to pursue personal excellences that put people at odds with the society in which they live. Better or not, however, such conflicts may occur. The reasonable approach is to recognize them, allow them to occur, and let the contest between defenders of public and private reasons decide the case. It must be emphasized, however, that this contest is *not* between morality and personal excellences, but between universal and social rules that protect the conditions in which personal excellences can be pursued and personal excellences that violate these universal and social rules.

It will perhaps be apparent by now how this approach can accommodate some of the important concerns of both Kant and Nietzsche. Kant is right: the art of life is a moral art; universal, impartial, and impersonal rules have an important place in it; and practical reason is the appropriate guide to participation in it. But Kant is also wrong: the art of life is not only a moral art but also a prudential and an aesthetic one; the place of universal, impartial, and impersonal rules is on the universal level, but there are also rules on the social and individual levels, which are particular; and practical reason is a guide to action on all three levels, but many of its requirements are particular, not universal or general, and its requirements, as expressed by private reasons deriving from ideals of personal excellence, may conflict with its requirements, as expressed by public reasons deriving from morality. Kant's approach to the art of life is thus most at home on the universal level and least on the individual level.

The opposite is true of Nietzsche's approach: it is most at home on the individual level and least on the universal one. The art of life is essentially concerned with the pursuit of personal excellences; moral rules may hinder their pursuit; living a good life often requires the rejection of the universal, impartial, and impersonal rules of the Kantian conception of morality and practical reason. Nevertheless, the pursuit of personal excellences should be constrained by morality and practical reason because they protect the conditions that make the pursuit of personal excellences possible; the art of life is not just an aesthetic art but also a moral and a prudential one; and the rejection of Kant's requirement that the rules of morality and practical reason must be universal, impartial, and impersonal is not the rejection of morality and practical reason because there are many moral rules and practical reasons that are particular and none the worse for that.

The argument in this chapter aimed to show the way in which the art of life can be practiced within the limits of morality. It is assumed in subsequent chapters that these moral limits are observed, that lives of personal excellence are good not only because they are satisfying but also because they are morally acceptable.

7 /

Individual Ideals and Projects

Men make for themselves pictures of ideal forms of life. Such pictures are various and may be in sharp opposition to each other. . . . The ideas of self-obliterating devotion to duty or to the service of others; of personal honour and magnanimity; of asceticism, contemplation, retreat; of action, dominance and power; of the cultivation of "an exquisite sense of the luxurious"; of simple human solidarity and cooperative endeavour; of a refined complexity of social existence; of a constantly maintained and renewed sense of affinity with natural things—any of these ideas, and a great many others too, may form the core and substance of a personal ideal.

PETER F. STRAWSON, "Social Morality and Individual Ideal"

7.1 Ideals and Projects

The art of life is to live according to a personally satisfying and morally acceptable ideal of personal excellence. This makes it obvious that the successful practice of the art of life depends on goal-directed activities. But there are important differences between the various activities and goals involved in living according to an ideal of personal excellence. A deeper understanding of the art of life requires, therefore, understanding these different activities and goals, as well as the various relations among them. This is the topic of the present chapter.

An indication of the relation between the activities and goals involved in personal excellences can be found by noticing a feature of some of the lives we have considered. More's self-direction led to his unwanted death; the decency of Countess Olenska and Archer stood in the way of the consummation of their love for each other; the old Oedipus's depth gave him only a good death, not a good life; and

Malesherbes's honor did not enable him to prevent the Revolution or save his king. There is a sense, therefore, in which the activities of these people failed to achieve their goals. It is noteworthy, however, that their failures actually enhanced, rather than diminished, their personal excellences. If personal excellences are essentially connected with goal-directed activities, then how could it be that the failure of the activities enhances, rather than diminishes, people's claim to personal excellences? What good are personal excellences if they may actually hinder people from getting what they reasonably want?

These questions point to a distinction that is centrally important to understanding personal excellences. Most everyday activities are straightforwardly goal-directed. We work in order make a living, take aspirin in order to stop a headache. But the activities that are constitutive of personal excellences are not means that enable people to reach the goals they reasonably pursue. Consequently, the failure of the activities to lead to the goals cannot be a defect. If the activities are not means, then they cannot be defective means. Activities can be goal-directed without being means: acts of loyalty are not means to friendship, scoring a touchdown is not a means to playing football, and being a conscientious taxpayer is not a means to patriotism. Each of these activities is a constituent of goals, not a means to them. Both kinds of activities have goals, but the goals of activities that are means are readily separable from the activities themselves. Their connection is contingent because it is incidental to the activities and the goals that the first leads to the second. The same goal may be achieved by different activities. The goals of constituent activities, however, are not separable from the activities because the activities constitute their goals. The goal of the activities that are constitutive of personal excellences is to be the kind of person who performs the appropriate activities in the appropriate situations. The connection between such activities and their goals is not contingent because the goals could not be what they are without the activities that constitute them.

The goals that many of the activities involved in personal excellences constitute are individual ideals: greatly valued ways of living and acting. They play a central role in the lives of those who hold them. But since they vary from person to person, they are individual. There is no ideal of personal excellence that any particular person is required by reason to hold. In civilized circumstances there are usually many reasonable ideals about how one might live and act, and reason allows people to choose among them. Indeed, reason allows people to live placid, conventional lives in which small pleasures, routine, and domestic comforts dominate and to avoid the turbulence, challenges, and disappointments involved in the pursuit of ideals. It is not contrary to reason, therefore, to have no ideal about how one should live and act or to hold any one of the usually many ideals available in one's context. What is contrary to reason is to hold an ideal, have the opportunity to act in conformity to it, and then fail to do so. Such failure violates one's conviction about how one should live.

All the people we have considered held individual ideals of personal excellence and acted in conformity to them. Montaigne's and More's was to reflect on how they live, achieve clarity about the hierarchy of their commitments, and navigate life's treacherous waters by judiciously compromising only when it left their deepest commitments intact. The *sophron*'s was to cope with the conflicts and adversities that beset his community by making skillful use of the resources of his Hellenic–Byzantine–Greek Orthodox tradition. Countess Olenska's and Archer's was to live according to the conventions of the society that sustained them and represented the best way of life they knew. Oedipus's was to achieve as much control over his life as possible by understanding and accepting its vulnerability to contingency. Malesherbes's was to live up to the responsibilities that followed from his high position regardless of the consequences for himself and his family.

The activities that are called for by an individual ideal of personal excellence are constituents of the goal of living and acting according to that ideal. Doing that is not a means to achieving the ideal but its exemplification. Such ideals, therefore, are not goals external to the activities that aim at them. They are internal to what people do when they act as they think they should. These activities are inseparable from the ideals that are their goals because the ideal *is* to act that way and the reason for acting that way is that it is the ideal. Such activities are referred to here as the pursuit of ideals of personal excellence.

These very same activities, however, also have goals other than the pursuit of ideals of personal excellence. They are performed in specific contexts, for specific reasons, to accomplish specific things. Montaigne's was to retire from politics and live a reflective private life; More's was to avoid the conflict between his religious and political loyalties; the *sophron*'s was to solve such practical problems as finding a husband for a pregnant girl; Countess Olenska's was to live separately from her husband; Archer's was to keep his love from ruining his coming marriage; Oedipus's was to come to terms with his incest and parricide; and Malesherbes's was to reform France and save the king. In this respect, some of them were successful and others not. These activities are referred to here as engagement in projects.

Being unsuccessful in one's engagement in a project is compatible with being successful in exemplifying the appropriate ideal. If engagement in projects is distinguished from the pursuit of ideals of personal excellence, then it becomes clear that activities can succeed or fail in two ways. Success or failure in one way does not determine success or failure in the other. So Montaigne and More, the *sophron*, Countess Olenska and Archer, Oedipus, and Malesherbes could succeed in exemplifying the ideals of self-direction, moral authority, decency, depth, and honor, respectively, and yet fail to achieve the specific goals to which their projects were means.

To have failed in their projects not only does not detract from their personal excellences but actually enhances them. For these people exemplified their personal excellences even though they failed to achieve the specific goals they had reason to pursue. They did not fail because they made a mistake or because they did not try hard enough. They did the best they could, and they could not be blamed for their failure. No one could have overcome the difficulties that defeated them. Their personal excellences were enhanced precisely by the way they faced the difficulties that defeated their projects. For it is much harder to act with self-direction, moral authority, decency, depth, and honor when one knows that one's efforts are being defeated than when the likelihood of success at one's project strengthens one's motivation. Personal excellences are more securely embedded in one's character if they continue to motivate regardless of whether they lead to successful engagement in one's projects. The reason for pursuing an ideal of personal excellence is not that it helps to get what one wants, but that it constitutes a way of living and acting that one regards as an ideal. A securely held ideal holds even in defeat, perhaps especially in defeat.

The upshot of this understanding of the connection between personal excellences and individual ideals is that the goal-directed activities involved in personal excellences can always be described in two equally legitimate ways. If this is recognized, if the two descriptions are not confused, and if the legitimacy of one is not taken to undermine the legitimacy of the other, then the confusion noted earlier is avoided. The source of the confusion is the failure to recognize that success and failure have different meanings in the two types of description. Projects succeed if they achieve their goals. The sign of failure is frustration caused by not getting what one wants. The same activities may be described as the pursuit of individual ideals of personal excellence. Success, then, means that one's activities exemplify the ideals. The sign of failure is damage to one's psychological identity and self-esteem caused by violation of one's ideal of how to live and act.

In the best lives, activities succeed in both ways. People live according to their ideals and succeed in their projects. Perhaps Montaigne and the *sophron* had such lives. In the worst lives, the activities fail in both ways. People violate their ideals and despise themselves, and they fail in their projects, so they are also frustrated. In lives that may be described as noble, people succeed in living according to their ideals even though they fail in their projects. Such were the lives of More, Countess Olenska and Archer, and Malesherbes. In lives that may justly be called base, people succeed in their projects but at the cost of violating their ideals. If More had sworn a false oath in order to stay alive, or if Countess Olenska and Archer had consummated their love, then they would have become base. It is now possible to identify as a further constitutive feature of personal excellences that the activities involved in them must exemplify individual ideals of how one should live and act. Success at this strengthens and failure weakens people's reasons to be satisfied with their lives.

The justified ascription of personal excellences may be done from the outside, by other people, or from the inside, when people say truly of themselves that they have a particular personal excellence. It is an interesting and revealing fact about personal excellences that people who have them are very unlikely to ascribe them to themselves. Just think of the immediate doubts that spring to mind upon hearing people claim of themselves that they are self-directed, morally authoritative, decent, deep, or honorable. The source of the doubt cannot be that it is immodest to ascribe a personal excellence to oneself. After all, immodest claims may be true, even if making them is unseemly. Furthermore, what is unseemly is to make such claims to others, to brag about one's personal excellence. But the fact is that people rarely ascribe personal excellences to themselves even privately, not even when in a quiet moment they take stock of how life is going for them.

There are several reasons that jointly explain why the self-ascription of personal excellences is unlikely. First, people may be genuinely committed to the pursuit of personal excellences, but few can have reached the point where they can truly claim to possess them, for the achievement is difficult and thus rare. On the one hand, people given to honest self-description are usually aware of their own contrary motives, of the difficulties and demands that may yet defeat their aspirations, and of the uncertainties and temptations that the future may bring. They are likely to be aware of their own weaknesses so they will be reluctant to lay claim to personal excellences. On the other hand, people with little interest in self-description will have little interest in ascribing personal excellences to themselves. Self-knowledge makes people diffident in predicting that they will do in the future what they see as the right thing now, although, of course, they mean and hope to do it. Not even saints, perhaps especially not them, regard themselves as saints.

A second reason is that people who actually have achieved personal excellences are unlikely to be aware of them. This is not because they are unreflective, but because their personal excellences have become so natural to them as to be part of the fabric of their lives. They have little reason, therefore, to take notice of them. They just go about their projects and spontaneously and effortlessly perform the appropriate activities. Their actions are self-directed, authoritative, decent, deep, or honorable without their awareness of them as such. Just as carpenters do not praise themselves for habitually hitting nails on the head, and first-class athletes just move gracefully without self-congratulation, so people with personal excellences feel no need to pay attention to the complimentary features of what comes naturally to them.

But perhaps the most illuminating reason for the rarity of the self-ascription of personal excellences is that neither the people who already have them nor those who are on their way to have them aim directly at personal excellences. They do not say to themselves, I want to be self-directed, morally authoritative, decent, deep, or honorable, so I had better take this action. What they say to themselves is: I have this specific goal (preventing the Revolution, not hurting my fiancée's feelings, finding a husband for this pregnant girl, and so forth), and this is the way to reach it. There are other ways as well, but they are inefficient, imprudent, or simply unthinkable because they are contemptible. So the direct motivation of people with personal excellences is a conjunction of their specific goals and the acceptable means available to them. Because they have the personal excellences, their actions reflect them. Their reason for their actions, however, is not to exemplify their personal excellences, but to achieve whatever specific goals they happen to have. Carpenters are not motivated by their skill to wield a hammer, athletes are not motivated to compete by their grace, and people's activities are not motivated by their personal excellences. There is, therefore, little reason, in the normal course of life, for people to be aware of the personal excellences they may have, and so they are unlikely to ascribe them to themselves.

The implication of this is that personal excellences are by-products of one's activities, not their specific goals. The way to develop personal excellences is not to aim at them directly but to engage in one's projects in a particular way. When doing it that way has come to form a consistent pattern, then one's activities exemplify the particular personal excellence. So the individual ideal that is constitutive of a personal excellence is not to be self-directed, morally authoritative, decent, deep, or honorable, but to achieve self-mastery, be an exemplary participant in one's tradition, live in harmony with one's society, come to understand the contingency of life, or do what one's station and its duties require. The extent to which people live up to these ideals is the extent to which they possess the corresponding personal excellences.

7.2 Personal Excellences and Virtues

It will take this account a step further to compare personal excellences and virtues. Much depends, of course, on what is meant by virtues. So let us take what is probably the best account of them—Aristotle's in *Nicomachean Ethics*—and ask whether personal excellences are moral virtues in the Aristotelian sense. The answer is that although they overlap in some ways, there are important differences between them. These differences point to further constitutive features of personal excellences, and that is the reason for comparing them with moral virtues.

It is clear that personal excellences are not cardinal moral virtues, that is, virtues required by all good lives, since good lives can be lived without any of the personal excellences. So the question is whether personal excellences can be identified with noncardinal moral virtues. According to Aristotle's well-known definition, a moral virtue is (a) a character trait that is (b) concerned with choosing actions, (c) based on reason, and (d) aiming at the mean between excess and deficiency.[1] It is questionable whether personal excellences meet these conditions. They are character traits, but the rest is doubtful.

To begin with the condition concerning choice, it is usually logically and empirically possible for people to have acted differently from the way in which they have actually acted. So this cannot be the sense of choice that matters because it would be extraordinary for conscious humans beings not to have chosen their actions. There is nothing in logic or in the laws of nature to prevent those who are insane, alcoholic, or addicted to drugs to commit suicide rather than perform their characteristic actions. In one sense, therefore, they are choosing their actions. And so do I if I have a gun pointed at me and I hand over my wallet. The sense of choice relevant to personal excellences is psychological. The question is whether it must be psychologically possible for people who possess personal excellences to act contrary to them. The answer surely is that sometimes it is not possible. If their personal excellence is deeply ingrained, if it is an essential part of their identity, if their self-esteem is fundamentally connected with it, if their action fits in with a habitual and predictable antecedent pattern of conduct that reflects the personal excellence, then it is psychologically impossible for them to choose a contrary action. They would regard it as unthinkable to act that way. As Luther said on another occasion, Here I stand, I can do no other. Their actions flow from their characters, so that when they act naturally and spontaneously, their actions are expressions of their personal excellences.

There is a perfectly good sense in which Montaigne and More could not have become craven camp followers, the *sophron* could not have told his fellow villagers to stop importuning him, Countess Olenska and Archer could not be indifferent to what their friends and family thought, Oedipus could not have been flippant about what happened to him, and Malesherbes could not have reveled in wine and women as France was going down the drain. They did not have a choice once their characters were formed in a certain way, because the very idea of acting contrary to their personal excellences appeared to them to be so contemptible, despicable, degrading, or distasteful that it was not a live option for them.

As Iris Murdoch puts it: "We are not free in the sense of being able suddenly to alter ourselves since we cannot suddenly alter what we see and ergo what we desire and are compelled by. In a way, explicit choice seems now less important: less decisive (since much of the 'decision' lies elsewhere) and less obviously something to be 'cultivated.' If I attend properly I will have no choices and this is the ultimate condition to be aimed at."[2] Choice becomes more important for people whose personal excellences are insecurely formed. The less they possess an excellence, the less unthinkable they find acting contrary to it, and then the more choices they have. In that case, however, choice becomes an indication of lack of excellence rather than a condition of it. If Aristotle is right and moral virtue must be concerned with choice of action, then many personal excellences are not moral virtues.

There is yet a further reason against trying to apply to personal excellences the Aristotelian view of the necessity of choice. Consider people who do not possess personal excellences and want to develop them. Choice is then important, yet its objects are not actions, as Aristotle says is the case for moral virtues. The usual situation of such people is not that they aim to acquire self-direction, moral authority, decency, depth, or honor and then decide to perform the actions that best further their aims. As Murdoch says, "The 'decision' lies elsewhere." It concerns the question what kind of person they want to be. They find in themselves various motives, and their decisions have to do with which of their motives they should or should not act on. And they decide on the basis of some ideal, which they want their lives and actions to approximate. Once that decision is made, there is not much need for choosing an action because the available actions will appear to them under the description that follows from their ideal. Some actions will seem admirable, others contemptible, and yet others irrelevant. They will then naturally perform the admirable action, and they will not have to make further choices. Complications, of course, may still occur. There may be equally admirable actions, but that is likely to be rare. Or their commitments to their ideals may be weak and their competing motives strong. Their problem then, however, is not what action to choose but which of their motives they should act on. So even where choice is involved in the development, although not in the possession, of a personal excellence, the choice typically concerns motives and ideals, not actions.

The next condition to which moral virtues must conform, according to Aristotle, is that the choice of appropriate action must be based on reason. Let us ignore the just-discussed difficulties about choice and concentrate on asking whether it is necessary for the possession of a particular personal excellence that either it, or the motives, ideals, and actions associated with it, should be based on reason. If being based on reason requires critical reflection, weighing various interpretations of one's situation, and adopting the one that seems to be the strongest in the light of logic and the relevant facts, then personal excellences need not be based on reason. This becomes obvious if internal and external questions about individual ideals are distinguished. Internal questions are prompted by complexities that occur and sought to be resolved, given commitment to an individual ideal. External questions are prompted by doubts about the individual ideal itself. If asking and answering internal questions were sufficient to support the claim that the resulting answers are based on reason, then the case for personal excellences being so based would be made out. The claims of reason, however, are not satisfied by keeping only to internal questions and answers. If they were, then those who hold noxious individual ideals of personal excellence would have to be regarded as reasonable just so long as they dealt with complexities in the light of their ideals. One wants to say, especially to adherents of Nazi, communist, racist, or terrorist ideals of personal excellence, that they ought to be more reasonable, more critical in their reflections, and they ought to ask external questions about their ideals. Reason calls for justification and criticism, not just casuistry. Personal excellences, then, are based on reason only if the critical reflection they involve goes beyond internal questions and answers and includes external ones as well. In that case, however, the personal excellences of More, the *sophron*, Oedipus, and Malesherbes were not based on reason. For More took for granted the Catholicism that formed him; the *sophron* had not reflected critically on his Hellenic–Byzantine–Greek Orthodox tradition; Oedipus did not ask external questions about the tragic view of life he came to hold; and Malesherbes did not question his aristocratic ideal, in which honor played a central role. Only Montaigne, and perhaps Countess Olenska and Archer, subjected their ideals to critical reflection. We may conclude, then, that personal excellences need not be based on reason. They need not, therefore, conform to a condition that according to Aristotle is necessary for being a moral virtue.

The last condition postulated in the Aristotelian conception of moral virtues is that reason should guide the choice of actions that reflect the virtues by aiming at the mean between excess and deficiency. The basic thought behind this condition is that the moral virtues control perfectly natural emotions. Control is needed because the emotions may lead to inappropriate actions. Fear of danger and desire for pleasure are natural, but they may be too strong or too weak. Courage and temperance make fears and desires appropriate to their objects; other moral virtues do the same for other emotions. Given this condition, personal excellences are not moral virtues because the emotions involved in them are very rarely excessive. Personal excellences may be said to control emotions, but only by strengthening weak ones.

Self-direction is motivated by an intense feeling of the importance of self-mastery; moral authority is accompanied by a feeling of loyalty and appreciation for the tradition in which one is an exemplary participant; decency involves the feeling of benevolence toward others in one's conventional context; depth goes with the strongly felt desire to penetrate below the surface and reach a better understanding; and honor is connected with feeling bound to fulfill obligations. There are, of course, other emotions as well. Perhaps the strongest are feelings of contempt, scorn, or distaste for the very possibility of acting contrary to one's individual ideal. The significance of these positive and negative emotions, in the present context, is that if the individual ideals involved in personal excellences are rightly valued, then the stronger people feel about them, the more admirable they are. And the corollary also holds: the weaker people's feelings are, the more likely it is that they will be deficient in the corresponding personal excellence.

If people are committed to lives of self-direction, moral authority, decency, depth, or honor, then it is hard to see how they could be said to feel too strongly their desire for self-mastery, love for the tradition that nourishes them, benevolence toward others in their context, passion for understanding, and sense of obligation. Strong feelings of this kind are parts of wholehearted commitment, of dedication to a way of living and acting that they value. It may happen, of course, that their strong feelings blind them to the defects of their ideals. But if their ideals are free of defects, then passionate feelings about them strengthen, rather than weaken, their personal excellences.

It could also be objected that if More had a weaker sense of integrity, if the *sophron* cared less about his tradition, if Countess Olenska and Archer had been less benevolent, if Oedipus's passion for understanding had been weaker, if Malesherbes had felt less conscientious, then they would have lived happier lives. That may be true. But it would not be true that they would then have been more self-directed, morally authoritative, decent, deep, or honorable.

People can live good lives without personal excellences, but lives dedicated to personal excellences are made better, not worse, by strongly felt commitment to the constitutive individual ideal. Personal excellences, therefore, are unlike Aristotelian moral virtues because the stronger are the emotions involved in personal excellences, the better it is, whereas stronger emotions may produce moral vices rather than virtues.

Personal excellences thus are character traits that need not be centrally concerned with choice of action; their development need not be based on reason; and it need not be necessary to control the strong emotions involved in them. They are certainly connected with choice, reason, and emotions, but this connection is not as close as Aristotle requires for virtues. The point of calling attention to these differences is neither to cast doubt on the Aristotelian account of moral virtues, nor to deny that there may be a sense in which personal excellences could be called virtues, but to understand better the nature of personal excellences. The understanding we have reached, however, is far from complete, as the following considerations show.

7.3 Styles of Life

There is a persistent sense of elusiveness about personal excellences that is not present about moral virtues. Each moral virtue is connected with a specifiable type of intentional object (*intentional* because the exercise of a virtue requires only the belief that the object is present, and the belief may be false). Courage is connected with danger, temperance with pleasure, honesty with nondeception, tact with the feelings of others, and so forth. To act virtuously, then, is to respond appropriately to the relevant intentional object. There may be a great variety of actions that represent a particular virtue because there is a great variety of dangers, pleasures, deceptions, and feelings. These complications, however, do not alter the fact that different instances of the same kind of virtuous action are identifiable with reference to the intentional object to which they are meant as responses. But what is the intentional object of self-direction, moral authority, decency, depth, or honor? What are the actual or imagined objects to which these personal excellences are responses? On what basis can actions be identified as self-directed, morally authoritative, decent, deep, or honorable?

These questions are puzzling, not because the intentional object that is connected with personal excellences may be instantiated in very many different ways but because, unlike the moral virtues, each personal excellence may involve countless very different *types* of intentional objects. Self-direction may lead to selfless sacrifices in defense of one's ideal or to quietly borne hardship and humiliation in order to keep one's ideal alive. In Stalinist Russia, Mandelstam may be thought to represent the first option, Akhmatova the second. To have moral authority may be to remain faithful to a tradition despite private qualms about it or to call for radical reforms because of one's qualms. Erasmus did the first, Luther the second. Decency may be scrupulous adherence to the letter of the prevailing conventions or the equally scrupulous violation of them in order to adhere to their spirit. The young American men who fought in Vietnam, regardless of their private disapproval of the war, did the first; those who became genuine conscientious objectors did the second. To have depth may be to regard appearances as superficial or to take them as the data that theories must explain. Plato was scornful of appearances, Aristotle wanted to save them. To have honor may be to earn high public esteem or to ignore it if it is at odds with a clear conscience. What anthropologists call shame cultures hold the former, guilt cultures the latter. The elusiveness of personal excellences, then, is a result of there being no clearly specifiable intentional objects or actions with which they must be connected. And that makes it puzzling how personal excellences could be identified and distinguished from one another.

The source of this puzzlement is that attempts to identify personal excellences are guided by the wrong expectation. If personal excellences were like moral virtues, then, the expectation is, they ought to have clearly specifiable intentional objects and actions connected with them. When it turns out that there are no such objects and actions, then personal excellences seem elusive. The way out of this difficulty is to abandon the expectation and recognize that personal excellences differ from moral virtues. This, of course, raises the question how personal excellences are to be understood if not by analogy with moral virtues. The answer leads to another of their constitutive features.

Personal excellences are not tendencies to perform particular actions but tendencies to perform actions in a particular way. They are ascribed to people not on the basis of *what* they do but on the basis of *how* they do it. They reveal something deep about people, something essential to their characters, something constitutive of their identity, and this something is an attitude that informs their conduct. The attitude is that their lives ought to be lived on certain terms. Personal excellences differ because the terms differ: for self-direction, it is to be in control of one's life and character; for moral authority, it is to be an exemplary adherent to one's tradition; for decency, it is to live in harmony with valued conventions; for depth, it is to understand human life and one's own life profoundly; and for honor, it is to discharge one's obligations faithfully.[3]

The underlying attitudes are connected with the positive and negative emotions discussed earlier. The positive ones are directed toward the individual ideals that people are committed to trying to realize in their lives. The negative ones regard acting in a manner that violates the ideals as contemptible, treacherous, shallow, dishonorable, base, or corrupt. Since adherence to the ideals is essential to living and acting in the way people want, these violations would be extremely serious. Their seriousness is not just a matter of the people's stumbling and endangering the goodness of their lives. Their commitment to acting in the appropriate manner is fundamental to their characters, and if they act inconsistently, their psychological identity and self-esteem are threatened. If More had sworn a false oath, the *sophron* had ignored the problems of his people, Countess Olenska and Archer had betrayed their promises, Oedipus had reverted to acting on unexamined impulses, and Malesherbes had failed to defend the king, then their whole conception of themselves would have been called into question.

It is convenient to have a single word to designate this feature of personal excellences, and the word that is used here, not without hesitation, is *style*.[4] A personal excellence is a style of life that characterizes a person. Style, of course, is inseparable from content because style can be expressed only by some content or another. Yet style is not connected with any particular content. Its content in the present case is activities. The same style can be expressed by different activities, and the same activities can be performed in quite different styles. That is why personal excellences are not connected with any specifiable action. Furthermore, since the activities that express the style of a particular personal excellence may be responses to quite different intentional objects, personal excellences are not connected with any specifiable intentional object either. Personal excellences are nevertheless not elusive because just as the style of artists is borne by their works, so the style of people is borne by their activities.

The style of activities must be distinguished from their manner.

That activities are performed in some manner is a grammatical, not a psychological, observation about them. What makes this observation true is that any activity can be characterized by adjectival and adverbial phrases, such as pedestrian, routine, imitative, common, or significant, exceptional, original, ingenious; activities can be done lethargically, dutifully, predictably, and boringly, as well as energetically, emotionally, provocatively, and surprisingly. The style of an activity is more than a grammatical feature; it is also an evaluation. Style makes activities distinctive; it implies that the activities bear the marks of the individuality of those who engage in them. This individuality, however, is not just a personal idiosyncrasy, a quirk, or a peculiarity but the expression of a particular and significant character trait. So the styles of people's activities cannot be rare or unusual episodes in their lives; their styles must express some lasting feature of their character. And this feature is not one they can come by without effort. Children, adolescents, fickle adults, people who imitate characters in soap operas or sentimental romances have no style.

Style requires the deliberate transformation of one's character to approximate some ideal. And it requires also that actions should form patterns of activities that reflect commitment to some ideal and express the relevant character trait. The individuality that is the hallmark of style emerges because this transformation of character and its expression in a lasting pattern of activity are always a matter of a reciprocal adjustment of the motivating ideal, the historically conditioned context in which people live and act, and the particular characters with which they grow out of childhood. The conjunction and the reciprocal influences of these three factors are bound to differ from person to person. This is the difference that produces the individuality that characterizes the style of a person.

Part of the great merit of the works in which the people who have been used to illustrate personal excellences appear is that they are shown acting in their characteristic style. At every important junction in their lives Montaigne and More acted self-directedly, the *sophron* authoritatively, Countess Olenska and Archer decently, the old Oedipus deeply, and Malesherbes honorably. But in so acting, they did not subordinate their individuality to a higher ideal. On the contrary, they expressed their individuality by consistently acting in the way self-direction, moral authority, decency, depth, and honor required in their contexts. And that context was made of their characters, societies, and the particular forms their ideals took in their circumstances.

Their achievement was to exemplify through consistent patterns of activities *their* interpretations of *their* ideals in the concrete terms of *their* contexts. Their interpretations were reasonable because they remained faithful to the ideals and expressed their individuality.

The manner of an activity, therefore, is a descriptive feature, whereas the style of an activity, if it has one, is a prescriptive one. Style is an achievement, but whether it is an admirable achievement depends on the character trait and the ideal that the style expresses. Thoroughly deplorable people, such as Göring and Napoleon, can have a style. But regardless of whether the achieved style is morally acceptable, having it is difficult. For there are numerous obstacles to the required self-transformation, such as self-deception, laziness, the comforts of conformity, the intrinsic difficulty of maintaining the necessary discipline, indecision or unclarity about ideals, and so—depressingly—on. Such difficulties prevent many people from developing personal excellences and make their lives drab, uninspired, and boring.

It must be stressed, however, that the achievement of style is not like solving a problem, becoming a grandmaster of chess, or understanding a complex book. These achievements aim at a specific goal, which is like a threshold, the crossing of which constitutes the achievement. The achievement is to *do* something difficult, and once one has done it, it need not, by oneself, be done again. The achievement of style is to *be* in a certain way, and being that way must be maintained. Not to maintain it is to lose it. It is like being healthy, even-tempered, or witty. The achievement *is* maintained by continuous activity, but it is not to keep doing some particular kind of thing but to keep doing whatever one does in a particular way. The doing is essential, but only as a vehicle of the style and just so long as it can be carried out in that style. It makes little difference to the achievement of style what the particular activity is. Of course, the nature of the activity matters greatly for moral reasons. As we have seen, morality excludes styles that violate the universal and social conditions of good lives.

7.4 Moral Education

It remains to be considered how people become acquainted with the individual ideals to which they commit themselves. In societies that are simple or highly structured, hierarchical, and stable, people occupy positions in which ideals are implicit. When Gary Cooper memorably mumbles in *High Noon* that a man has got to do what he has got to do, everybody knows what that is. If you are a good guy, you have got to shoot it out with the bad guys. Similarly, Homeric heroes must prove themselves in combat with other heroes; feudal landlords must pay fealty to those above them and expect it from those below; romantic artists must create in agony; English gentlemen in the colonies must hold a stiff upper lip and set an example to the natives; Jesuits must be the front-line troops of the pope; and so forth. Contemporary Western societies, however, are neither simple nor stable. Social mobility, moral ambiguity, rapid technological changes, and conflicts of responsibilities, loyalties, and roles are ever-present. Yet people are still motivated by individual ideals, and so the question arises how they become familiar with the available ideals among which they may choose some to make their own.

Personal experience may acquaint people with some admirable lives, which can then serve as ideals. But this cannot go very far. The personal experiences of most people are limited in range and variety. And it is typical of contemporary Western societies that people make a life for themselves by leaving behind the context in which they were born and raised and to which their personal experiences have given them access. So what, then, is the alternative?

The alternative is moral education, understood in a wide enough sense to go beyond the teaching of simple rules and to include admirable lives that serve as models to follow and contemptible lives that stand as warnings. Familiarity with these lives does not come from personal experience, but from literature, history, religion, philosophy, and ethnography. One of the several values of these subjects is that the great works that have formed them are repositories of admirable and contemptible lives. These works are the classics, and acquaintance with them provides an important part of the content of moral education. For the admirable lives represent possibilities of good lives, and the contemptible ones represent limits that good lives cannot transgress.

The great works are classics because the lives they depict are complex and flexible enough to serve as permanent ideals and dangers for human lives. The good lives depicted in the classics are not to be copied, and the bad ones are not specific pitfalls to be avoided. Their complexity and flexibility ensure that the general truths they contain about human lives can be applied to illuminate a great variety of very different contexts. Self-direction, moral authority, decency, depth, and honor have many different forms, and these forms vary historically, culturally, and individually. But they are united, as it were, by a common theme. A classic work is a classic because it gives enduring expression to one of these themes.

A central task of moral education is to make the classic works available and to explain their significance. This has been one of the traditional aims of the humanities, and it has been one of their contributions to the betterment of the human condition. It is a lamentable feature of our times that the humanities are under attack from both the outside and the inside. Outside attacks are largely the result of a failure to understand the importance of the humanities to moral education and the importance of moral education to good lives. The response to such attacks can only be a patient attempt to show, and show again, in concrete terms, the importance of what these attacks miss.

The attacks from the inside are attacks on the values of the Western tradition. It is supposed that the ideals and dangers of good lives as they have been depicted in the classic works of the Western tradition are somehow called into question by the existence of other possibilities. The response to this attack must be an equally patient attempt to explain that the existence of other possibilities does nothing to cast doubt on the tried and true values of the Western tradition. If there are classic works that depict these other possibilities, they add to our understanding of the ideals and dangers of good lives, and they should be welcomed. But to denigrate the values we have because there may be other possibilities we could value is a mistake that no reasonable person would wish to make.

Successful moral education leaves its beneficiaries with the task of connecting the ideals and dangers they have learned about with their own characters and circumstances. Making this connection depends on the possession of adequate moral imagination and practical wisdom. Through moral education people envisage what it would be like to live according to one of these ideals or to succumb to one of these dangers. Through practical wisdom they come to know how to apply their understanding of the ideals and dangers in their own context, formed of the particularities of their characters and circumstances. A large part of the art of life is to be skillful in making this connection.

7.5 Personal Excellences

The constitutive features of personal excellences that have so far been identified are, then, as follows. They are important character traits because they are essential to psychological identity and self-esteem. They are active tendencies directed toward two distinct types of goals: individual ideals of how one should live and act and projects that respond to the concrete circumstances of one's character and context. They are at once exemplifications of individual ideals and means to the achievement of specific goals. They are unlike Aristotelian moral virtues because they need not involve choice, they may not involve reasoned evaluation of the individual ideals that motivate them, and the emotions involved in them are rarely so strong as to be excessive. They are not tendencies to engage in particular activities, but tendencies to perform one's activities in one's individual style. These constitutive features taken together do not amount to a full account of personal excellences. Such an account must also include discussion of the dominant attitudes toward one's way of living and acting that are also constitutive features of personal excellences. It is to them that we now turn.

8/

Dominant Attitudes

Every person has a life of his own, his one and only life, and
that life he leads. But some more so than others. . . . My
point . . . concerns the varying degrees to which people . . .
manage to give to their lives a pattern, an overallness, or the
different degrees of success that they have in making their lives
of a piece. . . . Such integration of life . . . [is] something that, in
many ages, for many cultures, has been in the nature of an
ideal—a grace to be cultivated or a triumph to be won.

      RICHARD WOLLHEIM, "On Persons and Their Lives"

8.1 The Integration of Life

The grace and the triumph of an integrated life is a central theme in
contemporary moral psychology. There are several influential approaches to this elusive but highly desirable ideal. One is Wollheim's
own, according to which the key is the achievement of a mental connectedness that consists in bringing one's present under the influence
of one's past through the cultivation of memory that is cleansed of de-
fensive and self-aggrandizing falsifications.[1] Another approach is that
of Alasdair MacIntyre, who argues that the unity of the self is
achieved through the construction of a coherent narrative account of
one's past and present experiences, where the idiom in which the narrative is cast is the moral vocabulary of the tradition to which one belongs.[2] Stuart Hampshire's approach is to bring to consciousness one's
intentions and thereby understand more and more clearly what one
wants to do and why, and then act accordingly.[3] Harry Frankfurt regards as essential the control of one's first-order desires for various
satisfactions by subjecting them to the evaluations that follow from
one's second-order volition to be the kind of person who satisfies only

favorably evaluated desires and thus lives a certain kind of life.[4] Charles Taylor develops the notion of strong evaluation, which involves reflective self-examination, as the way to become a fully human and fully responsible agent.[5]

The approach described and defended in this chapter is indebted to those just listed, but it differs from them in three ways. One is that these psychoanalytically inspired approaches all suppose that the key to integrated lives is the individuals' conscious and realistic evaluation of their past experiences. Their supposition, therefore, is that integration is primarily a backward-looking and inner process.

This, however, cannot be quite right. The lives of Montaigne, More, the *sophron*, Countess Olenska, Archer, the old Oedipus, and Malesherbes were all integrated, yet backward-looking and inner-directed reflective self-evaluation played only a minor part in the lives of the *sophron*, Countess Olenska, Archer, and Malesherbes. Evaluations were certainly constant features of the latter lives, but these evaluations concerned what they should do to meet the demands of their ideals and projects, not what to make of their past experiences. The integrity of the *sophron*'s life depended on his dedication to solve the practical problems of his people in accordance with their shared tradition. The integrity of the lives of Countess Olenska and Archer had to do with the lifelong control of those unruly desires of theirs that were contrary to the conventions of their society. And the integrity of Malesherbes's life was the result of his subordination of his and his family's welfare to the welfare of France. The lives of all these people were of a piece, but only some of them made it so by concentrating on their inner lives and past experiences in order to decide how they ought to live.

It is, of course, beyond question that the integration of their lives is up to individuals and that it involves the evaluation of their past experiences. But that is not all it involves. Integration also involves the evaluation of one's life by appealing to standards set by one's ideal and projects. Part of the point of evaluating one's past experiences is to increase the likelihood in the future of approximating one's ideal and succeeding in one's projects. And since the ideal and projects must be pursued in circumstances that exist outside and independently of oneself, integration essentially involves looking both outward and toward the future. Consequently, while the present approach regards the development of personal excellences through the art of life as the key to an integrated life, it recognizes that success depends on both inner and outer conditions. The inner conditions include dominant attitudes, the topic of this chapter.

The second difference is that these other approaches, unlike the present one, make absolutist claims to having identified some essential condition that all good lives must meet.[6] Their absolutism becomes apparent when it is realized that they all advocate lives that have been described (in 1.1–4) as aiming at the personal excellence of self-direction. Now self-direction is certainly a form that good lives may take, but as we have seen, it is not an essential condition of all good lives. Lives of physical exertion by athletes and explorers, of selfless service by social workers and nuns; lives of soldiers and monks in strict hierarchical organizations; quiet conventional lives of ordinary people in ordinary occupations; lives of collectors, inventors, musicians, jockeys, farmers, and accountants may involve little reflection, self-examination, and self-evaluation; they may be unconcerned with the articulation of narratives or with the achievement of mental connectedness; and yet they may be good and responsible human lives. The present approach recognizes that self-direction is only one form that good lives may take; that the art of life is only one way of making lives good; and that there are many personal excellences, such as moral authority, decency, depth, and honor, in which self-direction need not have an important place and yet whose achievement through the art of life may lead to good lives.

The claim, then, is that the aim of the art of life is to make lives good. This may be done by developing personal excellences. Personal excellences are inspired by individual ideals, and they are shown by the style in which individuals engage in whatever projects they may have. But since the same ideals and projects can be pursued in different styles, understanding personal excellences requires more than what has been said up to now. It needs also to be understood what inner processes are involved in the development of one's style. These inner processes are referred to here as dominant attitudes. The third difference, then, between the psychoanalytically inspired approaches and the present one is that the former regard the inner processes upon which they take the integration of life to depend as some form of reflective self-evaluation, whereas the latter regards it as the possession of a dominant attitude in which reflective self-evaluation may, but need not, be particularly important.

The present approach to the integration of life is thus at once outward and inward directed, backward and forward looking, pluralistic in recognizing the legitimacy of other approaches; and it focuses on the development of a style in which individuals engage in their projects, a style that reflects their ideals and dominant attitudes. In short, personal excellences are to be understood in terms of individual ideals and dominant attitudes.

8.2 Attitudes

Understanding dominant attitudes requires understanding what kind of attitudes they are and what makes them dominant. The first will be done now, the second next. To begin with, to have an attitude of the relevant kind is to care about something that matters to oneself.[7] The attitude may be favorable, unfavorable, or an ambivalent mixture of both. Attitudes, therefore, are essentially evaluative. The evaluations may be moral, aesthetic, economic, scientific, horticultural, personal, medical, and so on and on. They may be private or public, important or trivial, reasonable or unreasonable, expressed or unexpressed, confident or hesitant, widely shared or idiosyncratic, correct or incorrect. But the evaluations are always made by individuals, and they consist in their favorable, unfavorable, or ambivalent reactions to some object, where the object is to be understood very generally as that toward which the attitude is directed. There is a sense, therefore, in which attitudes are necessarily subjective, since they are the attitudes of some subjects. This, of course, most emphatically does not mean that they are subjective in the quite different sense in which their correctness is entirely dependent on how the subjects evaluate some objects. Attitudes may be incorrect because their subjects may be mistaken in their evaluations of the objects of their attitudes.

The objects of the attitudes that concern us here are the lives of the subjects who have the attitudes. These attitudes consist in the subjects' evaluations of their own lives on the basis of how good their lives have been in the past and how good they are likely to be in the future. The evaluations are made in mid-course, when there is already a past of some duration behind and a realistic prospect of a future ahead; they are, therefore, not the prospective evaluations of adolescents or the retrospective evaluations of those near death.

These evaluative attitudes need not be expressed in a propositional form, they need not be reflective; indeed, the subjects may not even be aware of having them. The attitude may simply be an unarticulated feeling of satisfaction, dissatisfaction, or ambivalence regarding how life in general is going for oneself. It may just be an unconscious wish that the life should go on by and large the same way as it has been going, or it may be the inchoate wish that it should be changed in some important ways. The sign of satisfaction may be tranquillity, wholehearted engagement in one's projects, or a benign and generous view of other people. Dissatisfaction may show itself in boredom, irritable restlessness, unfocused anxiety, or what Nietzsche so perceptively described as *ressentiment*.

It is important to stress, as a corrective to the over-intellectualization characteristic of the psychoanalytically inspired views, that having a reasonable and realistic attitude toward one's life does not require knowing that one has the attitude, or the actual or potential verbalization of it. Of course, if people are seriously enough dissatisfied with their lives to actively want to change them, then getting clear about the source of their dissatisfaction becomes important. Because few lives are so fortunate as to be without serious dissatisfactions, clarity and articulation are often desirable. But they are desirable for remedying what has gone wrong, not as conditions of responsibility and full-fledged human agency that all good lives must meet. The desirability of correcting what has gone wrong should not be confused with the desirability of the state in which correction is unnecessary. Socrates, therefore, was wrong to say that the unexamined life is not worth living.[8] What he should have said is that examination may make many lives more worth living. The insistence on the necessity of reflective self-evaluation is the result of mistaking the kind of life intellectuals typically want to live for a model to which lives worth living must conform.

Regardless, however, of the degree of consciousness and articulation that is involved in people's attitudes toward their lives, the attitudes have cognitive, emotive, and motivational components. The cognitive component comprises the subjects' beliefs about themselves, their lives and circumstances, and the ideals and projects that motivate them. These beliefs may be true or false. If false, they may be so because some internal psychological obstacle, such as self-deception, fear, hope, stupidity, laziness, fatigue, and so forth, has interfered with accurate perception. Such obstacles range from reasonable defenses against the awfulness of one's circumstances, through nonculpable weaknesses and shortcomings, to culpable vices. It may or may not be reasonable to try to overcome such obstacles, for the effort may be futile or the false belief may help one cope with an unbearable truth. It is normally reasonable, however, to aim to hold true beliefs about one's life, for the successful pursuit of one's ideals and projects depends on the truth of the relevant beliefs. Only in exceptional cases do falsifications escape being unreasonable. The source of false beliefs, however, may also be the misperception of the facts that results from conditions other than psychological obstacles. Physiological limits, physical illness, deception by others, manipulation, adverse external conditions, the ambiguity or complexity of the facts may prevent or make difficult accurate perception.

It is not only factual mistakes, however, that account for having false beliefs about one's life. The mistake may be one of judgment, in which accurately perceived facts are ascribed the wrong significance. In this way people may over- or underestimate the importance of something they lack or have, such as money; or they may be beguiled by some features of their ideals or projects while overlooking other, no less important features, such as being attracted by the glamour of fame and missing the lack of privacy that goes with it; or they may be so wrapped up in their pursuit of ideals or projects that they lose sight of the moral and political implications of what they are doing.

The salient point about these and other mistakes of fact and judgment is that they reinforce the earlier argument that the sense in which the relevant attitudes are subjective (being the attitudes of subjects) is perfectly consistent with a sense in which the attitudes are also objective (aiming at the accurate perception and judgment of the relevant facts). In one sense, therefore, the attitudes are up to the subjects who hold them, for they may hold no attitudes of the relevant kind or hold any one of the wide range of relevant but different attitudes. In another sense, however, the attitudes are not up to the subjects, for they normally aim to hold attitudes based on true beliefs, and what those are is not up to them.

Turning now to the emotive component of attitudes, we should begin with the recognition that attitudes in general need not have an emotive component.[9] In the first place, the attitude may be one of indifference, neutrality, or disinterest, and these are normally marked precisely by the absence of emotions. Second, even favorable attitudes may be without emotions, as when an atheist approves of the judicious church reforms advocated by Erasmus or an empiricist finds Schopenhauer's clarity preferable to Hegel's obscurity. Such attitudes may involve no more than a cognitive reaction that is devoid of emotional investment. But indifference and a purely cognitive reaction usually mean that one does not much care about their objects. It is easy to have a dispassionate attitude toward them because they do not really matter to one.

If, however, we turn from attitudes in general to the attitude toward one's own life, then emotions are normally present. It is natural to feel optimistic or pessimistic, hopeful or fearful, pleased or apprehensive, proud or ashamed, satisfied or guilty, contented or frustrated, joyful or depressed, enthusiastic or bored about one's life. Such emotions being natural means that having them is readily understandable and it is their absence that requires explanation. If the explanation is given, it reveals that something has gone very wrong in the life of the person who has no emotional reaction to it. Extreme hardship, constant struggle, serious traumas, mental illness, recurrent humiliation, and the like may cause lives to be so hard to endure as to make it advisable or at least understandable for the subjects to focus their attention elsewhere. But if their lives are not grievously disturbed, people will have emotions about them.

Having emotions about one's life, however, is one thing; whether they are reasonable is quite another. In their origin, emotions are involuntary. They just happen. Strong ones assail us, weaker ones merely color our attitudes. They make us go up and down, they influence our judgments, and they affect how we regard our lives. Emotions thus tell us something that we may or may not welcome; strong ones do so insistently, weak ones softly. And when what they tell us is about our lives, they intimate something important. But their intimations are often obscure and unreliable. This leads many thoughtful people to distrust emotions in general, and their own emotions in particular. They try to think of them as noise that is the by-product of the workings of their mental machinery. If this distrust were warranted, it would cast doubt also on the attitude of which emotions are essential components, and the doubt would affect the art of life, whose successful practice depends on having a reasonable attitude to one's life. So we need to consider whether the distrust of emotions about one's life is reasonable.

As perceptively noted by L. A. Kosman, "Aristotle's moral theory must be seen as a theory not only of how to *act* well but also how to *feel* well; for the moral virtues are states of character that enable a person to exhibit the right kinds of emotions as well as the right kinds of actions. The art of proper living, we should say, includes the art of feeling well as the correlative discipline to the art of acting well."[10] The root of the distrust of emotions is that since they are involuntary, there does not seem to be a way of improving oneself in the art of feeling well. To know that one ought to have a certain emotion will not produce it; and to know that one ought not to have it will not dissipate it. Fear of things going wrong, enthusiasm about a project, guilt at not having tried hard enough, joy at success, shame at failure either come to one or not, but they cannot be summoned up. We cannot practice having them. They can certainly be faked by pretending to have them, but the pretense is for others; we cannot make ourselves feel the fear, enthusiasm, guilt, joy, or shame that we do not feel. What we should therefore do instead of trying to control the uncontrollable, skeptics say, is to concentrate on acting as we ought, regardless of whether emotions aid or hinder the effort.

This tendency to denigrate an essential component of the attitude to one's life is at once futile and unwarranted. Even if emotions do not lend themselves to direct control, it is possible to control them indirectly. There may be little that can be done about having or not having particular emotions, but there is much that can be done to correct them by strengthening reasonable emotions and weakening unreasonable ones. Such corrections are made possible by collateral beliefs. Reasonable emotions toward one's life are reactions to beliefs that are taken to be true: that one is loved, that one's project is the object of scorn, that a goal is within one's reach, that one has failed through lack of sufficient effort, that one has or lacks a necessary talent, that one's friend is true, that now nothing can go wrong, and so on. Then one feels joyous, angry, hopeful, ashamed, confident, or secure about one's life. Any of these beliefs may turn out to be false, and the realization of this is bound to affect the emotion, if it is a reasonable reaction to the false belief. The joy at being loved or the shame at failure cannot reasonably survive for long after the discovery that the love was simulated or the apparent failure was in fact a success. A reasonable emotion may linger then, like an aftertaste or the memory of a bad dream, but it will weaken and gradually dissipate.

Emotions, of course, may not be reasonable. Thinking of them as reactions to some particular collateral beliefs may just be a rationalization, not a reason. Their true sources are then hidden or disguised because they are too precious to be exposed, too threatening to face, or too shocking to admit. In that case, the realization that the collateral belief is false will not dispel the emotion. If the distrust of an emotion about one's life is based on the suspicion that the emotion is unreasonable in this way, then the distrust may be well founded. But the suspicion must itself be based on some reason, and that reason must be better than that what is suspected is an emotion. There is as little to be said for a global skepticism about emotions as there is for a global skepticism about beliefs or perceptions. They are all fallible, but only some of them are mistaken. If there is a reason to suspect that an emotion is unreasonable, then the very reason points to the way in which the suspicion may be confirmed or laid to rest, and thus the emotion may be brought under control. But if there is no reason to suspect its reasonableness, then there is no reason to distrust it.

The distrust of emotions about one's life, however, may be based not on their supposed imperviousness to reason but on the frequency with which they turn out to be unreasonable. People tend to have false beliefs and unreasonable emotions about their lives because it is often easier to nurture them than to face the truth they disguise. This is lamentable but true. Its truth, however, shows only that the art of life is difficult, not that it is impossible. And that is not exactly news.

The third component of the attitude toward one's life is the motivational one. The beliefs and emotions about one's life, as well as external circumstances, prompt motives and move one toward action. In the simplest cases, finding one's life bad motivates one to make it better and finding it good motivates one to continue to do whatever one has been doing. But people's attitudes toward their lives are rarely simple; the way in which motives are connected to actions is complex; and even in the simplest of cases, being moved toward action is not straightforward because, although the general goal of the action is then clear, the choice of the particular action that best serves the goal is not.

These complications are to a large extent the result of there being the two quite different types of goal-directed activities (see 7.2). The goal of one is to live and act according to one's ideal; the goal of the other is to do whatever the successful engagement in one's project requires. The ideal is to live and act so as to exemplify some particular personal excellence, such as self-direction, moral authority, decency, depth, or honor. The project is to engage in some particular form of activity that within the limits and possibilities of one's character and circumstances, represents one's chief concerns and interests. For Montaigne, it was reflection on life; for More, it was to be a good lord chancellor of England; for the *sophron*, it was to solve the moral problems of his people; for Countess Olenska and Archer, it was to discharge the duties of their station in life as members of the high society of New York; for Oedipus, it was to come to terms with his incest and parricide; and for Malesherbes, it was to do what he could for France during revolutionary times.

These two types of goal-directed activities are different. In the case of ideals, the activities are constitutive of their goals. The ideal just is to engage in the relevant activities. In the case of projects, the activities are means to achieving their goals. If other activities are better means, they will be chosen instead. In the first case, the goals are inseparable from the activities; in the second case, they are contingently connected. A further difference is that living according to an ideal does not require any particular activities; it requires that whatever the activities are, they be done in the way that the ideal requires. Engagement in projects, by contrast, does require particular activities, namely those that are most likely to achieve the goal of the project. Success in the first depends on *how* what is done is done; success in the second depends on *what* is done. That is why living according to an ideal is a matter of style, whereas engagement in a project calls for activities that give content to the style.

The differences between ideals and projects result in an unavoidable ambiguity in the identification of the motives that compose the motivational component of the attitude toward one's life, for the objects of the motives may be either the pursuit of an ideal or engagement in a project. In the case of good lives, this ambiguity makes no practical difference because one is succeeding at both. Pursuing an ideal is to engage in a project that combines successful activities and a particular style. But since few lives are as good as their subjects wish them to be, either the style or the activities, or both, are more or less deficient. The aim of the motives and actions must be to remedy their defects. Doing that, however, requires doing very different things. Making oneself increasingly self-directed, a better moral authority, more decent, deeper, or more honorable calls for quite different motives and actions than does the successful engagement in the projects that such people happen to pursue. There are many different ways in which these ideals of personal excellence can be exemplified, and although the activities involved in the relevant projects ought to exemplify the ideals in the background, the success of projects has little to do with success in the exemplification of ideals. Success in one is compatible with failure at the other. Of course, the desideratum is success at both, but neither guarantees the other. The necessity of having to succeed at two different types of activities in order to make one's life good accounts for much of the complexity of the motivational component of the attitude toward one's life.

These differences notwithstanding, there are also similarities between the two types of motives. They move one toward actions, and the actions aim to keep one's life good or to make it better. If the motives result in actions, they typically have both immediate and more remote consequences. The immediate ones concern how to do some particular thing or what particular thing to do. The more remote ones concern the effect of what or how it is done on the development of one's character. Actions form patterns, the patterns solidify into character traits, and character traits make one's character what it is. Both kinds of consequence have a bearing on the evaluation of actions.

The psychoanalytically inspired views discussed earlier carry the suggestion that full-fledged human agency and responsibility requires both the deliberate evaluation of motives and the assignment of primary importance to their more remote character-forming consequences. Neither suggestion seems to be right. Although the attitude to one's life is unavoidably evaluative, there are many customary, habitual, and problem-free areas of life in which one can afford to maintain a seamless connection between motive and action that is uninterrupted by deliberate evaluation. Nor is it always required that the immediate consequences should be ranked lower than the more remote ones. Reflective, responsible, fully human agents may reasonably judge that in responding to an emergency, a crisis, a unique opportunity, an exceptional situation, the immediate consequences are more important than the more remote ones, even if this affects the development of their characters in a way that is contrary to what they normally wish. The spontaneous emotions that may carry people away, and would not survive reflective evaluation, may actually lead them to act in morally better ways than they would do normally. People can be overcome also by love, generosity, and compassion, not only by hate, greed, and cruelty.[11]

A further similarity between the goal-directed activities involved in the pursuit of ideals and projects is that the connection between motive and action is often broken in both. This may happen for two reasons, one internal, the other external to the subject. The internal reason is that one may have more than a single motive, motives may conflict with one another, and only one of them can result in action. A benefit of integrated lives is that such conflicts are rare in them, and if they occur, then they have a ready resolution. Conflicting motives are characteristic of fragmented lives, and that is one reason for wanting to avoid them. The external reason why action may not follow from motive is that the obstacles in one's circumstances are formidable enough to make it too costly or too risky to act as the motive prompts. If the pursuit of ideals and projects endangers one's life, health, or other conditions of the possibility of future pursuits, then it may well be reasonable, although unheroic, to refrain from acting on one's motive.

In concluding this account of the attitude toward one's life, we may note that the following constitutive features of it have emerged. The attitude is *subjective*, in the sense that it is the attitude of a subject. The object of the attitude is one's life as a whole, viewed in the course of living it, when there is a substantial past behind and reasonable expectation of a future ahead. So the attitude is *reflexive* and *temporal*. The attitude is also *evaluative* because it reflects whether one views the life favorably, unfavorably, or ambivalently. If the evaluation is reasonable, it is based, in part, on one's success in pursuing some ideal of personal excellence and in engaging in some project. The *components* of the attitude are *cognitive*, *emotive*, and *motivational*: beliefs, emotions, and motives. The beliefs concern the facts and their importance in one's life. The emotions express how one feels about the life as a whole. And the motives, prompted by beliefs and emotions, move one toward actions. The attitude as a whole may or may not be reasonable, depending on whether the component beliefs, emotions, and motives are reasonable. Each can go wrong as a result of internal or external causes. Each can be corrected, although whether it should be corrected depends on the circumstances.

This account needs to be supplemented by three reminders. First, the attitude may be, but need not be, conscious, reflective, or verbalized. It may just be an inarticulate and generally favorable, unfavorable, or ambivalent reaction toward one's life. Second, given only what has been said up to now, the moral status of the attitude is open. No matter how favorably one may view one's life, it may still be immoral because it may violate the universal or social requirements of morality. Third, the general line of argument is that one way of making lives good is through the successful practice of the art of life; that involves the development of a personal excellence; that, in turn, depends, as we have seen, on one's individual ideal and, as we shall see, on one's dominant attitude. The just-completed account is intended to explain the nature of the attitude, but it leaves open the question why it should be dominant. We now turn to that question.

8.3 Dominant Attitudes

People's attitudes toward their lives may or may not be dominant. If dominant, they constitute the perspective from which they consistently view their lives. The relevant facts, of course, are what they are, but the dominant attitude influences what they make of the facts. It provides their standard for judging the relevance and the respective importance of the facts, their standard of salience. Such an attitude is necessarily evaluative because it is a favorable, unfavorable, or ambivalent reaction to their lives, depending on their success in living according to an ideal of personal excellence.

The attitude, however, may not be dominant, and there may be lives that have no dominant attitudes at all. People who see themselves not as individuals but as parts of a larger system (a family, a society, a temporary occupant of a role, a small segment of a providential order) may have their dominant attitude formed of the evaluative perspective of the system that includes them. This is not incompatible with their also having an individual attitude toward their lives, but their system's point of view is dominant and their individual perspective is recessive. Their touchstone of salience is what happens to their system, not what happens to them.[12] Still, these people have a dominant attitude, even if it is not directed toward their own lives, but there are others who lack a dominant attitude altogether. This may be because they live close to the subsistence level, all their energies must be concentrated on survival, and they do not have the leisure and luxury to evaluate much of anything. Or they may have a fleetingly dominant attitude toward their lives, but it is short-lived and keeps changing in the face of even negligible difficulties or faintly tempting new possibilities. Their attachment to individual ideals and projects is loose, their commitments are weakly held, and their concerns and interests are frequently changing. Yet others may be prevented from having a dominant attitude by doubt, despair, cynicism, superficiality, or fear of failure, and they live day to day without a coherent evaluative perspective.

Much may be said for and against these alternatives to having as dominant the attitude toward lives guided by an ideal of personal excellence. It is perhaps clear, however, that having a dominant attitude of this kind is an important feature of one conception of good lives. Part of the reason Montaigne's and More's lives were good is that they had a dominant attitude to self-direction, as the *sophron* had to moral authority, Countess Olenska and Archer to decency, Oedipus to depth, and Malesherbes to honor. But it is not clear exactly what a dominant attitude thus conceived contributes to good lives. Let us now try to make that clear.

If a good life is conceived in individualistic terms, if its goodness is thought to depend on living according to an ideal of personal excellence, then the dominant attitude forms the core of the agents' psychological identity. It is their deepest, most entrenched evaluative perspective. Approached from the outside, say from the point of view of a biographer, no description of such lives will be adequate unless it recognizes the centrality and comes to terms with the specific nature of its subject's dominant attitude. For to understand a dominant attitude is to understand the roots of a person's motivation: what it is that that person values above everything, for the sake of which everything is done, as well as what is unthinkable, psychologically impossible for that person. It is to know how someone ranks the available possibilities of life and sets the limits that are either inviolable or whose violation incurs the most serious psychological injury.

If the dominant attitude is approached from the inside, as it presents itself to oneself, it is experienced as the source of self-esteem. The surface of the dominant attitude is the favorable, unfavorable, or ambivalent evaluation of how successful one is in living according to an ideal of personal excellence. Reflection may prompt some people to go below the surface and try to identify the reasons for or against their evaluations. If the evaluations are more or less adverse or mixed, as they often are, then people may seek and find ways of correcting what is responsible for what has gone wrong. The dominant attitude, therefore, determines what really matters. It is not just the central but also a pervasive influence on the beliefs, emotions, and motives that constitute people's attitudes toward their lives.

Pervasiveness is an essential feature of dominant attitudes. People have many attitudes, not just dominant ones, and they have countless beliefs, emotions, and motives, some of which form parts of attitudes while others do not. Dominant attitudes are not discrete units that are regarded by their subjects as more important than the others. They *are* held to be more important, but one sign of that is that they affect very many of the less important attitudes. They spread over them, influence them, and they permeate much of people's sensibility.

This pervasiveness is possible because the beliefs, emotions, and motives that constitute the dominant attitude do not have the same recurring specific objects. They have, to be sure, specific objects, but what they are varies with the characters and circumstances of the people whose dominant attitudes they are. To have a dominant attitude toward living a self-directed, morally authoritative, decent, deep, or honorable life does not depend on having any particular beliefs, emotions, or motives. The requirements of these personal excellences vary individually, historically, and culturally. The subject must believe that living according to the personal excellence is important, must feel passionately about realizing the relevant possibilities and observing the limits, and must be strongly motivated to act according to the beliefs and the emotions. These requirements, however, concern *how* the subject holds the beliefs, feels the emotions, and is moved to action, and not *what* the specific beliefs, emotions, and motives ought to be. This is why to live according to a personal excellence is to have a certain style.

A person's style expresses something deep and essentially important, and we can now say that what it expresses is the person's dominant attitude. The attitude *is* composed of beliefs, emotions, and motives, but what makes it dominant is that that is how the subject tends to think, feel, and act, and not what in particular are the objects of the prevailing beliefs, emotions, and motives. The style of a person permeates many of the contingent aspects of the person's sensibility, and that is what endures throughout changes in character and circumstances. Self-direction, moral authority, decency, depth, and honor take radically different forms in ancient Greece, Confucian China, medieval Europe, revolutionary France, fin de siècle America, and the contemporary Western world, but something enduring makes these different forms the forms of the same thing. The unifying thread is the style that living according to the ideal of a particular personal excellence requires, and not any particular one of the ever-changing beliefs, emotions, and motives that the contingencies of a life lived at a certain time and place call for.

To make this attitude concrete, consider placing people who are committed to a life of self-direction, moral authority, decency, and depth in the same position in which Malesherbes actually was with his commitment to honor. Assume that all these people are French aristocrats, mature and reasonable men, who find themselves in the midst of the turmoil of the Revolution. How might their different styles express their dominant attitudes as they respond to the same events that confronted Malesherbes? They would agree with Malesherbes in finding the abuses of the ancien régime inexcusably stupid and the Terror of the Revolution a horrifying regression to barbarism, but they would have quite different reasons for their reactions.

The self-directed one will see the surrounding events as formidable obstacles to living the life he wants. He will see the murderous rampage of the mob as the predictable consequence of the sleep of reason. He will deplore what is going on for making it impossible to maintain a private sphere in which people can engage in their projects. The style that unifies his various responses will be that of beleaguered individuality. The one with moral authority will see the situation as the disintegration of a cherished but defective tradition. He will see the uselessness of trying to cope with the problems of revolutionary France by bringing to it the accumulated wisdom of her past tradition, for he will realize that the tradition no longer commands the allegiance of enough people to survive. The unifying style of his responses will be that of nostalgia for a valued but irretrievably lost tradition. The one committed to the ideal of decency will see his circumstances as the predicament of a conventional person during bad times. A life of decency presupposes a social context in which reciprocal goodwill and a spirit of cooperation generally prevail and in which the conventions provide the generally recognized forms for their expression. He will see that these are crumbling and that, although he can continue to conduct himself as he has hitherto, doing so has become as inappropriate and unreasonable as the efforts of a beached fish to swim. His style will reflect his bemused recognition that he has become a quixotic figure. The one dedicated to depth will see the brutality of the revolutionary upheavals as the latest manifestation of the contingency of life. He will see the delusions of those who think they are in control of the events, and he will recognize that the awfulness of the times is the unintended consequence of countless individual actions whose significance their agents have understood imperfectly or not at all. His style will be that of calm courage in the face of uncontrollable and unpredictable danger. If the ideal of the man is honor, then he will see it all as Malesherbes had done. He will do what he regards as his duty regardless of personal cost in a world gone mad. His response will be unified by the conscientiousness of a man who knows where he stands and who is unaffected by the moral uncertainties of his times.

As it happens, these styles of beleaguered individuality, nostalgia, bemused quixoticism, calm courage, and steadfast conscientiousness characterize responses to events that make the subjects' lives go badly. This is not surprising since the postulated events were those involved in the violent overthrow of a venal social order. The illustrations might have come from peaceful and settled times more conducive to good lives than revolutionary France. The suggestion intended by these illustrations is not that styles of life must be responses to adversity; they may also be responses to felicity. The important point is that whatever their coloring happens to be, styles of life pervade and unify people's responses by expressing their dominant attitude, which is informed by the commitment to an ideal of personal excellence.

It would be a gross oversimplification to think of the pervasiveness of dominant attitudes in the simple evaluative terms of having favorable, unfavorable, or ambivalent reactions to one's life as a whole. People do have such reactions, but they are made up of a cluster of beliefs, emotions, and motives, and the cluster occupies a considerable portion of their sensibility. People committed to an ideal of personal excellence hope to be able to live according to it and fear that they may fail; they are proud of their success in approximating it and ashamed of their failures; their efforts to impose discipline on themselves are motivated by it, and it is because self-indulgence would deprive them of it that they try to resist it; they see the pleasures they derive from living as they should as benign and deserved and the pleasures of deviation as dangerous and corrupting. This cluster of reaction includes not just responses that are directed toward themselves but also responses to others. They sympathize with those who are committed to the same ideal, resent those who denigrate it, envy or admire the ones who are conspicuously more successful than they are in approximating it, value being complimented for the progress they have made toward it, feel hurt or irritated if the nature of their efforts is misunderstood, become alienated from contexts in which there are no similarly committed people. It is this whole cluster of reactions that they try to convey to those by whom they wish to be understood;

this is what they try to teach their children; sharing it is what forms the basis of many of their friendships; its depiction in literature and art is what strikes a responsive chord in them; it is what they sentimentalize, what cheers them up, what they want to protect from ridicule, what largely animates their inner processes. And it is what is lacking in people who find their lives flat, uninspired, insipid, boring—people whose sensibility is pervaded by ennui, anomie, lassitude, by what the scholastics have called accidie.

Such clusters of reaction form part of the substance of the dominant attitudes and occupy the forefront of the sensibility of people who try to live according to an ideal of personal excellence. These ideals inspire and animate them both positively and negatively. Perhaps enough has been said about the positive influence of such ideals to make clear their connection with self-esteem and psychological identity. But it must now be emphasized again that the ideals also exert a negative influence that is at least as powerful as the positive one.

This influence is that people who are thus committed see the violation of their ideals as base, contemptible, corrupt, unworthy, despicable. If external circumstances or their own weaknesses cause them to incur these condemnations, not just for a few unfortunate episodes but for a consistent pattern of actions, then they have to convict themselves of an offense that they cannot but find extremely serious. They are then guilty in their own eyes, regardless of what others think of them. This is just what happened to the younger Oedipus when he discovered his parricide and incest. And it is what would have happened to Montaigne, More, the *sophron*, Countess Olenska, Archer, and Malesherbes if they had consistently betrayed their commitments.

If one were found guilty in the court where the presiding judge is oneself, it would result in the swift, severe, and unavoidable punishment of the destruction of one's self-esteem and psychological identity. For one's guilt would be for not being the kind of person one is committed to being. One would not merely have to admit to having done poorly; one would see oneself as having done so badly through living contrary to one's ideal as to make improvement most unlikely. What has been corrupted is the very character upon which improvement depends. The prospect of this happening to oneself is threatening enough to exert a powerful influence on people either to remain true to their ideals of personal excellence or to give up their commitments to them. But giving that up means losing what has been the focus of their lives, and that is nearly as bad as contempt for themselves.

The combined forces of the attraction of ideals of personal excellence and the contempt for living contrary to them explain why choice often plays no significant role in lives committed to such ideals. The important decisions, which may or may not have involved choice, have been made in past, and what remains is to see clearly the situation in which one has to act. Given that clarity, the dominant attitude composed of the relevant beliefs, emotions, and motives will prescribe what is to be done. This is why Murdoch is deeply right in saying, in opposition to the psychoanalytically inspired views, that "if I attend properly I will have no choices and this is the ultimate condition to be aimed at. . . . The ideal situation . . . is . . . a kind of necessity."[13] In most lives the ideal situation does not prevail. People may have an inkling of what they ought to do, but it does not strike them as a necessity because there are countervailing beliefs, emotions, and motives in their characters. They are thus fragmented. This is one reason so many lives are bad and the art of life is much needed.

There is a further feature that contributes to the dominance that the attitude toward one's life may have. If the art of life is to live in a style that exemplifies one's ideal of personal excellence, then the practice of that art is a task without an end. It is lifelong, it cannot be completed, and it must remain open-ended. Projects can be completed, but living according to an ideal can be completed only by dying. For to live that way is to do whatever one nontrivially does in the way that one's ideal prescribes. So to have a dominant attitude toward one's life is to have an attitude that overrides and pervades other attitudes both synchronically and diachronically. It dominates over past, present, and future alternatives by being the ruling principle of a life, which rules in the name of the ideal to which one is committed.

The recognition that living according to an ideal of personal excellence is an endless task, that its goal is not like a threshold that can be crossed but the maintenance of a style of life that informs one's important activities, helps deepen the explanation given earlier (in 7.2) of why people who are obviously living according to their ideal are unlikely to ascribe the personal excellence to themselves. Solon memorably said, Call no man happy until he is dead. His point was that what may happen to people before they die could alter the overall judgment of how well or badly their lives have gone, as Aristotle notes in connection with Priam's life.[14] The same is true of personal excellences. Even if one has so far lived in a self-directed, morally authoritative, decent, deep, or honorable way, it is unpredictable what adversities the future may hold and how well one may be able to respond to them. People with personal excellences tend to know this, as well as how difficult it has been for them in the past to adhere to their ideals. This is why they will be reluctant to lay claim to having a personal excellence.

It is now possible to add to the constitutive features of attitudes toward one's life (see 8.2) constitutive features that make the attitudes dominant. These additional features are that dominant attitudes are the core of *psychological identity* because they embody the subjects' *hierarchy of values* and thus form *the roots* of their *motivation*. Living in conformity to them is the source of *self-esteem*. They are *pervasive* influences on their subjects' beliefs, emotions, and motives. They influence them both *positively* by way of the attractions of their ideals of personal excellence and *negatively* through the threat consistent violations present to their psychological identity and self-esteem. Lastly, living in conformity to a dominant attitude is a *lifelong* task that cannot be completed so long as people remain active because it consists in performing their activities in the style of their ideal of personal excellence.

All this is true of those who conceive of a good life in terms of commitment to such an ideal and who live up to that commitment. There are other conceptions of a good life, and much can go wrong with lives aiming at personal excellence. External obstacles may make it impossible to act as the ideal requires, or internal conditions may prevent it. Perhaps the most frequent source of adverse internal conditions is the incoherence of the dominant attitude. It makes lives fragmented. Integrated lives are coherent, and that is why they are a grace and a triumph, whereas fragmented lives are seriously flawed. What has been said about dominant attitudes makes it possible to understand the conditions of integration and fragmentation.

8.4 Integration and Fragmentation

A life is integrated if the beliefs, emotions, and motives that compose the dominant attitude are congruous. This requires more than consistency, for beliefs, emotions, and motives are consistent if they are not incompatible. But they could be compatible and disjointed. They could constitute largely disparate and only marginally overlapping areas of a person's attitude toward life. The chief preoccupation of the beliefs may center on one's professional involvement with weather prediction, the focus of one's emotions may be a torrid love affair, and one's motives may concentrate on making a great deal of money. Such beliefs, emotions, and motives are consistent but not congruous. Congruity requires that there be a large area in which they overlap. Many of the beliefs, emotions, and motives should have the same object, so that actions flow from motives, motives reflect strongly felt emotions and reasonably held beliefs, and these beliefs make the strongly felt emotions reasonable. If it is added that the shared object of these beliefs, emotions, and motives is the life of the subject and that the subject evaluates the life in the light of an ideal of personal excellence, then it is possible to see why an integrated life, in which the beliefs, emotions, and motives are congruous, is a condition of a good life.

It must also be seen, however, that an integrated life is neither a necessary nor a sufficient condition of all good lives. It is not necessary because there are good lives other than those that aim at an ideal of personal excellence. Integration may be much less important in those lives. The most that can be justifiably claimed is that integration is a necessary condition of good lives that aim at an ideal of personal excellence. Nor is integration a sufficient condition even of good lives that do aim at personal excellence. For well-integrated lives of this sort may fail to be good because of obstacles external to them or because they are immoral.

The fact is, however, that many lives, aiming at perfectly reasonable ideals of personal excellence, are not integrated but fragmented because the beliefs, emotions, and motives that compose their subjects' dominant attitudes are incongruous. Such lives are full of serious conflicts. The beliefs, emotions, and motives that form the dominant attitudes pull their subjects in different directions. Here are three illustrations of fragmented lives.

In the first, John Stuart Mill describes the gaping hole between his beliefs and emotions.

All those to whom I looked up, were of the opinion that the
pleasure of sympathy with human beings, and the feelings
which made the good of others . . . the objects of existence,

were the greatest and surest sources of happiness. Of the truth of this I was convinced, but to know that a feeling would make me happy if I had it, did not give me the feeling. My education . . . had failed to create these feelings in sufficient strength to resist the dissolving influence of analysis, while the whole course of my intellectual cultivation had made . . . analysis the inveterate habit of my mind. I was thus left stranded . . . without any desire for the ends for which I had been so carefully fitted out to work for: no delight in virtue, or the general good.[15]

In the second, we are given a young man speaking to Jesus who cannot bring himself to be motivated by his beliefs and emotions.

One came up to him, saying, "Teacher, what good must I do, to have eternal life?" And he said to him . . . "If you would enter life, keep the commandments." . . . The young man said to him, "All those I have observed; what do I still lack?" Jesus said to him, "If you would be perfect, go, sell what you possess and give to the poor, and you will have treasure in heaven; and come, follow me." When the young man heard this he went away sorrowful; for he had great possessions. And Jesus said to his disciples, "Truly, I say to you, it will be hard for a rich man to enter the kingdom of heaven."[16]

In the third, André Gide locates the cause of his disenchantment with communism in his incapacity to make his beliefs follow his emotions and motives. He speaks, on the one hand,

of my love and admiration for the Soviet Union, where an unprecedented experiment was being attempted, the thought of which inflamed my heart with expectation and from which I hoped a tremendous advance, an impulse capable of sweeping along the whole humanity. It was certainly worth-while to be alive at such a moment to be able to witness this rebirth and to give one's whole life to further it. In my heart I bound myself resolutely . . . to the fortunes of the Soviet Union.

On the other hand,

> no question of Party loyalty can restrain me from speaking
> frankly for I place truth above Party. . . . I believe . . . that in so
> serious a matter it is criminal to lead others astray, and urgent
> to see matters as they are, not as we would wish them to be or
> had hoped that they might be. The Soviet Union has deceived
> our fondest hopes and shown us tragically in what treacherous
> quicksand an honest revolution can founder.[17]

Mill, the young man, and Gide had committed themselves to an ideal, tried to live according to it, but could not because their beliefs, emotions, and motives were fragmented, prompting them to move in different directions. Their ideals required them to have a dominant attitude, but their fragmented beliefs, emotions, and motives could not be joined in a dominant attitude. They had practiced the art of life badly. However one may judge the reasonability of the ideals they aimed at, it is clear that their inability to maintain an integrated dominant attitude made it impossible for them to live as they thought they should.

The explanation of their failures depends on their characters and circumstances. These, however, are so varied as to make it futile to try to formulate a general explanation of failure. Nevertheless, there are some patterns typical of an epoch or a culture. The prevailing circumstances in it make individual lives particularly vulnerable to failing in these ways. The next chapter considers some patterns to which we are vulnerable in our epoch and culture.

8.5 The Form and Content of Good Lives

Let us consider now some forms of good life. The first is the life of a painter. She discovered her talent early and spent many years learning the necessary skills and techniques and studying the great works of the past. She lived in poverty, resisted lucrative job offers to work as a commercial artist, and refused teaching positions. She saw the world in a particular way, and her life was a long preparation aimed at enabling her to put on canvas what she saw. She was unmoved by prevailing fashions, she stood outside the commercial life of the art world, and she felt herself get better and better at her art. She had a good marriage with a husband who understood what she was about and helped her. When she felt that she had reached maturity, that technique had become effortless, and that there were no obstacles between her vision and her expression of it, she had an exhibition that was a great success. Money, fame, and appreciation came to her, but she remained uncorrupted by them. She continued to paint, and when she died she left many works of lasting value to posterity. She lived a good life whose guiding ideal was self-direction and whose project was painting.

The second is the life of a historian who after a distinguished career was persuaded to become an academic dean at his university. He was reluctant to accept the position, but he was prevailed upon by many of his colleagues, who trusted him, his judgment, and who, like himself, felt that academic life was being corrupted by politics and self-serving special interests. He functioned as a dean by eloquently reminding other administrators, academics, and students of the traditional values of research and teaching that universities ought to serve. He consistently made decisions, coped with crises, and met opposition by reaffirming the centrality of the disinterested pursuit of truth and the imparting of it to the next generation. He was consistent, truthful, and trustworthy, and his personal example and articulateness made a convincing case for the values he stood for. After many years of distinguished service he retired and resumed his earlier work as a historian. The ideal of this good life was moral authority, and its project was the much-maligned work of academic administration.

The third is the life of a nurse who worked in the surgical ward of a large hospital. Her life was perfectly ordinary. She had a husband and children; they lived a middle-class life in a middle-class neighborhood. She fit comfortably into her life, the crises were manageable, the emergencies were not dire, the surrounding society was stable, the marriage was all right, and the children were healthy average kids with no worse than normal growing pains. In the midst of this she had a clear sense of her responsibilities. She was familiar with the conventional patterns of being a nurse, a wife, a mother, and a neighbor, and she did her best to conform to the patterns. She was kind, conscientious, and considerate, and she took pleasure in her life and in doing well at it. She was attentive to the needs of the patients in her care; she loved her husband and children; she coped with the frustrations of her life in a realistic way. She was recognized and respected as a pillar of strength by those around her, and she was loved by her family for being what she genuinely was. She was a sensible, competent, level-headed, kind woman. Her life exemplified the ideal of decency, and her projects were those of the normal pursuits of a quiet life.

The fourth is the life of an engineer who had suffered a series of misfortunes at the height of a successful career. His only child has disappeared; his wife became literally insane with grief; the company he worked for went bankrupt; his reputation was ruined by being wrongly blamed for the failure of a piece of equipment he had designed. He moved to a small town, took a job as a car mechanic, and started reading and reflecting on life in general and on his own life in particular. He resisted the easy answers and clichés of alien gurus, pop psychologists, media evangelists, and counterculture pleasure-seekers; he was repulsed by the pedantry, obscurity, and irrelevance of much of the writings of academic philosophers, theologians, psychologists, and sundry social scientists. But he had a clear mind, great respect for the truth, and impatience with humbug and self-deception. He came to understand the contingency of life, the human vulnerability to uncontrollable forces and accidents, the illusory nature of regarding the scheme of things as either benign or malign. He understood that his misfortunes were not his fault, that he just happened to have stumbled in the way of the indifferent course of impersonal events. And he finally found some peace. His was a life made good by the successful pursuit of the ideal of depth, a life whose successfully completed project was to come to terms with the misfortunes that had derailed it.

The fifth is the life of a politician. He got into politics because he was dissatisfied with the prevailing political arrangements. He thought that if people like him did not take a hand, then things would never get better. He ran on this platform and got elected. He realized that his first task must be to understand from the inside how legislation works. He found that it functioned as an informal system in which the participants provided reciprocal favors to one another. Having understood this, he refused to participate in it. He took every opportunity to expose it and to speak out against it both publicly and privately. He was threatened, he was offered bribes, he became intensely unpopular with his fellow politicians, but he persevered. His private life was of a piece with his political stance. He was a principled man of his word. He knew that being what he was, doomed him to isolation because in politics he could not count on cooperating with others, and personally he put people off by his unwillingness to be a party to the compromises that grease the skids of everyday life. He was not liked, but he was true. And eventually people who knew him developed a grudging respect for him and trusted him when they would not trust others. They came to see him as embodying a possibility they all thought was unattainable. He lived in this manner until he died. The goodness of his life was due to his successful pursuit of the ideal of honor, a pursuit that was made particularly difficult by his project's being political reform, which is among the areas least supportive of honor.

All these have been called *forms* of good life for two reasons. One is to imply that there are other forms, so that calling these forms good would not imply that other forms could not also be good. The other is to imply that, being forms, they need to be filled with detail. Many of the details vary from life to life, and describing them is a task of literature, not philosophy. But there are generalizations that can be made about *these* forms of good life, and the purpose of Chapters 6–8 was to make them. The time has come to restate them in a summary way.

Living a life of self-direction, moral authority, decency, depth, or honor involves two kinds of activities: the pursuit of ideals and engagement in projects. The ideals are personal excellences whose pursuit requires the transformation of one's character from what it happens to be as it emerges from adolescence to what the ideal prescribes that it ought to be. The projects are the activities involved in earning a living, following a profession, being part of a family, practicing a religion, working for a cause, improving one's society, as well as collecting, competing, exploring, gardening, teaching, inventing, and so on and on. The projects are the chief preoccupations of people; they are *what* they do in and with their lives. The ideals prescribe *how* they should do them, what the style of their lives should be. They perform the activities involved in their projects self-directedly, morally authoritatively, decently, deeply, or honorably. Their styles leave the imprint of their individuality on their important activities. Nevertheless, their individuality is not an idiosyncratic expression of personal peculiarities but a lifelong commitment to an ideal of personal excellence. And what makes that commitment individual is that the ideal is pursued in the context formed of their characters and circumstances, the combination of which varies with persons, societies, and ages.

In the best lives, both the pursuit of ideals and the engagement in projects conform to the requirements of morality (see 6.7) and they are successful. This felicity depends on sustained effort that individuals must make, but it also depends on fortunate external circumstances over which individuals typically have little control. Lives can be good, however, even if their projects are unsuccessful, provided their subjects have done what they could to make them successful in accordance with their ideals of personal excellence. For it can then be truly said of them that they embody a personal excellence and that the failure of their projects is the result not of personal defects, but of circumstances beyond their control.

The key to the effort individuals must make to pursue their ideals successfully is the development and maintenance of a well-integrated dominant attitude. Such an attitude is a perspective from which individuals evaluate their lives and actions. Its standard is the ideal of personal excellence to which they have committed themselves. It is the core of their psychological identity and the source of their self-esteem. It is a complex attitude composed of their beliefs, which are about the facts and their importance as they bear on how they live their lives; of their emotions, which concern how they feel about their lives; and of their motives, which reflect their beliefs and emotions and move them toward action. Dominant attitudes may be integrated or fragmented. They are integrated if their beliefs, emotions, and motives are congruous, that is, consistent and sufficiently overlapping so that many of the beliefs and emotions that compose them are harmonious and motivate unambiguous actions. In fragmented dominant attitudes, the incongruous beliefs, emotions, and motives leave people disjointed and thus without clear guidance about how they should act.

Well-integrated dominant attitudes define people's significant possibilities, which are inspired by their ideals of personal excellence, and significant limits, which are set by actions that violate their ideals. People who have such a dominant attitude decide what they ought to do in a particular situation on the basis of what the requirement of self-direction, moral authority, decency, depth, or honor is, given their characters and circumstances. They decide on the basis of how they believe and feel they ought to live.

Making reasonable decisions of this sort depends on the successful practice of the art of life. It is an art because it must go beyond the mechanical, or even the intelligent, application of rules. Living in accordance with an ideal of personal excellence cannot be merely a matter of following rules because the ideals must be adapted to the characters and circumstances of individuals, because how individuals evaluate their characters and circumstances is shaped by the ideals they have adapted to these very characters and circumstances, and because this reciprocal adaptation must take place in different contexts for different individuals because their contexts are composed of different characters and circumstances. The art of life, therefore, must be practiced by individuals in their particular ways, and the predictable results will be a few masterpieces, much kitsch, and a great many earnest but middling products.

This is as far as we can go in stating general conditions for forms of good life that are committed to the pursuit of ideals of personal excellence. But this is not the end of what can be usefully said about such lives. For lives that meet these general conditions may still be prevented from being good by various aberrations. Some of these aberrations have familiar forms, and they can be described and avoided. The present account of good lives may, then, be expanded by adding to it an account of some familiar forms of aberration and of what may be done to avoid them. This is the topic of the next chapter.

9/

Aberrations

It is possible to fail in many ways . . . while to succeed is possible only in one . . . to miss the mark easy, to hit it difficult.
ARISTOTLE, Nicomachean Ethics

9.1 Going Wrong

The aberrations discussed in this chapter are moralism, sentimentalism, and romanticism. They stand in the way of lives that aim at personal excellence even if the ideals and the ways in which they are pursued conform to the universal and social requirements of morality,
external circumstances are favorable, and the dominant attitudes are
integrated. What goes wrong is that one component of the dominant
attitude regularly overwhelms the others when they come into conflict. Going wrong consists in this occurring *regularly*. That from time
to time a particular belief, emotion, or motive becomes stronger than
the others is a condition of action and a necessity of life. But if one
component is regularly overwhelming, then the resulting life cannot
be good because a condition of its goodness excludes other conditions. The offending component is then aberrant because it has become *overriding*.

Each component of the dominant attitude may become aberrant in
many ways. The reason for focusing on just three of these ways is that
they are characteristic cultural pathologies of the present age. Moralism follows if the cognitive component is overriding; sentimentalism
results if the emotive component is overriding; and romanticism is a
consequence if the motivational component is overriding. Moralism,
sentimentalism, and romanticism, therefore, are used here as pejorative terms. They stand to cognition, emotion, and motivation as scien-
tism stands to science. Each component is fine in its place—indeed,

each is essential—but when it overrides the others, which are as essential as itself, it becomes aberrant.

9.2 Moralism

Moralism rests on two basic and false assumptions. The first is that the fundamental requirement of morality is expressible as a universal and impartial rule. The second is that all actions that violate this rule are immoral. Deontological moral theories that are committed to some version of the categorical imperative and consequentialist moral theories that regard the common good as the highest value are examples of moralism.[1] (It must be added that there are deontological and consequentialist approaches to morality that are free of this defect.)

The plausibility of moralism derives from an important element of truth in both of its assumptions. There *are* universal and impartial moral requirements, and there *are* actions that are immoral because they violate these requirements. The assumptions are false because they go beyond these important truths to insist that *all* moral requirements must be universal and impartial and that *all* actions that violate these requirements must be condemned as immoral. The result of moralism is that considerations essential to living a good life are excluded from morality and perfectly reasonable actions that most people routinely perform are condemned as immoral. Morality is thus undermined by the moralistic attempt to force on it a narrow interpretation that makes it irrelevant to essential aspects of human lives.

This point may be expressed in terms of the distinction among the three levels of morality (see 6.7). The universal level is concerned with the protection of the minimum requirements of all good lives. The social level is concerned with how a particular society provides that protection, as well as the protection of requirements beyond the minimum that make possible locally recognized forms of good lives. The individual level is concerned with people's efforts to make a good life for themselves, one way of doing which is to pursue some ideal of personal excellence. The appropriate context of universal and impartial rules is the universal level of morality. Moralism is an aberration because it insists on applying these rules in the inappropriate contexts of the social and individual levels of morality. Once the minimum requirements are met, good lives take many different socially and individually variable forms. It is detrimental to good lives to try to force them to conform to universal and impartial rules that not only fail to recognize this variety but condemn them as immoral unless they conform.

To make this concrete, suppose that the common good would have been better served if More had sworn a false oath (he was a good lord chancellor, and England was the poorer for losing his services) or if Malesherbes had cowered on his estate (the king was doomed in any case, so why go down with him?). The consequentialist version of moralism would then be committed to condemning as immoral their admirable actions that stand as inspiring examples to the rest of humanity. That More and Malesherbes remained true to their ideals in the face of great adversity would, on this view, worsen the immorality of their actions because their ideals led them to act contrary to the common good. And, it should be remembered, consequentialist moralizers are committed to condemning the actions of More and Malesherbes, even though they did not violate any minimum requirement of good lives and they acted according to ideals that were essential to their psychological identity, the source of their self-esteem, and constituted their aim in life. If this were what morality required, it would be reasonable to reject it.

The deontological version of moralism fares no better. Take Oedipus and the *sophron* before one acquired depth and the other moral authority. Oedipus was then struggling with his guilt for incest and parricide, and the *sophron* was struggling with the moral problems that confronted his people. Neither had achieved yet the personal excellence that made the successful resolution of their struggles possible. Deontological moralizers would advise them that unless they resolve their struggles by acting on a universal and impartial rule that they could wish everyone else in their situation to act on, they will stand condemned of immorality. This, however, would be an impossible requirement to lay on them. They were struggling precisely because they did not have a universal and impartial, or any other, rule they could follow, because Oedipus did not know how to cope with his guilt and the *sophron* could not find satisfactory resolutions of his people's moral problems.

It might be thought that this only shows that they are ignorant of the rule, which, if they but knew it, would tell them what to do. Consider, therefore, what such a universal and impartial rule would have to be to guide them in their situations. The *sophron* had to bring his moral tradition to bear on moral problems that were difficult because the existing rules did not cover them or because it was unclear which of the existing rules should cover them. He thus needed to rely on his judgment, and he struggled because his judgment was not yet sufficiently reliable. But there cannot be a rule that tells one how to apply rules to difficult situations because the application of that rule would also need a rule, and so on, ad infinitum. And if, per impossibile, there were such a rule, it would not be universal and impartial because there is no reason to suppose that what might be true of the application of the rules of the *sophron*'s Hellenic–Byzantine–Greek Orthodox moral tradition would also be true of the application of the rules of, say, a secular-liberal-pluralistic moral tradition. As for Oedipus, who was struggling with guilt for his unintentional incest and parricide, what would the universal and impartial rule be like that would help him? It would have to say, Whenever anyone is wracked by guilt for having slept with a woman who turned out to be his unknown mother and killed a man who turned out to be his unknown father, then. . . . Then what? How would deontological moralizers complete that rule? And if it was completed, what would it mean to say that it was universal and impartial? To whom would the rule apply apart from the unfortunate Oedipus?

Nor would deontological moralism be plausible if Oedipus and the *sophron* were supposed to have achieved depth and moral authority, for in that case the rule that they ought to be guided by could apply only to those who have achieved these personal excellences. Since the number of these is bound to be small, the rule, if there is one, that guides them cannot possibly have universal and impartial application. But then all those who lack the necessary personal excellence would have to be condemned for immorality by deontological moralizers. Any reasonable moral view must recognize that there are morally relevant social and individual differences among people, from which it follows that not all moral requirements can be universal and impartial.

These objections may appear to be so damning as to raise the question why reasonable people would defend moralism. The answer is that moralism rests on the further assumption that conformity to universal and impartial rules is a requirement of reason. Deviation from this requirement is thus not only immoral but also irrational. That people often have contrary emotions and motives is readily acknowledged by moralizers, but, it is said by them, these contrary tendencies ought to be overridden by the requirements of reasons, which are expressed by the universal and impartial rule. Moralizers thus claim that the cognitive component of dominant attitudes ought to override the emotive and motivational components when they come into conflict. The result is that moralism regards as a requirement of good lives that people may have to act contrary to some of their deepest emotions and motives. And this requirement is insisted on, not because the emotions and motives prompt actions that violate the minimum requirements of all good lives, but because they fail to conform to universal and impartial rules that, by their very nature, cannot take into account social and individual differences.

Moralizers offer two types of argument in defense of this amazing view. The first is formal: it is reason itself that requires that some consideration (e.g., the categorical imperative or the common good) should be overriding. Moral requirements are simply expressions of this overriding consideration. That such a consideration is overriding means, first, that reason requires that it should always take precedence over any other consideration that conflicts with it, so that it is universal. And it means, second, that the consideration holds for everyone equally and impersonally, so that it is impartial.

There are various closely related interpretations of the overridingness of moral requirements. One is that its requirements are nothing but the most important action-guiding considerations. Moral requirements, therefore, are bound to be overriding because they necessarily express what is most important. The reason, then, why moral requirements should override conflicting emotions and motives is that moral requirements are more important.[2] Another interpretation is that moral requirements are simply the universal and impartial requirements of reason applied to human actions. Since emotions and motives are individually variable, if they conflict with moral requirements, reason requires overriding them.[3] A further interpretation is that moral requirements are those that are arrived at after all relevant considerations have been taken into account. In any situation, after everything has been duly weighed, there follows a conclusion about what anyone in that situation should do. Acting on that conclusion becomes the universal and impartial moral requirement. If emotions or motives conflict with it, then either all things have not been adequately considered or acting on the contrary emotions or motives is irrational and immoral.[4]

All these formal arguments fail for several reasons. The first has to do with the force of the "should" in the formal claim that moral requirements should override incompatible emotions and motives. If the "should" is taken to express a moral requirement, then it is question-begging. It says that morality requires that moral requirements should be overriding. The same argument could be used to show that emotions or motives should be overriding. All that needs to be done is to interpret the "should" as expressing an emotive or motivational claim. Any consideration can be made overriding by this expedient. If, however, the "should" is not interpreted in this question-begging way, then how is it to be interpreted? Say it is the "should" of rationality. The claim, then, becomes that reason requires that moral requirements should override conflicting emotions or motives. But making this claim is not enough. It needs to be explained why reason requires this. Why does reason require that More should place his religious loyalty above his political one, that Countess Olenska and Archer should not consummate their love, that Oedipus should forgive himself, and that Malesherbes should endanger his own and his family's life? As soon as these questions are raised, however, the formal argument is confronted with a dilemma it can neither resolve nor avoid.

If, on the one hand, there are reasoned answers to such questions as these—to real moral questions as they occur in real life—they will have to be specific. They will have to show what particular moral requirements were followed or violated by these people. If that is shown, then the argument can no longer remain formal; it must be given content to make it applicable to the particular situations in which the questions arise. The argument thus must go beyond claiming that the moral requirement is to do what is most important, or what is rational, or what follows from the consideration of all things. It must say what these things specifically come to in that situation. But this is something that a formal argument, by its very nature, cannot do. If, on the other hand, the formal argument provides no reasoned answers to these questions, then there is no reason to accept it.

The second reason the formal argument fails also follows from its being formal: it must leave the content that may be given to it unspecified. Suppose the requirements of morality are the most important, or the rational ones, or those that are arrived at after all things have been considered. There is nothing in these formal considerations to prevent anyone from regarding crazy, vicious, trivial, perverse, or idiosyncratic requirements as moral and claiming that they are overriding, provided they are held consistently and followed in action. There must be a limit to what considerations can be reasonably regarded as important, universally and impartially action-guiding, or the result of the consideration of all things. Without such a limit all conflicts between reasons, on the one hand, and emotions and motives, on the other, could be resolved in favor of the latter by simply declaring that emotions and motives are the most important, or universally and impartially action-guiding, or the all-things-considered requirements. If people consistently acted accordingly, then the formal argument could not be used to fault them. For such absurdities to be avoided, limits must be imposed on what could be reasonably counted as overriding. As soon as that is done, however, the argument ceases to be formal. It must specify some content that makes moral requirements overriding.[5]

The third reason for the failure of the formal argument becomes apparent if it is recognized that claims about importance, universality and impartiality, and all things being considered are hopelessly vague unless much more is said about them. Moral requirements are not just important; they are important for something. What is it? Why does justice count but not a sense of humor? Universal and impartial moral requirements do not hold generally; they apply only to certain actions in certain contexts. What are these actions and contexts? Why exclude doing long division or playing chess? Moral requirements follow not from all things being considered but from all relevant things being considered. What things are relevant? Is it relevant if they are unpleasant, boring, hard to figure out, or calling for a great deal of tact? If such considerations are relevant, what makes them so? If they are not, why not?

There are, of course, answers to these questions. Moral requirements are important for good lives; universality and impartiality hold in contexts where actions can be right or wrong; and whether a consideration is relevant depends on whether it seriously affects the lives of people. But these are just empty phrases unless it is specified what lives are good and what actions are right or wrong. Without specifying them, people are free to claim that their emotions and motives are the most important considerations in their context, that they should be most important universally and impartially, and that the relevant considerations bear on what enhances or detracts from their satisfaction. If there is an argument that provides these necessary specifications, it cannot be formal.[6]

The formalist argument for moralism, therefore, fails. But it is not hard to reformulate it in order to avoid the objections just discussed. If it is understood that what motivates defenders of moralism is not attachment to formal arguments as such, but the assumption that moral requirements must be universal and impartial, then the reformulation can readily introduce substantive considerations provided they can be shown to have universal and impartial application. If the goodness of all human lives depends on certain conditions, then there is a very strong reason for having a universal and impartial rule that protects those conditions, condemns actions that violate them as immoral, and overrides any contrary emotion or motive. This very strong reason is that it would be unreasonable if these universal and impartial moral requirements did not override moral requirements that reflect individual differences because the requirements protect the conditions in which individual differences could exist. Let us call this reformulated argument for moralism *minimally substantive*. The question, then, is whether moralism can be defended by the minimally substantive argument.[7]

There are two reasons for thinking that the answer is no. One is that the minimally substantive argument is too strong, and the other is that it is too weak. The trouble with the argument on account of its strength is that if it were correct, then reasonable people, insofar as they were reasonable, could not find themselves in a real conflict between their reasons, on the one hand, and emotions and motives, on the other. Montaigne could not be genuinely conflicted if his distaste for constant compromises led him to opt out of politics and his reason led him in the opposite direction. Oedipus could not be in a real predicament if his guilt prompted him to blame himself while his reason insisted on his innocence. Malesherbes could not be seriously split between the promptings of his love for his family and the promptings of his reason to defend the king. The reason the minimally substantive argument gives for these implausible claims is that such conflicts could not occur because acting according to reasons is a necessary condition of living a life of personal excellence. These people, like everyone else, would be irrational if they were committed to a life of personal excellence but violated a necessary condition of it. They should see that their reasons should always override their contrary emotions and motives because reasons lead them to conform to universal and impartial rules that protect the minimum requirements of all good lives, including those of their own. This, however, is plainly not so. Montaigne became self-directed precisely because he quit politics. Oedipus achieved depth only after he admitted his guilt. And Malesherbes was honorable even though he endangered his family. Something, therefore, must be wrong with the minimally substantive argument from which it follows that these actualities are impossible.

What is wrong is that the reasons that conflict with the emotions and motives of Montaigne, Oedipus, and Malesherbes are not the reasons that undoubtedly exist in favor of the overriding claims of the minimum requirements of all good lives. Those latter reasons *should* override contrary emotions and motives. But the minimum requirements would not be violated if Montaigne went against his reason and opted out of politics, if Oedipus did likewise and admitted his guilt, and if Malesherbes's love of his family proved stronger than his reason to defend the king. If their emotions and motives led these people to murder, mayhem, or extortion, then they would violate the minimum requirements as a means to pursuing personal excellences. If they were reasonable, they would not be conflicted about that. The outcome of their actual conflicts, however, leaves the minimum requirements unaffected. No doubt they ought to weigh what their reasons tell them, but the minimally substantive argument has not shown that such conflicts are always unreasonable, that the claims of reasons should always override the contrary claims of emotions and motives. And even if reasons should prove stronger than emotions and motives, the explanation of that is not that they protect the universally and impartially applicable minimum requirements but that they make the pursuit of a personal excellence more likely to succeed. The minimally substantive argument, therefore, is too strong in claiming that all the requirements of morality must be universal and impartial, that reasons should always override conflicting emotions and motives, or that reasons must be universal and impartial.

The other reason moralism cannot be defended by the minimally substantive argument is that the argument is too weak. It shows something, but not enough to support the claim that reasons should always override conflicting emotions and motives. What it shows is that any acceptable view of morality must recognize the necessity of protecting the minimum requirements of all good lives. It also shows that the minimum requirements set some limits to what can be reasonably counted as an important, or as a universal and impartial, or as an all-things-considered requirement of good lives. But it does not show that it follows from the necessity of the minimum requirements that reasons should always override emotions and motives. For good lives require more than the minimum, and the minimally substantive view is silent on the subject of what the requirements beyond the minimum are. It may be that good lives sometimes require that emotions and motives should override reasons, once the minimum requirements are met.

That good lives require more than the protection of the minimum requirements becomes obvious once it is seen that lives whose minimum requirements are met may still be immoral, frustrating, pointless, boring, or futile; that they may be full of pain, drudgery, shame, anger, guilt, humiliation, and fear; and that people themselves may take this view of their lives. The requirements beyond the minimum may be such things as an interesting job, a rich emotional life, a lively imagination, appreciation of beauty, solidarity with a worthy community, intimate and loving personal relationships, moderation, intelligence, a satisfying sex life, self-respect, fulfilling projects, a sense of humor, physical fitness, financial security, a pleasing appearance, public recognition of one's achievements, and so forth.[8]

These additional requirements of good lives make it an unavoidable question for the minimally substantive argument for moralism how the conflicts among reasons, emotions, and motives should be settled on the individual level of morality. This question is particularly pressing because in lives of personal excellence, as indeed in most lives that have a chance of being good, such conflicts are routine. It is no answer at all to say, as the minimally substantive argument does, that all good lives have minimum requirements, that the additional requirements presuppose that the minimum ones have been met, and that the reasons in favor of meeting them should always override conflicting emotions and motives. One can and should acknowledge that and go on to insist that the minimally substantive argument for moralism does not show that the universal and impartial requirements of reason should always override conflicting emotions and motives once the minimum requirements are met. So that even if moralism holds on the universal level of morality, there is no reason to suppose that it also holds on the individual level.

The upshot of this criticism of moralism is that the standard arguments for it fail to show that the cognitive component of dominant attitudes should always override the conflicting emotive and motivational components. That the cognitive component should sometimes be overriding is true. But the same is true of the emotive and the motivational components. There is no reason to suppose that this necessarily leads to immorality. Passionate commitment to an ideal of excellence and uncompromising motivation to live in a certain way may be morally admirable, as the examples we have been using show. Emotions and motives, of course, can go wrong, but so can reasons. It is part of the art of life to prevent this from happening. Doing that, however, is an art for which no general, and certainly no universal and impartial, rules can be given. The absence of such rules, however, does not mean the absence of reasons. The art can be practiced well or badly. Those who practice it well are good at making decisions in particular cases in which the comparative importance of relevant considerations must be weighed. This is always a matter of judgment. It concerns how one should live one's life, within the constraints of the universal and social levels of morality. This is the central question that must be answered on the individual level of morality.

How one answers it depends on the ideal of personal excellence whose achievement is the goal of one's life, on the nature and success of one's projects, on one's character and circumstances, on the adversities one faces, and on the nature and comparative strength of one's beliefs, emotions, and motives. Such answers are always individual, complex, fallible, and difficult. But there are good answers. It is hard to know at the time an answer is given whether it is good. In the long run, however, one will know because the life lived on its basis will turn out either well or badly. And it may turn out badly even if the answer is good because not even the greatest skill in the art of life is guarantee against misfortune. Still, one should endeavor to answer it as well as one can, for otherwise the misfortune will be self-inflicted.

9.3 Sentimentalism

Sentimentalism is the aberration that follows if the emotive component of dominant attitudes regularly overrides the cognitive and the motivational components when they come into conflict. The emotions of sentimentalists overwhelm their contrary beliefs and motives so that they respond to the world on the basis of how they feel about it. There would be nothing wrong with this if emotions were reliable guides to how the world was, but they are not. Emotions tend to get out of hand; they are often too strong or too weak; they are directed toward inappropriate objects; they respond not to what is there but to what is hoped, feared, imagined, or fantasized is there. Life without emotions cannot be good, but life with emotions can be good only if the emotions are controlled. Sentimentalism is an aberration because it spurns control. It thus leads to the systematic falsification of the objects of emotions.

The falsification, however, does not just happen, as errors of perception usually do. Sentimentalists take an active part if getting the objects of their emotions wrong. They falsify the objects to make them appropriate to their emotions even though they are not. The psychological mechanism of sentimentalism is the inflation of the importance of some relatively insignificant feature of an object at the expense of a truly significant one. The root of sentimentalism, therefore, is the fault of trying to make the world fit one's emotions rather than the other way around. A film, novel, play, or painting is sentimental if it emphasizes some comforting feature of an otherwise distressing situation, such as focusing on instances of heroism in death camps at the expense of the surrounding horror. The attitude to terrorists is sentimental if it concentrates on their selfless dedication, but not on the suffering they inflict on innocent people. Love is sentimental if it exaggerates the attractions and ignores the defects of its recipient.

As these examples show, sentimentalism typically idealizes the objects of emotions. It makes the past appear better than it was, people more lovable or deserving than they are; it sees hope in gross inhumanity, heroism in miserable victims. It falsifies human suffering by treating it as an opportunity for growth. What makes this sort of falsification so insidious and resistant to criticism is that it contains an element of truth, for the feature that it falsifies is indeed there. It is just that its significance is small in comparison with what else is there. What if Hitler loved dogs, a terrorist had polio as a child, or a gangster is devoted to his mentally defective child?

The kind of sentimentalism that concerns us here exaggerates the significance of a particular emotion by taking it to be the key to good lives and the foundation on which morality rests. This emotion has a wide range, and it may be referred to as love of humanity, fraternity, fellow feeling, kindness, charity or *caritas*, compassion, altruism, *agape*, or sympathy. All these more or less overlapping but distinguishable emotions are referred to here collectively as *benevolence*. Sentimentalists suppose that the more benevolent people are, the better lives in general will be. They take moral improvement to consist in the spread of benevolence. The bearing of this on good lives is that sentimentalism imposes on them as a matter of morality the requirement that when personal excellence conflicts with benevolence,

benevolence should override it. It will be argued that this involves a falsification of the facts of moral life and makes lives of personal excellence impossible.

The relevant definition of benevolence in *The Oxford English Dictionary* is, "Disposition to do good, kindness, generosity, charitable feeling (toward mankind)." It is thought by many people, holding a wide range of often incompatible moral views, that benevolence is the foundation of morality. Many Christians regard Jesus' Sermon on the Mount as such, and they rely on the second of the two "great commandments" on which "depend all the law and the prophets": "You shall love your neighbor as yourself."[9] Kierkegaard, writing in the dominant exegetical tradition, interprets this as "your neighbour is every man. . . . He is your neighbour on the basis of equality before God: but this equality absolutely every man has, and has it absolutely."[10]

Many secular utilitarians think the same. Mill says that there is "a natural basis of sentiment for utilitarian morality. . . . This firm foundation is that of the social feeling of mankind—the desire to be in unity with our fellow creatures, which is already a powerful principle in human nature, and happily one of those which tend to become stronger, even without inculcation. . . . [It is] so habitual to man that . . . it give[s] to each individual a stronger personal interest in practically consulting the welfare of others, it also leads him to identify his *feelings* more and more with their good."[11] According to Sidgwick: "Utilitarianism is sometimes said to resolve all virtues into universal and impartial Benevolence . . . we should aim at Happiness generally as our ultimate end, and so consider the happiness of any one individual as equally important with the happiness of any other."[12] John J. C. Smart says: "The utilitarian must appeal to some ultimate attitudes. . . . The sentiment to which he appeals is generalized benevolence, that is, the disposition to seek happiness, or at any rate, in some sense or another, good consequences, for all mankind."[13] Or as Geoffrey Warnock puts it: "Rationality in fact seems . . . to be something that can be used to do harm . . . what is ultimately crucial is *how* it is used. Nothing in the end, then, seems to be more important, in the inherent liability to badness of the human predicament, than limited sympathies. . . . The general object of morality . . . is to expand our sympathies, or, better, to reduce . . . their natural tendency to be narrowly restricted."[14]

Hume, speaking for the moral sense school that includes Shaftesbury, Francis Hutcheson, Joseph Butler, and Adam Smith, among others, says: "I am of the opinion that tho' it be rare to meet one, who loves any single person better than himself; yet 'tis rare to meet with one, in whom all the kind affections, taken together, do not overbalance all the selfish. . . . No man is absolutely indifferent to the happiness and misery of others. The first has a natural tendency to give pleasure; the second pain. This every man finds in himself."[15] Schopenhauer, who was no utilitarian, thinks: "Only insofar as an action has sprung from compassion does it have moral value; and every action resulting from any other motive has none. . . . All satisfaction and all well-being consists in this."[16]

Superficial appearance notwithstanding, these views diverge on the crucial question whether the moral requirement of benevolence is interpreted in a limited or a general sense. They agree that benevolence is the morally fundamental emotion to care about the good of others, but they are split over how inclusively they interpret the "others" about whom morality requires caring. Hume and Butler interpret it in a limited sense; many Christians, Mill, and Schopenhauer in a general sense. This difference is central to the topic of sentimentalism.

To the question, Who is our neighbor? Butler replies, "That part of mankind, that part of our country, which comes under our immediate notice, acquaintance and influence, and with which we have to do."[17] And Hume says that "there is no such passion in human minds, as the love of mankind, merely as such, independent of personal qualities, of services, or of relation to ourself." Further, "the generosity of man is very limited, and . . . it seldom extends beyond their friends and family, or, at most, beyond their native country. Being thus acquainted with the nature of man, we expect not any impossibilities from him; but confine our view to that narrow circle, in which any person moves."[18] Kierkegaard, however, thinks that the others are our neighbors, who include everybody. Mill thinks that the standard of morality "is not the agent's own greatest happiness, but the greatest happiness altogether," and that "one person's happiness . . . is counted exactly as much as another's."[19]

Limited benevolence is the view that there is a natural human disposition to care about the good of some of those people with whom one shares a context. Champions of this view regard limited benevolence as the basis of morality. They may be right or wrong about its being *the* basis, but even if wrong, they cannot be accused of sentimentalism. To claim, as they do, that limited benevolence is important to morality is an accurate observation about human psychology. It does not falsify the relevant facts.[20] General benevolence, in contrast, is the view that morality requires the expansion of limited benevolence to include all human beings, and it requires also that one should be equally benevolent to everyone. Christians give as a reason for this that there is an absolute equality before God, and utilitarians base it on each person's happiness counting exactly as much as any other person's happiness. It is champions of general benevolence who are guilty of the aberration of sentimentality. They falsify the facts of moral life, facts of which no person possessing at least average intelligence and modest information can be ignorant.

There are strong factual, practical, psychological, and moral reasons for rejecting general benevolence as the foundation of morality. The factual reason is that there is no such universally felt emotion as general benevolence. There may be a few saintly people who are actually motivated by it, but in the lives of the majority of humanity general benevolence has no part. Certainly, Montaigne, More, the *sophron*, Countess Olenska and Archer, Oedipus, and Malesherbes were without general benevolence. If they felt benevolent at all, it was restricted to a narrow context. But the implausibility of regarding general benevolence as a widespread human emotion increases manifold when it comes to the billions of semi-literate Chinese and Indian peasants, members of African tribes, South American slum dwellers, Russian laborers, Indonesian island dwellers, and so on who are kept fully occupied with obtaining the necessities of life. It takes a very special kind of perversity to suppose that in the hearts of these needy masses there lurks the general benevolence that counts the happiness of everyone equally.

Human nature is so constructed that people's benevolence begins within their families. In favorable circumstances it expands a bit wider. But it gradually weakens as the connection between themselves and others becomes more remote and impersonal. And when it concerns the vast majority of human beings to whom they are not connected by family ties, shared customs, language, or culture, it peters out. The injunction that people should go against their natural dispositions and try, artificially, to fan the flames of their limited benevolence to embrace total strangers about whose lives and circumstances they are largely ignorant is wildly unrealistic and unrealizable. Christian and utilitarian rhetoric no doubt urges people to do otherwise, but what that really amounts to is a misleadingly expressed wish that human nature were other than it is. A reasonable approach to morality must respect facts, yet defenders of general benevolence ignore them. As Hume says, moral thinkers "must take mankind as they find them, and cannot pretend to introduce any violent change in their principles and ways of thinking. . . . The less natural any set of principles are . . . the more difficulty will a legislator meet with in raising and cultivating them."[21]

The practical reason against general benevolence is that the only effective way of translating into helpful action such benevolence as people have is to restrict it to familiar contexts. The desire to improve the welfare or to diminish the suffering of others is not enough. It must be known how to go about achieving it. The more remote needy people's contexts are, the less can one know what form of help is likely to be effective. The reasonable policy is to act in contexts where it is clear what would be helpful and not to waste chronically scarce resources through dubious action based on inadequate knowledge. It is, for instance, less than useless to donate money for the relief of suffering in distant parts of the world if it is not known, as it rarely is, what causes the undoubted suffering, how the money will be used, and whether there are dependable safeguards against inefficiency, corruption, and stupidity in its distribution. The point of these doubts is not merely to deplore the waste of scarce resources but also to urge the alleviation of suffering close to home. The choice is not between wasteful general benevolence and withholding all help but between general benevolence in distant lands, which is likely to be ineffective, and limited benevolence in one's own bailiwick, which has a far better chance of achieving its object.

The psychological reason against general benevolence is that it misdirects people's moral attention. The moral lives of most people consist in participation in a network of more or less personal relationships. Their obligations are dictated by family ties, the jobs they have, the various groups to which they belong, and the customs and laws of their society. It is not easy to discharge these obligations. The difficulty is not merely that personal defects often lead people to violate these obligations, but also that the more intimate the personal relationships are, the more active must be people's participation in them. Intimate relationships are far more demanding and complex than impersonal ones. It is much more difficult to be a good parent or spouse than it is to be a good citizen. Intimate relationships place heavy demands on people's sustained attention. Caring for another person requires nearly as much knowledge, understanding, and seriousness as people devote to themselves. And, of course, they often fail. Benevolence may lead them to fail less, but it is limited benevolence that may do this, for it is not a general and impersonal caring that intimacy calls for. It is attention precisely to their personal qualities that intimates need. Love is personal and partial; it is not love if it does not favor its recipient. One problem with general benevolence is that it directs people's attention away from the immediate context of their lives, relationships, and the resulting obligations and toward general and impersonal attention to strangers and their troubles. The more general benevolence becomes, the less of it is left for intimate relationships, for attending to the individuality of others that personal relationships require. Just think of what would have happened if Countess Olenska and Archer had averted their attention from each other and their families, the *sophron* from his villagers, Malesherbes from saving what he could in France, and they had devoted themselves instead to world hunger. What would have happened to their personal excellences that rightly command our admiration?

The moral reason against general benevolence is that there are central moral requirements that could not be met if people were motivated by general benevolence. Consider, first, blame directed at wrongdoers. It is an absolutely central moral phenomenon: the appropriate response to the violation of some moral requirement. Its point is to express disapproval. It is intended to cause pain to the wrongdoers, and that is not benevolent. It may be thought that blame is nevertheless benevolent in the long run because the wrongdoers will eventually benefit from the painful experience. But this is a mistake. For blame would be justified even—and especially—if the wrongdoers were incorrigible or their conduct remained unaffected by it. Nor can the benevolence of blame be made to rest on its strengthening morality for the common good. It is true that blame strengthens morality and that morality serves the common good. But it is not true that blame must be based on benevolence. The source of blame is often a commitment to justice, indignation on behalf of the victim, reluctance to let the wrongdoer get away without punishment, or a sense of fairness. So that blame for wrongdoing is justified, it is often nonbenevolent, and if benevolence were the foundation of morality, it would exclude much justified, necessary, and morally important blame.

A second phenomenon that is incompatible with general benevolence is the requirement to meet onerous obligations. These obligations are difficult and unpleasant for the agent, and no one benefits from meeting them. One should pay debts even to the very rich, keep promises although no one remembers them, not lie to save general embarrassment, and do one's share regardless of there being no urgent need for it. Morality requires the discharge of onerous obligations, but it is conscientiousness and a sense of duty rather than benevolence that motivates people. Those who are moved by general benevolence will be indifferent to their onerous obligations.

This discussion of blame and onerous obligations relies on the obvious truth that people are motivated by various moral considerations, among which benevolence is only one. People can act in morally commendable ways without being motivated by benevolence, and nonbenevolent actions are often morally right. The same, of course, can be said of benevolence and benevolent actions. This leads to moral conflict, which is the third moral reason indicating that neither general nor limited benevolence is the foundation of morality. The relevant form of moral conflict occurs within people who are moved by commendable motives to act in incompatible ways. It is a ubiquitous feature of moral life that commitments to justice and forgiveness, fairness and friendship, loyalty and love may conflict.

The significance of this kind of conflict in the present context is that it cannot be reasonably resolved by simply asserting that benevolence should override contrary moral requirements. On the one hand, there has to be an argument that establishes that morality requires this. If there is one, it must appeal to some consideration that is deeper than either benevolence or whatever conflicts with it. But then the consideration that is appealed to would have a better claim than benevolence to be the foundation of morality. If, on the other hand, no argument is given in support of resolving such conflicts in favor of benevolence, then the arbitrariness of the sentimentalism that rests morality on such a questionable foundation stands exposed.

There are, then, strong factual, practical, psychological, and moral reasons against the sentimentalist view that morality requires general benevolence, that the emotion of general benevolence should override conflicting beliefs and motives. These reasons do not show that general benevolence is morally wrong. They show that its moral status is open to question. Like everything else, it too can go wrong. But if this is so, if the reasons that have been adduced against its being the foundation of morality are as obvious and strong as they appear to be, then why is it that the sentimentalist aberration that idealizes general benevolence has been so influential?

The answer is that the root of this form of sentimentalism is faith in the essential goodness of human beings. According to this faith, if human beings were not corrupted by poverty, ignorance, crime, injustice, war, persecution, exploitation, and repression, if they had sufficient freedom and resources to live as they please, then they would live good rather than bad lives. They would, then, naturally and spontaneously live morally, not immorally, like Rousseau's Emile. In other words, goodness is natural to human beings, and whatever is bad is a corrupting external interference with their essential nature. This, of course, is a highly comforting faith, for it licenses optimism about the future, suggests policies whose implementation would improve the human condition, and warrants general benevolence on account of the essential goodness of all human beings. If humanity were like that, we would all have cause for feeling good about ourselves and benign toward everyone else. Even the most evil people can then be regarded as being underneath it all good. But there is no reason to accept this comforting faith, and there are good reasons to reject it as a sentimental falsification of reality.

The most superficial glance at history reveals that bad times were far more frequent and lasting than good ones. Slaves, serfs, and laborers have always been more numerous than their masters; there have always been more who lived close to the subsistence level than those who enjoyed luxuries; life expectancy has been low, disease rampant; civil, religious, ethnic, and national wars have been ever-present; the good in power have been the exception and the bad ones the rule; justice has been arbitrary; and for the majority, life has been nasty, brutish, and short even in civil societies whose putative justification is to avoid life's being like that. If this lamentable spectacle implies any inference, it is that bad lives are the norm and good ones the deviation from it.

Sentimentalists, of course, will not accept this. They will interpret the historical record as a confirmation of their faith. They will say that if the admittedly bad political arrangements did not corrupt people, then they would have lived good lives. And this farrago of an argument will lead them to redouble their efforts to make political arrangements that increase everyone's freedom and share of resources. But they ought to ask the question that they shy away from, the question that will present itself to those who can and will think clearly: What made political arrangements bad? Political arrangements are made by people, and they reflect the dispositions of their makers. Bad political arrangements show that there are bad people who make and perpetuate them. Are these people made bad by bad political arrangements? And if so, what made those political arrangements bad? Sooner or later the conclusion will have to be drawn, first, that there are bad people who have not been corrupted but are bad naturally and, second, that, given what history shows, there must be many of them. From which it follows that human nature is not essentially good. It does not follow that human nature is essentially bad. What follows is that human nature is essentially ambivalent. Whether it develops in good or bad ways depends, in part, on the prevailing political arrangements. Morality requires that political arrangements should favor the good, but it also requires that they should suppress the bad. Realistic political arrangements that avoid the sentimentalist aberration will aim to increase the freedom and share of resources not of everyone but only of those whose conduct have not shown them to be undeserving.

Leaving political arrangements aside, the reason sentimentalism is so influential and resistant to obvious criticisms is that it rests on the comforting faith in the essential goodness of human beings. Although the faith is indefensible, its devotees cherish it because they are unwilling to question their unwarranted optimism about the future and syrupy sentiments about humanity.

There is, therefore, no good reason to suppose that the beliefs and motives of lives of personal excellence should be overridden by the emotion of general benevolence when they conflict. Lives of self-direction, moral authority, decency, depth, and honor would be impossible if instead of aiming at these ideals people were obliged to work for the equal distribution of happiness throughout humanity. Such lives will have an indirect effect on human welfare, but that is an incidental by-product, not their aim or justification. The absence of general benevolence from such lives does not mean that the people who live them are selfish or heartless. The projects of self-directed, morally authoritative, decent, deep, and honorable people typically benefit others, but the ways in which they do so is not impersonal or equal. The repudiation of general benevolence is the repudiation of a sentimental illusion that falsifies the facts by ascribing to people an emotion that few of them have, diverts scarce resources from useful local to wasteful remote purposes, undermines personal relationships by directing people's attention away from their intimates who are entitled to it toward the plight of distant strangers who have done nothing to deserve it, and encourages immorality by weakening the legitimacy of blame, the requirement to meet onerous obligations, and the possibility that the claims of justice may in some cases be more important than the claims of benevolence.

9.4 Romanticism

Unlike moralism and sentimentalism, romanticism has no clearly pejorative connotation. There are, indeed, few things clear about the meaning of romanticism. Philosophically informed accounts of it typically begin with Arthur Lovejoy's surely correct observation that "the word 'romanticism' has come to mean so many things that, by itself, it means nothing."[22] Those who still wish to say something about romanticism must, therefore, make clear what they mean by it. Three passages help locate the sense in which the term is used here.

> Bernard Knox: The hero offered . . . the assurance that in some chosen vessels humanity is capable of superhuman greatness, that there are some human beings who can imperiously deny the imperatives which others obey in order to live. . . . He is a reminder that a human being may at times magnificently defy the limits imposed on our will by the fear of public opinion, of community action, even of death, may refuse to accept humiliation and indifference and impose his will no matter the consequences to others and himself.[23]
> Kenneth Clark: The heroic in life or art is based on the consciousness that life is a struggle; and that in this struggle it is courage, strength of will, and determination which are decisive, not intelligence, nor sensibility. The heroic involves a contempt for convenience and a sacrifice of all those pleasures which contribute to what we call a civilized life. It is the enemy of happiness. . . . It is a struggle with Fate.[24]
> Isaiah Berlin: A new and immensely influential image began to take possession of the European mind. This is the image of the heroic individual, imposing his will upon nature or society: of man not as the crown of a harmonious cosmos, but as a being 'alienated' from it, and seeking to subdue and dominate it. . . .

The noblest thing a man can do is to serve his own inner ideal no matter at what cost. . . . The question of whether an ideal is true or false is no longer thought important, or indeed wholly intelligible. The ideal presents itself in the form of a categorical imperative: serve the inner light within you because it burns within you, for that reason alone. Do what you think right, make what you think beautiful, shape your life in accordance with those ends which are your ultimate purpose, to which everything else in your life is a means, to which all else must be subordinated. . . . The only principle which must be sacredly observed is that each man shall be true to his own goals, even at the cost of destruction, havoc, death. That is the romantic ideal in its fullest, most fanatic form.[25]

Romanticism, therefore, is here taken to mean the ideal that the will should be the overriding element in the dominant attitudes of lives of personal excellence. In conflicts with beliefs and emotions, the will should prevail. Romanticism is thus the aberration that assigns priority to the motivational component over the cognitive and emotive ones. It needs to be stressed that this is not the only way in which romanticism may be understood, but it is the way in which it is understood here. In this sense, Fichte, Schopenhauer, Nietzsche, and the early Sartre were romantics but Kant was not, since although he assigned priority to the will in his moral outlook, he insisted that it had to be good and then it was identical with practical reason.

There is general agreement that romanticism is at once a reaction and an alternative to the world view that has dominated Western thought from the Greeks to the Enlightenment. This world view, of course, was not without challenge, and it was never homogeneous. Even its adherents disagreed profoundly about numerous fundamental questions. But they also agreed on a point that was deeper than their disagreements: the world external to them had a discernible order, the best guide to understanding it was reason, and good lives for human beings depended on understanding and living in accordance with this order. Their disagreements were about whether the order was created by God, whether reason was a priori or empirical, whether it yielded certainty or only fallible hypotheses, and whether the control human beings could exercise over their lives was sufficient to make them good. The romantic reaction was to reject the fundamental point that underlay these disagreements. The world is chaotic, not orderly; reason is not a guide to truth, but a rationalization of the will; and good lives must be made by creative individual efforts, not found by conforming to external requirements.

Out of this reaction came the alternative that romanticism juxta-posed to the old world view. Good lives are achieved, if at all, by way of a struggle in the course of which some exceptional individuals suc-ceed in transforming themselves, in creating an identity, in imposing their will on the world, and thus enlarging the stock of human possi-bilities. Few will succeed, but the very attempt is admirable; indeed, it is the only undertaking that has genuine worth. A central conse-quence of this view is that overriding importance must be ascribed to human motivation, whose engine is the will. For everything depends on individuals' having the will to enter into and carry on the arduous struggle in which most of the admirable few will nevertheless fail.

It would be contrary to the spirit of romanticism to provide rea-sons in defense of it. For reasons are disguised appeals to the will, and they will convince only those who have the will. So reasons are either futile or unnecessary. If you are not one of the exceptional few, it is useless to waste time trying to convince you. The point of the volumi-nous writings of romantics, therefore, is not to convince the uncom-mitted and the unexceptional, but to inspire the like-minded by artic-ulating a vision of life that they share but have not yet expressed for themselves.

This is not an entirely satisfactory state of affairs, especially since what is at stake has profound implications. The will that overrides reason and emotion may be immoral and irrational. And lives domi-nated by the will may be as insipid, futile, self-destructive, or boring as other lives. If romanticism is to be taken seriously, there must be an explanation of how good and bad lives dominated by the will can be distinguished. Numerous friends and foes of romanticism have at-tempted to provide such an explanation, even if the romantics them-selves would scorn their efforts. One of the most distinguished of these attempts is Harry G. Frankfurt's, which is expressed in the aus-tere medium of analytic philosophy.[26] His message, as we shall see, is quite different from the medium in which it is expressed. Frankfurt does not connect what he says with romanticism, but the connection is there, and it will be made obvious.

Frankfurt sets out to "capture those attributes which are the subject of our most humane concern with ourselves and the source of what we regard as most important and most problematical in our lives."

And he says that what he is looking for "is to be found in the structure of a person's will." He distinguishes between "first-order desires . . . which are simply desires to do one thing or another" and "second-order desires."[27] "Someone has a desire of the second order when he wants simply to have a certain desire or when he wants a certain desire to be his will. In situations of the latter kind, I shall call his second-order desires 'second-order volitions.' . . . It is having second-order volitions . . . that I regard as essential to being a person." He uses "the term 'wanton' to refer to agents who have first-order desires but are not persons because . . . they have no second-order volitions."[28] He goes on to say that "the essence of being a person lies not in reason but in will," and he explicitly disavows the view that "volitions of the second order, or of higher orders, must be formed deliberately and that a person characteristically struggles to ensure that they are satisfied. . . . The conformity of a person's will to his higher-order volitions may be far more thoughtless and spontaneous than this."[29]

Frankfurt's view may be summed up as the claim that what is most important in the lives of persons is to shape their characters by willing themselves to have and act to satisfy some of their desires but not others. Frankfurt deliberately leaves unspecified what these desires should be, for what matters, according to him, is the act of identifying the will with some desires, not the nature of the desires. Those who fail to do this are wantons, who thereby fail to be persons. Moreover, this most important act of identification is an act of will, not of reason, and it may be thoughtless and spontaneous. Although it is doubtful that Frankfurt intends it, what emerges from this view is indistinguishable from "the image of the heroic individual" that has been described above by Berlin as "the romantic ideal in its fullest, most fanatic form."[30] But there is a great difference between Frankfurt's and the romantics' approach: Frankfurt attempts to justify his claims, whereas the romantics disdain the effort. Frankfurt considers the questions that cry out for answers: Why is the will the source of what people regard as most important in their lives? Why does its lack disqualify human beings from being persons? Why is the will not subject to reason?

Frankfurt answers these questions by way of considering a "fundamental preoccupation of human existence—namely, *what to care about*. . . . We . . . need to understand what is *important* or, rather, what is *important to us*." There are "wide variations in how strongly and how persistently people care about things. . . . In certain instances, however, the person is susceptible to a . . . kind of necessity, in virtue of which his caring is not altogether under his control. There are occasions when a person realizes that what he cares about matters to him not merely so much, but in such a way, that it is impossible for him to forbear from a certain course of action."[31] Frankfurt calls this impossibility "volitional necessity." He says that a "person who is constrained by volitional necessity . . . accedes to it because he is *unwilling* to oppose it and because, furthermore, his unwillingness is *itself* something which he is unwilling to alter. . . . Therefore he guides himself away from being critically affected by anything—in the outside world or within himself—which might divert or dissuade him either from following that course or from caring as much as he does about following it." Volitional necessity "is generated when someone requires himself to avoid being guided in what he does by any forces other than those by which he most deeply wants to be guided. In order to prevent himself from caring about anything as much as he cares about them, he suppresses or dissociates himself from whatever motives or desires he regards as inconsistent with the stability and effectiveness of his commitment."[32]

Frankfurt thus answers the question why the will is the source of what people regard as most important in their lives in terms of volitional necessity. Its presence reveals what they care about most, what it is that they must or cannot do no matter what reasons, emotions, or other motives they may have. Volitional necessity thus follows from having overriding commitments, and having them is a matter of will that involves people's identification with certain of their desires. Furthermore, the possession, or being possessed by, volitional necessity is what makes human beings into persons. Those without it are wantons, ruled by desires they fail to control. And that is his answer to the question why the lack of volitional necessity disqualifies human beings from being persons.

There can be no doubt that Frankfurt has provided a psychologically acute description of the inner lives of some people who are appealing because they have taken control over their lives. But one should be more careful than Frankfurt is in unqualifiedly approving of such lives. It should be recognized that people living such lives include those who make themselves deaf to anything but the inner voice that tells them what they must and cannot do. They train themselves to ignore all countervailing cognitive, emotive, or motivational considerations, regardless of whether their sources are external or internal. They make themselves invulnerable to criticism, and thus they may do whatever they do no matter how immoral, irrational, or self-destructive it may be. They include the people whom romantics cele-brate as the heroic individuals. A more accurate characterization of them, however, is that they are fanatics. But Frankfurt goes even fur-ther than many romantics, who merely regard the unheroic with con-tempt. Frankfurt denies that they are persons. They are, according to him, wantons. It is hard to see how Frankfurt could be sanguine about the probably unintended consequence of his position that the major-ity of human beings, who at least occasionally allow their reasons and emotions to oppose their will, fail to be persons.

Unpalatable as these answers are, perhaps they are justified. Let us see, therefore, how Frankfurt tries to justify his view that the will is not subject to reason. On this point, Frankfurt's customary clarity deserts him. He says: "In maintaining that the essence of being a per-son lies not in reason but in will, I am far from suggesting that a crea-ture without reason may be a person. For it is only in virtue of his ra-tional capacities that a person is capable of becoming critically aware of his own will and of forming volitions of the second order. The structure of a person's will presupposes, accordingly, that he is a ra-tional being."[33] But if the essence of a person lies in the will, not in rea-son, then how could the structure of a person's will presuppose that he is a rational being? Surely, what is presupposed is deeper, more es-sential than what is presupposing it. Moreover, this passage cannot be reconciled with what Frankfurt says elsewhere: volitional necessity "is generated when someone requires himself to avoid being guided in what he does by any forces other than those by which he most deeply wants to be guided ... he suppresses or dissociates himself from whatever motives or desires he regards as inconsistent with ... his commitment."[34] What about people whose deepest commitment is to the rejection of constraints on them so that they can live a life of pleasure, adventure, artistic creativity, power, revenge, and so forth? Are these people rational beings? Does their will presuppose reason? If Frankfurt answers yes, then what is excluded by being rational? Frankfurt thus faces a dilemma. If he allows that reason and the will may conflict but insists that the will must prevail, then the will cannot presuppose reason. If he denies that reason and the will may conflict because reason is but the exercise of the will, then the absurdity fol-lows that whatever a person most deeply wills to do becomes rational.

Frankfurt, forthright as he is, struggles with what to make of rationality. He asks, "What does it mean to say that an action is for a certain person unthinkable?"[35] His answer is that it "means that there are no circumstances in which he would be willing to perform it," and he goes on: "It is quite possible for someone to anticipate realistically . . . that there are matters with respect to which he is incapable of acting rationally."[36] Frankfurt makes clear that "the unthinkability of the action is so decisive that it constitutes for him a limit not only on what he can do but also on what he can be . . . it is a constitutive element of his nature or essence as the person he is."[37] People for whom nothing is unthinkable are not persons. But if the existence of limits that the unthinkable expresses is essential to being a person, and if the unthinkable expresses the respect in which a person is incapable of acting rationally, then the conclusion is unavoidable that the incapacity to act rationally in some respects is essential to being a person. And the respects in which the incapacity holds are those that concern the person's deepest commitments, the ones the person cares most about, commitments that are most important in the life of that person.

Nevertheless, Frankfurt claims that "rationality belongs distinctively to the essential nature of a human being."[38] How can he hold both this and that the incapacity to act rationally is essential to being a person? The answer is that he thinks the first kind of rationality is not the same as the second kind. By the first kind of rationality, he means sanity. To be irrational in this sense is to be insane. "The terms 'insane,' 'unnatural,' and 'irrational' are convergent. The insane are irrational, and irrationality is unnatural for a creature to whose nature reason is essential." By the second kind of rationality, he means "a mode of rationality that pertains to the will itself . . . it has to do with the inviolability of certain limits."[39] It is easy to see that rationality-as-sanity is indeed essential to being a person, and in that sense no one could seriously opt for irrationality. But rationality-as-inviolability-of-limits is not essential to being a person, and in that sense it may be right to opt for irrationality. Whether or not it is right depends on the nature of the limit that a person holds to be inviolable. If people find it unthinkable to risk their lives, forgive their enemies, act against their self-interest, or let justice rather than love guide their actions toward their children, then it may be right and proper to say to them that they ought to violate what they wrongly hold as inviolable. To call that irrational, as Frankfurt does, is a highly misleading use of the word, and it commits him to the absurdity of holding that people who violate what they wrongly regard as inviolable cease to be persons. If

Frankfurt were right, all people who are led by moral or political considerations to abandon a strongly held commitment would be irrational non-persons. It must be emphasized, however, in fairness to Frankfurt, that these criticisms are directed against probably unintended consequences of his position. Perhaps a more careful reformulation would allow Frankfurt to avoid these consequences.

Be that as it may, the conclusion that follows is that as they stand, Frankfurt's arguments do not help acquit romanticism of the charge that it may foster irrational, immoral, and self-destructive lives. If the romantics hold, as they do, that the will should always override conflicting reasons, emotions, and other motives, then romanticism is an aberration that endangers the possibility of good lives. To say that the romantic will is constrained by the requirements of sanity is of little avail, since many irrational, immoral, and self-destructive people are perfectly sane. Good lives require that the will be open to the possibility of control by reason, emotion, and other motives, for only then is it possible to avoid the unacceptable consequences of romanticism.

9.5 Getting It Right

The art of life is to make a good life for oneself. One of the ways of doing that is to pursue an ideal of personal excellence. This involves the development of an attitude that becomes dominant in the life of a person. A condition of the goodness of lives of personal excellence is that the components of the dominant attitude must be integrated. The beliefs, emotions, and motives that compose the dominant attitude must harmoniously direct the agents toward their ideals of personal excellence. If the other conditions of a good life are also met—if, that is, the universal and social requirements of morality are observed, external circumstances are favorable, and the ideals and the ways in which they are pursued are reasonable—then the resulting lives will be good. Getting it right means living a life of personal excellence that meets these conditions.

One of the ways in which such lives can go wrong is if their dominant attitudes are fragmented rather than integrated. Their cognitive, emotive, and motivational components conflict with one another, and the agents resolve their conflicts by making one component always override the others. The result is the aberration of meeting one requirement of good lives by violating another requirement. For good lives require that the agents' beliefs about their lives be reasonable, their emotions largely favorable, and their motives strong enough to lead them to engage in the appropriate activities. If one of these components always overrides the others when they conflict, then the life will be fragmented because the agents' beliefs, or their emotions, or their motives will be contrary to their ideals of personal excellence.

The three aberrations that have been discussed in this chapter involve fragmentation caused by making overriding the universal and impartial requirements of reason, or benevolence, or the will. The resulting moralism, sentimentalism, and romanticism are widespread contemporary obstacles to lives of personal excellence in the Western world. But they are not, of course, the only forms aberrations may take. Overriding status may be assigned to any one of many beliefs rather than to the universal and impartial requirements of reason, any one of many emotions rather than to benevolence, and any one of many motives rather than to the will. The number of possible aberrations, therefore, is large, probably large enough to make it impossible to enumerate them.

This has an unavoidable implication for any attempt to specify the conditions of good lives of personal excellence: it can be stated as a general requirement of all good lives of personal excellence that they must be free of the aberration of making some belief, emotion, or motive always overriding, but it cannot be specified what forms the aberrations may take. The ways in which lives can go wrong by fragmentation are therefore many, whereas the only way in which they can be integrated is by not allowing any component of their dominant attitudes to become overriding. This is the point of the epigraph to this chapter. Its practical consequence is that there can be no blueprint for good lives of personal excellence, for there can be no specification of what component may be made overriding. People, therefore, must make their own lives good by becoming skillful in avoiding the aberrations that tempt—and threaten—them. For the development of that skill, they need the art of life.

10/

Good Lives

Philosophers have usually tended to seek universal formulae . . . but when we leave the domain of the purely logical we come into the cloudy and shifting domain of the concepts which men live by—and these are subject to historical change. This is especially true of moral concepts. . . . We should, I think, resist the temptation to unify the picture by trying to establish . . . what these concepts *must be*. . . . Can the moral philosopher, once he stops being critical and begins to be positive, establish anything at all in the nature of a universal truth? . . . I think the answer is no. . . . Man is a creature who makes pictures of himself and then comes to resemble the picture. This is the process which moral philosophy must attempt to describe and analyse.

IRIS MURDOCH, "Metaphysics and Ethics"

10.1 Good Lives and the Art of Life

The art of life is the art of making a good life for oneself. It is a moral art because practical reason requires good lives to be lived within the limits set by the universal, social, and individual requirements of morality. But the art of life is also an aesthetic art because it depends on the creative efforts of individuals to live and act in accordance with their ideals of personal excellence. These efforts involve the reciprocal adaptation of ideals of personal excellence to the characters and circumstances of the people who pursue them and the transformation of their characters and circumstances to approximate more closely the personal excellences they pursue. This makes the art of life unavoidably particular, concrete, and individualistic. It is nevertheless possible to identify some general requirements on which the successful practice of the art of life depends. The aim of Chapters 6–9 has been to set out these requirements.

It must be emphasized, however, that the connection between good lives, the art of life, and personal excellences is not claimed to be necessary. One can live a good life without having mastered the art of life, and neither good lives nor the art of life have to take the form of the pursuit of personal excellence. The purpose of the argument has been merely to explain and defend the much more modest claim that one way of making one's life good is to practice the art of life well and that one way of doing that is to try to achieve personal excellence. This is just what Montaigne and More, the *sophron*, Countess Olenska and Archer, the old Oedipus, and Malesherbes were shown to do in Chapters 1–5. The explanation and defense of this approach to good lives leaves open the possibility that there are other approaches.

Personal excellences are traits of character, lasting tendencies to live and act in certain ways. Some traits are important, others less so. Important ones are essential to people's being what they are. If these traits were different, those who had them would thereby also be different in a fundamental way. Montaigne and More without self-direction, the *sophron* without moral authority, Countess Olenska and Archer without decency, the old Oedipus without depth, and Malesherbes without honor would be radically different people. Personal excellences, however, are only one kind of important character trait. Others are formed by significant experiences, such as religious conversion or years spent in a concentration camp; or by vocation, such as being a politician or a priest; or by having some great talent, for instance, for music, eidetic imagery, or languages; or by living through some momentous event, such as the Second World War or the Black Death; and so forth. In order to understand personal excellences, it is necessary, therefore, to understand the features that make them important and distinguish them from other important character traits.

Personal excellences are important character traits because they are essential components of the psychological identity of those who have them. This distinguishes personal excellences from habits that can be broken without seriously altering one's character, such as smoking; from physiognomic features, such as having a beard; or from taste, for instance, for Chinese cuisine. Personal excellences are deep, formative elements of character rather than superficial, changeable ones. They are active rather than passive: tendencies to live by trying to change one's character and circumstances rather than tendencies to be favorably or unfavorably affected by certain experiences. They involve doings rather than undergoings. They are connected with patterns of publicly observable actions, not just with inner states. They are like being a writer, an athlete, or an inventor, which are inseparable from appropriate overt activities, and unlike being a connoisseur, an ironic spectator of politics, or the possessor of a rich fantasy life, which can be largely covert.

A personal excellence involves not just a lasting tendency to live and act in a certain way but also a particular motive for doing so. This motive is that living and acting that way is valued because it is inspired by commitment to an ideal. People may have a variety of motives for developing lasting tendencies, such as hypocrisy, fear, manipulation, self-deception, stupidity, imitation, and so forth. These tendencies may actually bear marked similarities to personal excellences, yet since they are not based on the right motive, they are not the real thing. Patterns of apparently self-directed, morally authoritative, decent, deep, and honorable actions are counterfeit unless a prominent motive for performing them is the intrinsic value people attach to acting that way. People, of course, typically have more than one motive for doing most things, but in the case of personal excellences, one of their important motives must be that they are inspired to act that way by an ideal of personal excellence. It follows that the activities involved in living according to personal excellences are goal-directed. But since there are two quite different types of activities and goals involved, understanding personal excellences requires understanding what these activities and goals are and how they are related.

The activities are pursuing an ideal of personal excellence and engaging in a project. The goal of the first is to live a life that exemplifies the relevant personal excellence, and the goal of the second is to achieve some concrete result. Pursuing an ideal of personal excellence is a lifelong activity because its goal is to live and act in a certain way. The goal is coterminous with the life that aims at it. Success requires people to give a particular style to their lives by imprinting their activities with the individual form of their self-direction, moral authority, decency, depth, or honor. The goal in this case just is consistent activity of the relevant kind. By contrast, engagement in a project does not require any particular kind of activity; the activity it requires is whatever is most likely to achieve the concrete result that is the goal of the activity. If the result is achieved, the activity is successful. In typical lives, there are many projects, and engagement in them requires many different activities.

The goodness of this form of life depends on the extent to which people succeed in pursuing an ideal of personal excellence. To have succeeded is for it to be true that they have lived as they reasonably think they ought to live. And that means both having an ideal of personal excellence that defines how they ought to live and actually living that way. To have failed is to have lived in violation of their own reasonable ideals. The resulting lives, therefore, will be neither personally satisfying nor morally acceptable. The goodness of this form of life is not dependent on the success or failure of people's projects, however. Lives can be good even if all their projects have failed, provided the failures were not the people's fault and the relevant activities were performed in conformity to their ideals of personal excellence.

This last point makes it evident that despite the differences between ideals and projects, they are closely connected. For engagement in various projects is essential to all lives, and in this form of good life the activities and the goals of the projects reflect people's ideals of personal excellence. Good lives of this form exemplify personal excellences *by* engaging in projects. The projects are the contents of which the styles of life are the form. People pursue their ideals of personal excellence by consistently engaging in their projects in a way that is self-directed, morally authoritative, decent, deep, or honorable. The adjectives expressing styles qualify the verbs that designate the activities of the projects.

When people consistently pursue an ideal of personal excellence for the right motive, their emotions are engaged, both positively and negatively. Their positive emotions derive from the importance that their ideals of personal excellence have in their lives. Such ideals give meaning and purpose to their lives, form central components of their psychological identity, and guide their important decisions, so of course they elicit strong positive emotions. It would be unnatural not to have them about such an important aspect of their lives. These people desire to live and act according to their ideals; they feel good about themselves if they succeed; their hopes for the future are connected with them; and they are objects of their ambitions. They also have negative emotions of frustration if they are prevented from acting as they think they should; they feel shame and/or guilt if they try and culpably fail; and they despair if they see their ideals recede from their lives.

Commitment to an ideal of personal excellence thus informs people's sensibility. It makes them view the world in a particular way because it gives direction and focus to a central portion of the evaluative dimension of their lives. Their sensibility is characterized by a dominant attitude to their lives and actions, which spreads much wider than the immediate context in which they have to make decisions about what to do. These attitudes influence their dealings with other people, have a formative effect on what they see as a live option or as being beyond the pale, and inform their judgments about what is important and trivial, inspiring and depressing, interesting and boring, supererogatory and contemptible.

Dominant attitudes are complex mixtures of cognitive, emotive, and motivational components. People have beliefs about the ways they live and act, about the ways they ought to live and act, and about how close the first comes to the second. These beliefs give rise to positive and negative emotions about how their lives are going. And the beliefs and emotions motivate them to continue living as they have been or change their lives in big or small ways.

The dominant attitudes in good lives are integrated. This means that the beliefs and emotions people have about their lives and their motives for action are overlapping and harmonious to a considerable extent. Their motives reflect their beliefs and emotions, their emotions are informed by their beliefs, and their beliefs take into account their emotions and motives. These components of dominant attitudes may be fragmented, however, and then the beliefs, emotions, and motives are incongruous. They are disjointed, and they give rise to activities that take people in different, often incompatible, directions. Many lives aiming at an ideal of personal excellence are bad because they are fragmented in this way.

There are many reasons lives may become fragmented. A frequent one is that one of the components of dominant attitudes regularly overwhelms the others. If people's lives and actions are governed by one of these components to such an extent as to regularly deprive the other components of their normal scope, then the resulting lives are bound to be frustrated because people are prevented from heeding their beliefs, emotions, or motives. They will be compelled to go against their own deepest psychological propensities and thus be forced to deny an important part of their nature. These aberrations may take countless forms because there are countless beliefs, emotions, and motives that may overwhelm the others. We have considered only three of them, one each for a particular way in which the cognitive, emotive, and motivational components can go wrong: moralism, sentimentalism, and romanticism.

The resulting view is that one way of making lives good is the successful practice of the art of life. This requires living and acting in conformity to a reasonable ideal of personal excellence and developing a well-integrated dominant attitude. Lives that meet this requirement will be personally satisfying. But good lives must also be morally acceptable, and that requires that their ideals, dominant attitudes, and corresponding activities conform to the universal, social, and individual requirements of morality.

10.2 Is Boredom a Problem?

The aim of the argument throughout this book has been to describe, analyze, and commend good lives that take the form of the pursuit of personal excellence through the art of life. That argument is now complete, and it should speak for itself. It should lead those who understand it to conclude that this form of life is indeed good. Reaching this conclusion does not require that one should live and act accordingly. If there is a plurality of forms that good lives may take, then it can be perfectly reasonable to recognize that a particular form of life is good and simultaneously adopt another. It is possible, however, that understanding the argument will not remove doubts about the goodness of this form of life. The object of such doubts may be not that this life is not good for oneself but that it may not be good at all. It may be thought that it is just a mistake to take personal satisfaction in such a life, that people should have higher or different standards.

One way of articulating this sort of doubt is to apply to the form of life we have been considering a test question that Nietzsche has formulated. He asks: "What, if some day or night a demon were to steal after you into your loneliest loneliness and say to you: 'This life as you now live it and have lived it, you will have to live once more and innumerable times more. . . . ' Would you . . . have answered him: . . . 'never have I heard anything more divine.' . . . How well disposed would you have to become to yourself and to life *to crave nothing more fervently* than this ultimate confirmation and seal."[1] Put plainly, Nietzsche's test question about the goodness of a life is whether the person living it would welcome it if the present form of life were continued into the indefinite future. One's life cannot be good, Nietzsche suggests, unless one is prepared to answer this question affirmatively. Any other answer would indicate less than wholehearted satisfaction with one's life. Let us, then, see whether a life that involves the successful practice of the art of life would prove to be good if this test question were put to it.

One significant attempt to struggle with this question is Karel Capek's in *The Makropulos Case*.[2] This is the title of a play which he—probably ironically—calls a comedy but which is in fact as authentic a tragedy as any that has been written since those of ancient Greece. It is comic only in the sense that some of its lines are very funny. The same theme is treated in Leon Janacek's opera *Makropulos*.[3] The theme then is taken up and discussed from a philosophical point of view by Bernard Williams in "The Makropulos Case: Reflections on the Tedium of Immortality."[4] In all these treatments the answer to the test question is that the lives that interest us here would not be good because their continuation into the indefinite future would be unbearably boring. Consequently, no reasonable person could or would be satisfied with such a life. Since personal satisfaction is a necessary condition of the goodness of this form of life, the successful practice of the art of life, as it has been conceived in the course of the argument, would not lead to good lives. In defending this form of good lives, we must show, therefore, that all these people are mistaken and their doubts misplaced. First, however, we need to understand the reasons behind their doubts.

Capek's play is about an unsurpassable opera singer, Emilia Marty. It is revealed in the course of the play that she is three hundred thirty-seven years old. In fact, she has been thirty-seven years old for three hundred years. Her longevity and arrested aging is the result of an elixir, discovered by her father, Makropulos. One drop of the elixir prolongs life in its present state for three hundred years. Emilia Marty spent her years as a singer in the guises of Elsa Mueller, Ellian MacGregor, Ekaterina Myshkina, Eugenia Montez, and the original Elina Makropulos. She has been perfecting her art all this time, and when we encounter her she has achieved an unprecedented of state of excellence. Her three hundred years are just about up, and she has to have another drop of the elixir if she is to live on.

She is asked about her state of mind, and she describes it as "boredom. . . . Everything is so pointless, so empty, so meaningless. . . . One finds out that one cannot believe in anything. Anything. And from that comes this cold emptiness. . . . You realize that art is useless. It is all in vain. . . . People are never better. Nothing can ever be changed. Nothing, nothing, nothing really matters. If at this moment there were to be . . . the end of the world, or whatever, still nothing would matter. Even I do not matter." And she says to her quotidian interlocutors: "You disgust me. . . . You believe in everything: in love, in yourselves, in honor, in progress, in humanity . . . in pleasure . . . faithfulness . . . power . . . you fools." As for her, "everything tires me. It tires one to be good, it tires one to be bad. The earth itself tires me. . . . We . . . we old ones . . . we know too much . . . in us all life has stopped. . . . And it goes on, goes on, goes on. Ah, this terrible loneliness."[5] Janacek has her sing: "I've grown tired of good things,/I've grown tired of evil things./Tired of earth,/tired of the heavens!/And then one knows that the soul has died in him."[6]

Emilia Marty was forced by her extraordinary circumstances to put to herself Nietzsche's test question: Would you want it if "this life as you now live it and have lived it, you will have to live once more and innumerable times more"?[7] Her eventual answer is that she would not want it because it would involve the endless repetition of familiar activities that have become meaningless. Such an existence would become a tiresome burden that no one who understood it would want to bear. The implication is that it is a failure of understanding to regard lives of personal excellence—lives pursuing love, honor, progress, pleasure, faithfulness, power—as good. It is only because we lack understanding that we find this form of life good. If we understood what Emilia Marty had come to understand, we would arrive at the same conclusion as she did. We would see that lives committed to the pursuit of some personal excellence only appear to be good because their shortness prevents us from discovering their meaninglessness. We would then do as Emilia Marty had done: refuse to take the elixir and, as a benefit to humanity, destroy the formula.

Let us ask, however, why it should be supposed that the indefinite prolongation of a life would have to involve endless repetition. If it did, it *would* become tiresome, meaningless, and overwhelmingly boring, but why could it not involve an endless variety of different activities? Why would Emilia Marty have to remain a singer throughout her three hundred thirty-seven years? Williams argues that this way of relieving the tedium of immortality is not open because if the activities were different, then the person who performed the activities would also be different, and the continuity necessary for immortality would be lost. Williams claims that the conception of an unending life is coherent only if it meets two conditions: First, "that it should clearly be *we* who lives for ever," and second, "that the state in which I survive should be one which, to me looking forward, will be adequately related, in the life it presents, to those aims which I now have in wanting to survive at all."[8]

In order to meet the first condition, it must be supposed that there is a physical and psychological continuity between the different phases of the life of the person who lives endlessly. Williams calls this condition "the constancy of character." If EM's (Emilia Marty's) character is constant, then "everything that could happen and make sense to one particular human being . . . had already happened to her." If, however, "the pattern of her experiences [is] not repetitious in this way, but varied . . . then the problem shifts to the relation between these varied experiences, and the fixed character: how can it remain fixed, through an endless series of very various experiences? The experiences must surely happen to her without really affecting her; she must be, as EM is, detached and withdrawn."[9] Thus, either the condition of constancy of character is not met or boredom is inevitable.

According to Williams, the second condition, call it the *constancy of aim*, fares no better. He says that "some philosophers have pictured eternal existence as occupied in something like intense intellectual enquiry." This would avoid boredom because the "activity is engrossing . . . and by being engrossing enables one to lose oneself."[10] But the more one succeeds in losing oneself, the less is left of the person who "will be adequately related . . . to those aims which I now have in wanting to survive at all."[11] Thus, either the condition of constancy of aim is not met or boredom would not be avoided.

In sum, Williams poses the following dilemma: If the two conditions of continuity are met, then the tedium of immortality is inevitable; whereas if the conditions are not met, then there is no person there to whom immortality could be ascribed, so the idea of immortality becomes incoherent. The claim that lives of personal excellence are good can be defended only if this dilemma is avoided.

The key to avoiding it, however, is readily at hand. Recall the central importance of the distinction between ideals and projects that was drawn in Chapter 7 and developed subsequently. The implied claim of Capek, Janacek, and Williams that Nietzsche's test could not be met by successful lives of personal excellence is plausible only if the difference between the two aims of pursuing ideals and engaging in projects is ignored. The continuity, which Williams rightly insists is necessary, is provided by enduring commitment to an ideal of personal excellence. And the variety, which he rightly insists a good life requires, and thus the avoidance of debilitating boredom and meaninglessness, is provided by the many different projects in which reasonable people pursuing an ideal of personal excellence may be reasonably engaged.

The conditions of the constancy of character and aim are met by commitment to living a self-directed, morally authoritative, decent, deep, or honorable life. That is what is essential to the psychological identity of the people who live this form of life. But that commitment can be maintained by engagement in a wide variety of projects, which may succeed or fail, continue or come to an end, command one's interest or become tedious. The trouble with EM's life was that she mistook her project of being a singer for an ideal of personal excellence. When she grew tired of singing, she grew tired of her life. If people do not make her mistake—if Montaigne, More, the *sophron*, Countess Olenska, Archer, and Malesherbes were to grow tired of their present projects—then they could readily engage in another project without its affecting the continuity of their characters and aims to live according to their ideals of personal excellence. It is true that there may be lives whose projects are so central as to preclude abandoning them. Oedipus's project of coming to terms with his incest and parricide was of this sort. If he had abandoned that project, he would have lost the continuity of his character and aim. His project was imposed on him by the tragedy that befell him. But if Montaigne grew tired of mediating between the warring Protestant and Catholics and took up horse breeding, if More gave up the lord chancellorship to devote himself to philosophy, if the *sophron* became a monk, if Countess Olenska put an end to her volunteer work for various charities for painting, if Archer switched from law to working as an art critic, if Malesherbes left politics for botany, then they could all have remained constant to their ideals of personal excellence while changing from a project that has come to bore them to one they found interesting. In most cases, there is no reason people could not be constant to their ideals and vary their projects.

In fact, it is one of the attractions of the conception of a good life that the successful practice of the art of life makes possible that it is open to as wide a variety of projects as people can reasonably engage in. Life is often frustrating because it is too short to satisfy people's craving to learn languages, immerse themselves in cultures, have adventures, acquire depth and breadth of knowledge, make friendships, appreciate the arts, climb mountains, understand history, keep up with scientific developments, commune with nature, play serious chess, or live for a while on each of the continents. An endless life would be wonderful because this frustration would not occur in it. One wants to say to EM, If singing bores you, become an arctic explorer, learn to juggle, practice law, study astronomy, and stop complaining. If, to adopt a line from Gertrude Stein, there had been a there where EM's character was supposed to be, then she might have rejoiced in her longevity.

What the Makropulos case shows is not that endless life would be boring and meaningless, but that the riches of an endless life could be enjoyed only by those who have a securely established character. One of the benefits of the successful practice of the art of life is that it enables people to maintain their psychological identity throughout the vicissitudes of their changing projects. The mistake Capek, Janacek, and Williams make is to suppose that it is a consequence of people's projects' becoming boring and meaningless that their lives also become boring and meaningless. The supposition is false, however, because lives are made good by the successful pursuit of ideals of personal excellence, not by engagement in any particular project, and because a project that grows tiresome can be left behind for one that is interesting. The Makropulos case, therefore, does not show that lives of personal excellence are not good because they would fail Nietzsche's test question.

10.3 Making Life Good

It will perhaps be helpful to conclude by making explicit some distinctive features of the account of good lives that has formed the subject matter of this book. These features are pluralism, individuality, balance, and particularity.

The pluralism that characterizes the account of lives of personal excellence pertains to good lives in three respects. First, it insists that since there are many different personal excellences, lives that are made good by the successful pursuit of a personal excellence may be good in many different ways. Self-directed, morally authoritative, decent, deep, and honorable lives are all both good and different, and of course, there are many different personal excellences in addition to these. Second, although the good lives that have been discussed are all the products of the art of life, pluralists reject the view that lives can be made good only by the art of life. The art of life requires people to take an active role in shaping their characters, circumstances, and ideals. This, however, does not mean that lives cannot be good unless they are centrally concerned with this inner-directed activity. The unreflective lives of athletes, the conventional lives of people in traditional or tribal societies, the highly disciplined lives of nuns or soldiers can be good even though their activities are directed outward toward the world, their characters duplicate unquestioned patterns, and their circumstances are severely restricted to narrow contexts. That the present account has concentrated on a particular form of good lives leaves room for there being other forms. Third, pluralists avoid the mistake of supposing that there is some one ideal, or some few of them, conformity to which determines the goodness of all lives. Lives of personal excellence may be good, but lives of self-denying service to others, lives devoted to some cause that requires minimizing the importance of individuals, lives spent in occupying traditional roles, lives of simplicity and hard work in which most of people's time and energy is spent on coping with their natural environment may also be good.

In being committed to pluralism in these three ways, the present approach is at odds with both the absolutist and the relativist approaches to good lives. Absolutists—such as Plato, Kant, Mill, and their followers—are committed to holding that there is a pattern or a principle to which all good lives must conform. They hold that in their essential aspect all good lives are alike. The obvious differences among different forms of life concern only the much less important matter of how people, given their different characters and circumstances, must go about conforming to the pattern or principle. If pluralism is correct, then there is no such pattern or principle. As there is a plurality of good lives, so there is a plurality of patterns and principles conformity to which may make lives good. In this respect, pluralists agree with relativists.

The rejection of absolutism, however, does not lead pluralists to embrace relativism—different versions of which are held by Nietzsche, historicists, existentialists, postmodernists, and multiculturalists—according to which there are no objective grounds on which lives can be evaluated. Lives are good, according to relativists, if they conform to whatever standard is accepted in the context in which the lives are lived. The evaluation of lives, therefore, can only be internal and context-dependent because there are no external, context-independent standards that reasonable people could reject only if they make a mistake or lapse into unreason. Pluralists think, in agreement with absolutists, that there are such standards. The requirements of moral acceptability and personal satisfaction cannot be met merely by a society or an individual thinking that they have been met. Societies and individuals may be mistaken in thinking about good lives as they do. They may regard ways of living as morally acceptable or personally satisfying, and they may be wrong. There are many ways of living that ought not to be regarded as good. Whether the universal and social requirements of morality are met and whether the art of life is practiced well is determined by objective considerations and not by what anyone thinks. These considerations, however, establish only some conditions that all good lives must meet, and so they fall short of what absolutism requires.

Individuality is the second distinctive feature of lives of personal excellence that has emerged in the course of the argument. Lives of personal excellence require people to play a very active part in making their lives exemplify ever more closely the ideal they aim at. This, in turn, depends on people's transformation of their characters from what they are as they emerge from adolescence to what enables them to live as they are committed to living. And it depends also on how people interpret their circumstances, on what they see as obstacles or opportunities, limits or possibilities, important or trivial, problematic or expected, challenging or irrelevant, and so forth. Their individuality emerges, therefore, in the course of what they themselves do in shaping their characters and interpreting their circumstances so as to approximate their ideals.

The source of their individuality is not that they invent their ideals, make their circumstances, or create their characters. Ideals are adopted, not invented; circumstances are the products of political, economic, technological, and historical influences that affect people, rather than being made by them; and characters are formed by genetic inheritance and upbringing, not created by those who have them. The individuality that is a distinctive feature of lives of personal excellence consists in people's attempts at reciprocal adaptation of their ideals to their characters and circumstances and of their transformation of their characters and interpretation of their circumstances in the light of their ideals. This is an individual process because it requires the adaptation of characters and circumstances that vary with individuals; because it can be done only by individuals for themselves; and because individuals must be the judges—albeit fallible ones—of whether, all things considered, they find their lives personally satisfying.

Successful lives of personal excellence are, then, characterized, among other things, by their individuality. This, however, does not mean that people living such lives must do some particular things. True, they must be engaged in the process of reciprocal adaptation, but that is merely a very general description that, given some limits, leaves unspecified what can be included under it. The interpretation that has emerged from the argument is that individuality depends, not on engagement in any specifiable activity, but on performing whatever activities are required by the pursuit of ideals in a particular way. Individuality consists in *how* people do what they do, not in *what* they do. Individuality is thus a matter of style. The style reflects the ideal that guides a life, not the idiosyncrasies of the person whose life it is. The style is an evaluative stance, not a mannerism. To have a style is to engage in whatever projects are appropriate to one's character and circumstances in a self-directed, morally authoritative, decent, deep, or honorable way. The mark of individuality is not the project, but the ideal that prescribes how that project of that person in those circumstances ought to be pursued. People living lives of personal excellence show their individuality by their interpretations of what self-direction, moral authority, decency, depth, honor, and so forth require, given their unique contexts composed of their reciprocal adaptations between their characters and circumstances and their ideals.

If individuality is understood in this way, it lends support to and deepens the reasons for a pluralistic view of good lives and for the rejection of absolutism. For absolutism is committed to there being patterns or principles that set universal, impartial, and impersonal requirements that make all lives good. Pluralists deny that there are such requirements. We can now see that an additional reason for that denial is the unavoidable individuality of lives that are made good by the successful pursuit of ideals of personal excellence. Since the requirements of self-direction, moral authority, decency, depth, and honor vary with individuals and depend on their various personal circumstances, conformity to universal, impartial, and impersonal prescriptions cannot be sufficient for a good life. There are some prescriptions that it is necessary for all good lives to meet, but meeting them is not enough to make a life good. If a life of personal excellence is good, it is so because its individual requirements are also met. The present account, therefore, is incompatible with all accounts that suppose that the conditions of good lives can be given a universal, impartial, and impersonal specification.

The third distinctive feature of successful lives of personal excellence is balance. The balance is achieved if the attitude that dominates such lives is well integrated, if, that is, the cognitive, emotive, and motivational components of the attitude coexist harmoniously and none of them regularly overwhelms the others. This means that the beliefs and emotions people have about their lives and their motives for relevant actions largely overlap and reinforce one another. If their beliefs about their lives take account of the emotions their lives elicit and the motives they prompt; if their emotions reflect their beliefs and influence their motives; if their motives prompt actions based on their beliefs and emotions, then they can live in a wholehearted way. They are not then frustrated by their failure to express some essential part of themselves; they are not pulled in different directions by a fragmented inner life; and their sensibility is not dominated by one aspect of their essential selves at the expense of another no less essential aspect. In successful lives of personal excellence, cognitive, emotive, and motivational considerations all play a central role. When one takes temporary precedence over the others, it is not because a pattern has been or is being established, but because the exigencies of a particular situation make it reasonable.

If this balance is upset, an aberration follows. One condition of the goodness of lives of personal excellence is the avoidance of such aberrations. Avoiding them, however, is, once again, an unavoidably individual matter because only individuals can do it for themselves and because whether an aberration threatens them depends on the economy of their inner lives, to which only they have a privileged access.

The recognition of the importance of each of the components that should be balanced is a distinctive feature of successful lives of personal excellence. It also points to a contrast with some highly influential views. The Platonic view regards the domination of the cognitive component over the others as the key to good lives. The Humean view places the emotive component at the center and insists on the subordination to it of the cognitive and motivational ones. The Kantian view holds that the motivational component—the will—should be dominant, and it denigrates emotions, regards theoretical reason as irrelevant, and views practical reason as merely the working out of the implications of what the will demands if it is to be good. The Platonic, Humean, and Kantian views have dominated arguments about good lives. If the present account is correct, then these alternatives either lead to aberrations or must be reinterpreted to remedy the imbalance they cause.

The three distinctive features of the account of good lives—pluralism, individuality, and balance—have focused on personal satisfaction with one's life. But good lives must also be reasonable and morally acceptable. The fourth distinctive feature—particularity—is a view about the requirements of reason and morality as they pertain to successful lives of personal excellence. The moral requirements will be discussed first, the requirements of reason second.

According to the present account, there are universal, social, and individual requirements of morality. The universal requirements protect the minimum conditions of good lives, and they are independent of how good lives are conceived beyond that basic level. These conditions are the satisfaction of elementary physiological and psychological needs that all normal human beings have merely in virtue of being human. Examples of these conditions are the physiological needs for nutrition and rest and the psychological needs for the absence of terror in one's life and for some form of companionship. The social requirements emerge in the course of the history of a society. They protect the conventional ways in which the universal requirements are met in that context and regulate the routine interactions of people living in it. These requirements prescribe appropriate attitudes to food, sex, illness, child rearing, work, authority, commercial dealings, and so forth. The individual requirements have to do with the limits that must be observed and the possibilities that may be explored by individuals who try to make good lives for themselves in the framework protected by the universal and social requirements. This is the context in which individuals must evaluate the various ideals and projects that are open to them.

Particularity is a distinctive feature of this three-level conception of morality because the moral requirements of good lives cannot be given a general description. The universal requirements are general because they apply to everyone; the social requirements are less so because they apply only to those who live in a particular society; and the individual requirements are not general at all because the moral demands of particular ideals, such as those of self-direction, moral authority, decency, depth, or honor, apply only to those who have committed themselves to living according to them, and what that requires varies with their characters and circumstances.

All three of these requirements are moral because they protect conditions of good lives, but the social and individual requirements are particular, not general. They cannot be formulated as universal, impartial, and impersonal prescriptions to which morality requires everyone to conform. The reason for stressing this point is to make evident the distinctiveness of the feature of particularity that characterizes successful lives of personal excellence. It is distinctive because it rejects the view shared by most deontological and consequentialist approaches to morality that moral requirements must be universal, impartial, and impersonal. The present account acknowledges that the requirements on the universal level of morality are like that, but it denies that the requirements on the social and individual levels are as many deontologists and consequentialists insist all moral requirements must be. And this, of course, deepens the explanation of the pluralism and individuality of the present account.

Particularity characterizes the requirements of reason as well. Successful lives of personal excellence are reasonable, but there is no single standard conformity to which makes them so. Reason requires being logically consistent, taking account of the relevant facts, trying to find the most feasible solution to whatever problem is at hand, and remaining open to criticism. When we try to determine whether a life of personal excellence is reasonable, however, these general requirements must be made particular because what facts are relevant, what counts as a solution and as the most feasible solution, and what openness to criticism requires one to do are questions that do not lend themselves to general answers. This is most emphatically not to deny that reasonable answers are available. It is to deny that the reasonable answers, in this context, are general. Reasonable answers will be particular because the characters, circumstances, projects, and ideals of different people are unavoidably different as a result of variations in facts and in the outcomes of their reciprocal adaptations of their inner and outer conditions. Consequently, a life that may be found to be reasonable or unreasonable for one person to live may or may not be so for another. But that, of course, presupposes that a life *can be* found to be reasonable or unreasonable.

According to the present account, a life is reasonable if the person living it cannot be blamed if it falls short of being good. In favorable conditions, reasonable lives will be good. If a reasonable life fails to be good, it must be either because unfavorable conditions have prevented it or because the person has made mistakes that were unavoidable in those circumstances. If nothing goes wrong, a reasonable life of personal excellence is good because it is personally satisfying and morally acceptable. But we have seen that, because of the pluralism, individuality, balance, and particularity of such a life, there will be systematic variations in what makes it personally satisfying and morally acceptable. And that is why there will also be systematic variation in what makes individual lives of personal excellence reasonable.

The judgment that a life of personal excellence is or is not reasonable is objective, not subjective; hard, not soft; aims at the truth, not at what anyone happens to think. But it is a particular judgment that holds only in the context of a particular life, and it is not generalizable to other lives and contexts. It is a distinctive feature of the present account that it is committed to there being reasonable judgments of this kind. Many absolutists and relativists deny that such judgments can be reasonable. If what has been said about pluralism, individuality, balance, and particularity is correct, then this denial is mistaken.

These distinctive features characterize lives of personal excellence, but they also exert a formative influence on the kind of book that can be written about them. Such a book cannot contain a general theory, a blueprint for all good lives, or a set of principles to which all good lives must conform. The subject matter permits some generalizations, but they fall far short of a general account. The gap must be filled, to the extent to which it can be, with concrete cases that exemplify, but neither define nor exhaust, the forms good lives may take. Lives of personal excellence were proposed as one such form. The proposal, however, was made with full acknowledgment both that there are other forms and that there are many other lives of personal excellence apart from the ones that have been discussed.

The result of this way of proceeding has been a degree of selectivity that has introduced an unavoidably personal element into the argument of the book. For the cases that have been selected were cases that have seemed to be admirable to the author. Someone else writing the same sort of book is likely to have selected different cases. This should be recognized. Given the plurality, individuality, balance, and particularity of lives of personal excellence, however, this is not a weakness that calls for apology but a consequence of the subject matter. It follows from it that there is at least one form of good lives that is open-ended and hospitable to new and untried experiments in living, thus permitting the modest hope that the contingencies of life may present in the future not just dangers but also valuable possibilities.

Notes

INTRODUCTION: THE MOST IMPORTANT OF ALL HUMAN ACTIVITIES

1. Lawrence A. Blum, *Moral Perception and Particularity* (New York: Cambridge University Press, 1994); Harry G. Frankfurt, *The Importance of What We Care About* (New York: Cambridge University Press, 1988) and *Necessity, Volition, and Love* (New York: Cambridge University Press, 1999); Peter A. French, *The Virtues of Vengeance* (Lawrence: Kansas University Press, 2001); Pierre Hadot, *Philosophy as a Way of Life*, trans. Michael Chase (Oxford: Blackwell, 1995); Joel J. Kupperman, *Value ... And What Follows* (New York: Oxford University Press, 1999) and *Learning from Asian Philosophy* (New York: Oxford University Press, 1999); Alexander Nehamas, *The Art of Living* (Berkeley: University of California Press, 1998); Richard Shusterman, *Practising Philosophy: Pragmatism and the Philosophical Life* (New York: Routledge, 1997); and Susan Wolf, "Moral Saints," *Journal of Philosophy* 79 (1982): 419–39.

1. SELF-DIRECTION

1. Plato, *The Republic*, trans. Robin Waterfield (Oxford: Oxford University Press, 1993), chap. 2.

2. David Hume, *Enquiries Concerning the Principles of Morals*, ed. L. A. Selby-Bigge (Oxford: Clarendon Press, 1961), p. 276.

3. Isaiah Berlin, "Two Concepts of Liberty," in *Four Essays on Liberty* (Oxford: Oxford University Press, 1969), p. 131.

4. Aristotle, *Eudemian Ethics*, trans. J. Solomon, in *The Complete Works of Aristotle*, ed. Jonathan Barnes (Princeton: Princeton University Press, 1984), 1214b.

5. Michel de Montaigne, *The Complete Essays of Montaigne*, trans. Donald M. Frame (Stanford: Stanford University Press, 1958). The references are to the pages of this edition.

6. The source of these facts is Donald M. Frame, *Montaigne: A Biography* (San Francisco: North Point Press, 1984).

7. Robert Bolt, *A Man for All Seasons* (New York: Random House, 1965), p. xiii. The references are to the pages of this edition. The historical accuracy of Bolt's portrayal of More has been seriously questioned by G. R. Elton, "The Real Thomas More?" in *Reformation Principle and Practice*, ed. Peter Newman Brooks (London: Scolar Press, 1980), pp. 23–31, and Richard Marius, *Thomas More* (New York: Knopf, 1984). But the doubts raised in these works have been laid to rest in Louis L. Martz, *Thomas More: The Search for the Inner Man* (New Haven: Yale University Press, 1990). The present account follows and is indebted to Martz's interpretation of More's character.

8. The cited passages refer to the volumes and pages of *The Yale Edition of The Complete Works of St. Thomas More*, R. S. Sylvester, executive ed. (New Haven: Yale University Press, 1963), 14 vols.; abbreviated CW. Thus CW 14:359 refers to volume 14, page 359 of the *Complete Works*.

9. From More's letter to his daughter Margaret in *The Correspondence of Sir Thomas More*, ed. Elizabeth Frances Rogers (Princeton: Princeton University Press, 1947), p. 514.

10. Ibid., pp. 514–15.

11. Hume, *Enquiries*, p. 209; Jane Austen, *Sense and Sensibility* (Harmondsworth: Penguin, 1969), p. 338.

12. William Butler Yeats, "The Second Coming," in *The Collected Poems of W. B. Yeats* (London: Macmillan, 1982).

13. For a history of this idea, see, e.g., Robert E. Norton, *The Beautiful Soul: Aesthetic Morality in the Eighteenth Century* (Ithaca: Cornell University Press, 1995), and Isaiah Berlin, *The Roots of Romanticism*, ed. Henry Hardy (Princeton: Princeton University Press, 1999).

14. Friedrich Nietzsche, *Untimely Meditations*, trans. R. J. Hollingdale (Cambridge: Cambridge University Press, 1983), III. 1., p. 127. See also Alexander Nehamas, *Nietzsche: Life as Literature* (Cambridge: Harvard University Press, 1985), chap. 6.

15. See Lionel Trilling, *Sincerity and Authenticity* (Cambridge: Harvard University Press, 1971).

16. The locus classicus is Immanuel Kant, *The Groundwork of the Metaphysics of Morals*, trans. H. J. Patton (New York: Harper, 1964). Influential interpretations are Thomas E. Hill, *Autonomy and Self-Respect* (New York: Cambridge University Press, 1991), and Christine M. Korsgaard, *Creating the Kingdom of Ends* (Cambridge: Cambridge University Press, 1996). For the egalitarian liberal view of autonomy, see, e.g., John Rawls, *A Theory of Justice* (Cambridge: Cambridge University Press, 1971), especially section 78.

17. Hill, *Autonomy and Self-Respect*, pp. 45–46.

18. For this interpretation, see Gerald Dworkin, "The Concept of Autonomy," in *The Theory and Practice of Autonomy* (Cambridge: Cambridge University Press, 1988); Harry G. Frankfurt, "Freedom of the Will and the Concept of a Person," in *The Importance of What We Care About* (Cambridge: Cambridge University Press, 1988); and Charles Taylor, "Responsibility for Self," in *The Identities of Persons*, ed. Amelie Rorty (Berkeley: University of California Press, 1976).

19. Plato, *Symposium*, trans. Michael Joyce, in *The Collected Dialogues of Plato*, ed. Edith Hamilton and Huntington Cairns (Princeton: Princeton University Press, 1961).

20. David L. Norton, *Personal Destinies* (Princeton: Princeton University Press, 1976).

21. Ibid., p. 358.

22. See W. H. Bruford, *The German Tradition of Self-Cultivation* (Cambridge: Cambridge University Press, 1975).

23. Quoted in ibid., p. 2.

24. Michael Oakeshott, "Rationalism in Politics," in *Rationalism in Politics* (Indianapolis: Liberty Press, 1991), p. 7.

2. MORAL AUTHORITY

1. The account is based on J. G. Peristiany, "The Sophron—A Secular Saint? Wisdom and the Wise in a Cypriot Community," in *Honor and Grace in Anthropol-*

ogy, ed. J. G. Peristiany and Julian Pitt-Rivers (Cambridge: Cambridge University Press, 1992), pp. 103–27. Parenthetical references in the text are to the pages of this work. Peristiany was an anthropologist, and his description is based on fieldwork conducted between 1954 and 1983.

2. E.g., Hannah Arendt, "What Is Authority?" in *Nomos I: Authority*, ed. Carl J. Friedrich (Cambridge: Harvard University Press, 1958), and Carl J. Friedrich, *Tradition and Authority* (New York: Praeger, 1972).

3. E.g., Robert P. Wolff, *In Defense of Anarchism* (New York: Harper & Row, 1970).

4. E.g., Stanley I. Benn and Richard S. Peters, *Social Principles and the Democratic State* (London: Allen & Unwin, 1959), chap. 14; Richard E. Flathman, *The Practice of Political Authority* (Chicago: University of Chicago Press, 1980); Richard B. Friedman, "On the Concept of Authority in Political Philosophy," in *Concepts in Social and Political Philosophy*, ed. Richard E. Flathman (New York: Macmillan, 1973); and Joseph Raz, *The Morality of Freedom* (Oxford: Clarendon Press, 1986), chaps. 2–4.

5. Wolff, *In Defense of Anarchism*, p. 18.

6. Flathman, *Political Authority*, p. 90.

7. See Stanley I. Benn, "Authority," in *The Encyclopedia of Philosophy*, 8 vols., ed. Paul Edwards (New York: Macmillan, 1967); Steven Lukes, "Power and Authority" and "Perspectives on Authority," both in *Moral Conflicts and Politics* (Oxford: Clarendon Press, 1991); Richard S. Peters, "Authority," *Proceedings of the Aristotelian Society*, supp. vol. 32 (1958): 207–20; Raz, *Morality of Freedom*, chaps. 2–3.

8. See Lukes, "Perspectives on Authority," and Peters, "Authority."

9. Max Weber, *Economy and Society*, 2 vols., ed. and trans. G. Roth and C. Willick (New York: Bedminster, 1968).

10. See Lukes, "Power and Authority" and "Perspectives on Authority."

11. Lukes, "Power and Authority," p. 92.

12. See Friedrich, *Tradition and Authority*.

13. One notable exception is Samuel Fleischacker, *The Ethics of Culture* (Ithaca: Cornell University Press, 1994), chap. 4.

14. The account is in Richard Wollheim, "The Sheep and the Ceremony," in *The Mind and Its Depths* (Cambridge: Harvard University Press, 1993), p. 1. Wollheim's account draws on Confucius, *Analects*, trans. James Legge (New York: Dover, 1971), book III, chap. XVII. It must be said that the text does not quite support Wollheim's interpretation, but that may be ignored for the present purposes.

15. For a fuller treatment, see John Kekes, *Moral Wisdom and Good Lives* (Ithaca: Cornell University Press, 1995).

16. Peter F. Strawson, "Freedom and Resentment," in *Freedom and Resentment* (London: Methuen, 1974), p. 29.

17. Plato, *The Republic*, trans. Robin Waterfield (Oxford: Oxford University Press, 1993), 514a–518c.

18. Plato, *Republic*, 518a.

19. See Peter Winch, "Authority," *Proceedings of the Aristotelian Society*, supp. vol. 32 (1958): 221–40.

3. DECENCY

1. The description is in a letter from Olga Friedenberg to Boris Pasternak. Eliot Mossman, trans. and ed., *The Correspondence of Boris Pasternak and Olga Friedenberg, 1910–1954* (New York: Harcourt, 1982), pp. 303–4.

2. Aristotle's account of friendship is in *Nicomachean Ethics*, books VIII and IX; *Eudemian Ethics*, book VII, chap. 12; *Rhetoric*, book II, chap. 3; and several scattered remarks in *Politics*. For all of them, see *The Complete Works of Aristotle*, ed. Jonathan Barnes (Princeton: Princeton University Press, 1984).

3. Aristotle, *Politics*, 1295b23–25.

4. John M. Cooper, "Aristotle on Friendship," in *Essays in Aristotle's Ethics*, ed. Amelie Rorty (Berkeley: University of California Press, 1980), p. 302. See also Cooper, "Aristotle on the Forms of Friendship," *Review of Metaphysics* 30 (1977): 619–48. The whole discussion of civic friendship is indebted to Cooper.

5. Aristotle, *Nicomachean Ethics*, 1160a11–30.

6. Ibid., 1162b25–33.

7. Ibid., 1155a23–28.

8. The discussion of Hume's moral theory is indebted to John L. Mackie, *Hume's Moral Theory* (London: Routledge, 1980); Philip Mercer, *Sympathy and Ethics* (Oxford: Clarendon Press, 1972); and David Miller, *Philosophy and Ideology in Hume's Political Thought* (Oxford: Clarendon Press, 1981).

9. David Hume, *Treatise of Human Nature*, ed. L. A. Selby Bigge (Oxford: Clarendon Press, 1960), p. 317.

10. Ibid., pp. 493, 413.

11. Ibid., p. 367.

12. David Hume, *Enquiries Concerning Human Understanding and Concerning the Principles of Morals*, ed. L. A. Selby-Bigge (Oxford: Clarendon Press, 1961), p. 270.

13. Hume, *Treatise*, p. 488.

14. Ibid., p. 489.

15. Ibid.

16. Ibid.

17. Hume, *Enquiries*, p. 44.

18. Hume, *Treatise*, pp. 575–76.

19. Hume, *Enquiries*, p. 229.

20. Hume, *Treatise*, p. 489.

21. Edith Wharton, *The Age of Innocence* (New York: Scribner's, 1920). Since the book has many different editions, references are to its chapters.

22. Ibid., chap. 12.

23. Ibid., chap. 18.

24. Ibid., chap. 25.

25. Ibid., chap. 18.

26. Ibid.

27. Ibid.

28. Ibid., chap. 24.

29. Ibid., chap. 28.

4. DEPTH

1. Immanuel Kant, *Critique of Pure Reason*, trans. Norman Kemp Smith (London: Macmillan, 1953), A805.

2. Sophocles, *Oedipus the King*, in *The Three Theban Plays*, trans. Robert Fagles (New York: Viking, 1982). Passages from this work, abbreviated K., are cited in the text by line number.

3. William Wordsworth, "The Prelude," in *Poetical Works*, ed. Ernest de Selincourt (Oxford: Oxford University Press, 1969), book XII, lines 3–7.

4. Kant, *Critique of Pure Reason*, A810.

5. Georg W. F. Hegel, *Reason in History*, trans. Robert S. Hartman (New York: Liberal Arts, 1953), pp. 26–27.

6. Anthony Savile, *The Test of Time* (Oxford: Clarendon Press, 1982), chap. 7, appears to be the only contemporary treatment of the subject. It contains a useful survey of some historical discussions of depth, but it concentrates on depth as an aesthetic notion. The present discussion is indebted to Savile's.

7. See the title essay in Max Black, *The Prevalence of Humbug and Other Essays* (Ithaca: Cornell University Press, 1983).

8. It is only in this tenuous sense that the present account agrees with Savile's claim that depth involves the approximation of truth. See Savile, *Test of Time*, pp. 126–27.

9. Some of these emotive reactions are illuminatingly discussed in Nicholas Rescher, *Ethical Idealism* (Berkeley: University of California Press, 1987), chap. 4.

10. Sophocles, *Oedipus at Colonus*, in *The Three Theban Plays*, trans. Robert Fagles (New York: Viking, 1982). Passages from this work, abbreviated C., are cited in the text by line number.

11. The claim on behalf of this interpretation is very modest. It is only a possible interpretation of one aspect of these two plays. There are many other aspects not touched upon by this interpretation, and even of the aspect considered other interpretations are possible.

12. Henry Sidgwick, *The Methods of Ethics* (Indianapolis: Hackett, 1981), p. 382.

13. Thomas Nagel, *The View from Nowhere* (New York: Oxford University Press, 1986), p. 208.

14. Thomas Nagel, *Mortal Questions* (Cambridge: Cambridge University Press, 1979), p. 23.

15. Leo Tolstoy, *The Death of Ivan Ilych*, trans. A. Maude (New York: Signet, 1960), pp. 121–22.

16. Bertrand Russell, *A History of Western Philosophy* (New York: Simon & Schuster, 1945), p. xiv.

5. HONOR

1. Peter Berger, "On the Obsolescence of the Concept of Honor," in *Revisions*, ed. Stanley Hauerwas and Alasdair MacIntyre (Notre Dame: University of Notre Dame Press, 1983), p. 172; Frank Henderson Stewart, *Honor* (Chicago: University of Chicago Press, 1994), pp. 9, 33n; Nicholas Fotion and Gerard Elfstrom, "Honor," in *Encyclopedia of Ethics*, 2 vols., ed. Lawrence C. Becker and Charlotte B. Becker (New York: Garland, 1992), 1:554; Charles Taylor, *Sources of the Self* (Cambridge: Harvard University Press, 1989), p. 214; Curtis Brown Watson, *Shakespeare and the Renaissance Concept of Honor* (Princeton: Princeton University Press, 1960), pp. 12–13; John Casey, *Pagan Virtue* (Oxford: Clarendon Press, 1990), p. 83.

2. Julian Pitt-Rivers, "Honour and Social Status," in *Honour and Shame*, ed. J. G. Peristiany (Chicago: University of Chicago Press, 1966), pp. 21–22.

3. See, e.g., Stewart, *Honor*; Taylor, *Sources of the Self*; Watson, *Shakespeare and the Renaissance Concept of Honor*; and Alexis de Tocqueville, *Democracy in America*, 2 vols., trans. Henry Reeves (New York: Schocken, 1961), vol. 2, chap. 18.

4. The literature on the Greek hero is voluminous. Some excellent accounts are J. K. Campbell, "The Greek Hero," in *Honour and Grace in Anthropology*, ed. J. G. Peristiany and J. Pitt-Rivers (Cambridge: Cambridge University Press, 1992), pp. 129–49; Bernard M. W. Knox, *The Heroic Temper* (Berkeley: University

of California Press, 1964); and James M. Redfield, *Nature and Culture in the Iliad* (Chicago: University of Chicago Press, 1975).

5. For the shift from competitive to cooperative excellences, see Arthur W. H. Adkins, *Merit and Responsibility* (Chicago: University of Chicago Press, 1960).

6. As the ever-perceptive Tocqueville put it: "They gave a generic name to what was only a species." *Democracy in America*, 2:284.

7. James Collins, "Honor," in *World Book Encyclopedia* (Chicago: Field Enterprises Educational Corporation, 1968), 9:289; Stewart, *Honor*, p. 51; Cora Diamond, "Integrity," in *Encyclopedia of Ethics*, 1:619.

8. See J. M. S. Allison, *Lamoignon de Malesherbes, Defender and Reformer of the French Monarchy* (New Haven: Yale University Press, 1938).

9. John Rawls, *A Theory of Justice* (Cambridge: Harvard University Press, 1971), p. 440.

10. Ibid., p. 62.

11. Gregory Vlastos, "Justice and Equality," in *Social Justice*, ed. Richard B. Brandt (Englewood Cliffs, N.J.: Prentice-Hall, 1963), p. 43.

6. THE ART OF LIFE

1. All quotations are from John Stuart Mill, *A System of Logic* (London: Longmans, 1872), book VI, chapter XII, sections 6–7.

2. Ibid.

3. Ibid.

4. These phrases occur so frequently in Mill's *Utilitarianism* that it would be pedantic to document their uses.

5. John Stuart Mill, *Utilitarianism* (Indianapolis: Hackett, 1979), pp. 16, 17, 31, 32.

6. Mill, *System of Logic*, book VI, chapter XII, section 7.

7. John Stuart Mill, *On Liberty* (Indianapolis: Hackett, 1978), pp. 54–55.

8. Ibid., p. 56.

9. Immanuel Kant, *Groundwork of the Metaphysics of Morals*, trans. H. J. Paton (New York: Harper, 1964), p. 80.

10. Ibid., p. 114.

11. Ibid.

12. Ibid. Kant gives several formulations of the categorical imperative, and relations among them are exceedingly complicated. These complications are irrelevant for the present purposes so they will be ignored. For a discussion of them, see H. J. Paton, *The Categorical Imperative* (London: Hutchinson, 1947), book III.

13. The precise nature of the inconsistency involved in violating the categorical imperative is a controversial question. Perhaps the most convincing account of it is given by Christine M. Korsgaard, *Creating the Kingdom of Ends* (New York: Cambridge University Press, 1996), essays 3 and 5.

14. Kant, *Groundwork*, p. 112.

15. Ibid., p. 81.

16. Ibid., p. 84.

17. Ibid.

18. For a very interesting discussion of the aesthetic approach to the art of life, see Alexander Nehamas, *The Art of Living* (Berkeley: University of California Press, 1998). See also Robert E. Norton, *The Beautiful Soul: Aesthetic Morality in the Eighteenth Century* (Ithaca: Cornell University Press, 1995), for part of the history of this idea. For a contemporary defense of the aesthetic approach, see Richard

Shusterman, *Pragmatist Aesthetics* (Oxford: Blackwell, 1992) and *Practicing Philosophy* (New York: Routledge, 1997).

19. See Friedrich Nietzsche, *On the Genealogy of Morals*, trans. Walter Kaufmann, in *Basic Writings of Nietzsche*, ed. Walter Kaufmann (New York: Modern Library, 1966), third essay, section 6.

20. Plato, *The Republic*, trans. Robin Waterfield (New York: Oxford University Press, 1993), 607b.

21. Isaiah Berlin, "The Romantic Revolution," in *The Sense of Reality*, ed. Henry Hardy (London: Chatto & Windus, 1996), pp. 169–70.

22. Friedrich Nietzsche, *The Gay Science*, trans. Walter Kaufmann (New York: Vintage, 1974), p. 125.

23. Nietzsche, *Genealogy*, pp. 453, 456.

24. Friedrich Nietzsche, *The Will to Power*, trans. Walter Kaufmann and R. J. Hollingdale (New York: Random House, 1967), p. 353.

25. Nietzsche, *Genealogy*, p. 456.

26. Friedrich Nietzsche, *Beyond Good and Evil*, trans. Walter Kaufmann, in *Basic Writings of Nietzsche*, ed. Walter Kaufmann (New York: Modern Library, 1966), section 5.

27. Nietzsche, *Will to Power*, p. 361.

28. Friedrich Nietzsche, *Twilight of the Idols*, trans. Walter Kaufmann, in *The Portable Nietzsche* (Harmondsworth: Penguin, 1954), part V, section 6.

29. Friedrich Nietzsche, *Thus Spoke Zarathustra*, trans. R. J. Hollingdale (Harmondsworth: Penguin, 1961), part 1, "Of the Afterworldsmen," p. 60.

30. Nietzsche, *Will to Power*, p. 361.

31. Nietzsche, *Gay Science*, p. 270.

32. Ibid., p. 335.

33. Ibid., p. 290.

34. Friedrich Nietzsche, *Untimely Meditations*, trans. R. J. Hollingdale (Cambridge: Cambridge University Press, 1983), essay 2, section 9.

7. INDIVIDUAL IDEALS AND PROJECTS

1. Aristotle, *Nicomachean Ethics*, 1106b36–1107a3, in *The Complete Works of Aristotle*, ed. Jonathan Barnes (Princeton: Princeton University Press, 1984).

2. Iris Murdoch, "The Idea of Perfection," in *The Sovereignty of Good* (London: Routledge, 1970), pp. 39–40.

3. What Oakeshott calls self-enactment is close to this view. See Michael Oakeshott, *On Human Conduct* (Oxford: Clarendon, 1975), pp. 7–80.

4. This is a difficult and obscure concept, hence the hesitation. It has its home in aesthetics, but it is unclear and controversial there as well. For some interesting discussions of it, see Antonio S. Cua, *Dimensions of Moral Creativity* (University Park: Pennsylvania State University Press, 1978), chap. 7; Joel J. Kupperman, *Learning from Asian Philosophy* (New York: Oxford University Press, 1999), especially part 1; Berel Lang, ed., *The Concept of Style* (Philadelphia: University of Pennsylvania Press, 1979); Alexander Nehamas, *Nietzsche: Life as Literature* (Cambridge: Harvard University Press, 1985), especially chap. 6; Michael Oakeshott, "Learning and Teaching," in *The Voice of Liberal Learning*, ed. Timothy Fuller (New Haven: Yale University Press, 1989); and Jenefer M. Robinson, "Style and Personality in the Literary Work," *Philosophical Review* 94 (1985): 927–47.

8. DOMINANT ATTITUDES

1. Richard Wollheim, "On Persons and Their Lives," in *Explaining Emotions*, ed. Amelie Rorty (Berkeley: University of California Press, 1980); *The Thread of Life* (Cambridge: Harvard University Press, 1984); and *The Mind and Its Depths* (Cambridge: Harvard University Press, 1993), essays 2–7.

2. Alasdair MacIntyre, *After Virtue* (Notre Dame: University of Notre Dame Press, 1981), especially chap. 15.

3. Stuart Hampshire, *Thought and Action* (London: Chatto & Windus, 1960) and *Freedom of the Individual* (Princeton: Princeton University Press, 1975), expanded edition.

4. Harry Frankfurt, *The Importance of What We Care About* (Cambridge: Cambridge University Press, 1988), especially essays 1–7.

5. Charles Taylor, *Human Agency and Language* (Cambridge: Cambridge University Press, 1985), essays 1, 2, and 4; and *Sources of the Self* (Cambridge: Harvard University Press, 1989).

6. Mental connectedness is "the foundation stone of human culture" (Wollheim, "On Persons and Their Lives," p. 321); "the only criteria for success and failure in a human life as a whole are the criteria of success or failure in a narrated or to-be-narrated quest" (MacIntyre, *After Virtue*, p. 203); "a man becomes more and more a free and responsible agent the more he at all times knows what he is doing, in every sense of this phrase, and the more he acts with a definite and formed intention" (Hampshire, *Thought and Action*, p. 177); "the concept of a person is not only, then, the concept of a type of entity that has both first-order desires and volitions of the second order. It can also be construed as the concept of a type of entity for whom the freedom of its will may be a problem" (Frankfurt, *What We Care About*, p. 19); "the capacity for what I have called strong evaluation is an essential feature of a person" (Taylor, *Human Agency and Language*, p. 43).

7. See Joel J. Kupperman, *Value . . . And What Follows* (New York: Oxford University Press, 1999), especially chap. 2; L. W. Sumner, *Welfare, Happiness, and Ethics* (Oxford: Clarendon Press, 1996), especially chap. 2; and for a very helpful review of the psychological literature, Gerald F. Gaus, *Value and Justification* (Cambridge: Cambridge University Press, 1990), especially chap. 8.

8. Plato, *Apology*, in *The Collected Dialogues*, ed. Edith Hamilton and Huntington Cairns (Princeton: Princeton University Press, 1989), 38a.

9. The discussion of emotions here and subsequently is indebted to Bennet Helm, "Emotional Reason: How to Deliberate about Value," *American Philosophical Quarterly* 37 (2000): 1–22; Rosalind Hursthouse, *On Virtue Ethics* (Oxford: Clarendon Press, 1999), part 2; Kupperman, *Value . . . And What Follows*, chap. 2; Richard Wollheim, *On the Emotions* (New Haven: Yale University Press, 1999); and to several of the essays in Rorty, ed., *Explaining Emotions*.

10. L. A. Kosman, "Being Properly Affected: Virtues and Feelings in Aristotle's Ethics," in Rorty, ed., *Explaining Emotions*, p. 105.

11. A phenomenon perceptively described as "inverse akrasia" by N. Arpaly and T. Schroeder in "Praise, Blame, and the Whole Self," *Philosophical Studies* 93 (1999): 161–88.

12. For a suggestive account of such an attitude, see Clifford Geertz, " 'From the Native's Point of View': On the Nature of Anthropological Understanding," in *Local Knowledge* (New York: Basic Books, 1983).

13. Iris Murdoch, "The Idea of Perfection," in *The Sovereignty of Good* (London: Routledge, 1970), p. 40.

14. Aristotle, *Nicomachean Ethics*, in *The Complete Works of Aristotle*, ed. Jonathan Barnes (Princeton: Princeton University Press, 1984), 1100a10–1101a7.

15. John Stuart Mill, *Autobiography* (New York: Columbia University Press, 1924), chap. 5.

16. Matthew 19:16–23.

17. André Gide, "André Gide," in *The God That Failed*, ed. Richard Crossman (New York: Bantam Books, 1952), pp. 177, 197.

9. ABERRATIONS

1. Kant says, "Moral laws hold for every rational being as such." This law "is an imperative which, without being based on, and conditioned by, any further purpose to be attained by a certain line of conduct, enjoins this conduct immediately. This imperative is *categorical* . . . the imperative of *morality*." There is "only a single categorical imperative and it is this: *'Act only on that maxim which you can at the same time will that it should become a universal law.'* " Immanuel Kant, *Groundwork of the Metaphysics of Morals*, trans. H. J. Paton (New York: Harper, 1964), pp. 79, 84, 88.

Mill says: "Happiness is the sole end of human action, and the promotion of it the test by which we judge of all human conduct; from which it necessarily follows that it must be the criterion of morality." But that criterion "is not the agent's own greatest happiness, but the greatest amount of happiness altogether." "One person's happiness . . . is counted for exactly as much as another's . . . 'everybody to count for one, nobody for more than one.' " John Stuart Mill, *Utilitarianism* (Indianapolis: Hackett, 1979), pp. 38, 11, 60.

2. See Neil Cooper, *The Diversity of Moral Thinking* (Oxford: Clarendon Press, 1981), and Richard M. Hare, *The Language of Morals* (Oxford: Clarendon Press, 1952) and *Moral Thinking* (Oxford: Clarendon Press, 1981).

3. This is the Kantian view. Some contemporary versions of it are Christine M. Korsgaard, *The Sources of Normativity* (New York: Cambridge University Press, 1996) and *Creating the Kingdom of Ends* (New York: Cambridge University Press, 1996), and Thomas Nagel, *The View from Nowhere* (New York: Oxford University Press, 1986) and *Equality and Partiality* (New York: Oxford University Press, 1991).

4. See Kurt Baier, *The Moral Point of View* (Ithaca: Cornell University Press, 1957), and Lawrence C. Becker, *Reciprocity* (London: Routledge, 1986).

5. See Philippa Foot, "Morality as a System of Hypothetical Imperatives," in *Virtues and Vices* (Los Angeles: University of California Press, 1978).

6. See W. David Falk, "Morality, Self, and Others" and "Morality, Form, and Content," in *Ought, Reasons, and Morality* (Ithaca: Cornell University Press, 1986), and William K. Frankena, "The Concept of Morality," *Journal of Philosophy* 63 (1966): 688–96.

7. Versions of this argument are advanced by many people, but for particularly influential ones, see Alan Gewirth, *Reason and Morality* (Chicago: University of Chicago Press, 1978), and John Rawls, *A Theory of Justice* (Cambridge: Harvard University Press, 1971) and *Political Liberalism* (New York: Columbia University Press, 1993).

8. This point has been made, and made again, by many people, including Harry G. Frankfurt, in "The Importance of What We Care About," in *The Importance of What We Care About* (Cambridge: Cambridge University Press, 1988); Stuart Hampshire, *Morality and Conflict* (Cambridge: Harvard University Press, 1983); John Kekes, *The Morality of Pluralism* (Princeton: Princeton University

Press, 1993); Charles Taylor, "The Diversity of Goods," in *Philosophy and the Human Sciences* (Cambridge: Cambridge University Press, 1985); Bernard Williams, "Persons, Character, and Morality," in *Moral Luck* (Cambridge: Cambridge University Press, 1981), and *Ethics and the Limits of Philosophy* (London: Collins, 1985); and Susan Wolf, "Moral Saints," *Journal of Philosophy* 79 (1982): 419–39.

9. Matthew 22:37–40.

10. Søren Kierkegaard, *Works of Love*, trans. H. Hong and E. Hong (New York: Harper, 1962), p. 2.

11. Mill, *Utilitarianism*, pp. 30–31.

12. Henry Sidgwick, *The Methods of Ethics* (Indianapolis: Hackett, 1981), p. 241.

13. John J. C. Smart and Bernard Williams, *Utilitarianism: For and Against* (Cambridge: Cambridge University Press, 1973), p. 7.

14. Geoffrey J. Warnock, *The Object of Morality* (London: Methuen, 1971), pp. 25–26.

15. David Hume, *Enquiry Concerning the Principles of Morals*, ed. L. A. Selby-Bigge (Oxford: Clarendon Press, 1960), pp. 219–20.

16. Arthur Schopenhauer, *On the Basis of Morality*, trans. E. F. J. Payne (Indianapolis: Bobbs-Merrill, 1965), p. 144. In the quotation the original sentence order has been changed.

17. Joseph Butler, *Fifteen Sermons* (London: Bell, 1953), p. 187.

18. Hume, *Enquiry*, pp. 481, 602.

19. Mill, *Utilitarianism*, pp. 11, 60.

20. See Richard B. Brandt, "The Psychology of Benevolence and Its Implications for Philosophy," *Journal of Philosophy* 73 (1976): 429–53.

21. David Hume, "Of Commerce," in *Essays Moral, Political, and Literary* (Indianapolis: Liberty Press, 1985), p. 260.

22. Arthur O. Lovejoy, "On the Discriminations of Romanticism," in *Essays in the History of Ideas* (Baltimore: Johns Hopkins University Press, 1948), p. 232. For general surveys, see Crane Brinton, "Romanticism," *Encyclopedia of Philosophy*, ed. Paul Edwards (New York: Macmillan, 1967), and Franklin L. Baumer, "Romanticism," *Dictionary of the History of Ideas*, ed. Philip P. Wiener (New York: Scribner's, 1973). Illuminating philosophical discussions are Isaiah Berlin, "The Apotheosis of the Romantic Will," in *The Crooked Timber of Humanity*, ed. Henry Hardy (London: Murray, 1990), and *The Roots of Romanticism*, ed. Henry Hardy (Princeton: Princeton University Press, 1999); and Edward Craig, *The Mind of God and the Works of Man* (Oxford: Clarendon Press, 1987), chap. 5.

23. Bernard M. W. Knox, *The Heroic Temper* (Berkeley: University of California Press, 1964), p. 57.

24. Kenneth Clark, "The Young Michelangelo," in *Renaissance Profiles*, ed. J. H. Plumb (New York: Harper, 1965), p. 43.

25. Isaiah Berlin, "European Unity and Its Vicissitudes," in *Crooked Timber of Humanity*, pp. 185, 187, 192.

26. See Harry G. Frankfurt, "Freedom of the Will and the Concept of a Person," "The Importance of What We Care About," and "Rationality and the Unthinkable," in *The Importance of What We Care About* (New York: Cambridge University Press, 1988), and "Concerning the Freedom and Limits of the Will," in *Necessity, Volition, and Love* (New York: Cambridge University Press, 1999).

27. Frankfurt, "Freedom of the Will," p. 12.

28. Ibid., p. 16.

29. Ibid., pp. 17, 22.
30. Berlin, "European Unity," p. 192.
31. Frankfurt, "Importance of What We Care About," pp. 80–81, 85–86.
32. Ibid., pp. 87–88.
33. Frankfurt, "Freedom of the Will," p. 17.
34. Frankfurt, "Importance of What We Care About," pp. 87–88.
35. Frankfurt, "Rationality," p. 181.
36. Ibid., p. 184.
37. Ibid., pp. 187–88.
38. Ibid., p. 186.
39. Ibid., pp. 186 n. 8, 190.

10. GOOD LIVES

1. Friedrich Nietzsche, *The Gay Science*, trans. Walter Kaufmann (New York: Vintage, 1974), 341. Nietzsche repeats what is virtually the same question in "Why I Am So Clever," in *Ecce Homo*, trans. Walter Kaufmann (New York: Modern Library, 1966). The question is illuminatingly discussed in Alexander Nehamas, *Nietzsche: Life as Literature* (Cambridge: Harvard University Press, 1985), chap. 5.
2. Karel Capek, "The Makropulos Secret," trans. Yveta Sinek and Robert T. Jones, in *Toward the Radical Center* (Highland Falls, N.J.: Catbird Press, 1990), pp. 110–77.
3. See Michael Evans, *Janacek's Tragic Operas* (London: Faber & Faber, 1977), pp. 168–203, 259–64.
4. Bernard Williams, "The Makropulos Case: Reflections on the Tedium of Immortality," in *Problems of the Self* (Cambridge: Cambridge University Press, 1973), pp. 82–100.
5. Capek, "Makropulos Secret," pp. 173–75.
6. Evans, *Janacek's Tragic Operas*, 44b.
7. Nietzsche, *Gay Science*, 341.
8. Williams, "Makropulos Case," p. 91.
9. Ibid., p. 90.
10. Ibid., p. 96.
11. Ibid., p. 91.

Index

aberrations, 205–33
aesthetic approach, 129–32, 142–49, 157
Archer, 72–83, 123, 158, 160–62, 165, 167, 168, 171, 178, 186, 190, 194, 210, 219, 221, 235, 243
Aristotle, 9, 14, 63–67, 71, 91, 164–69, 205
attitudes, 177–204
Austen, 24, 61
authenticity, 30–31
authority, 39–45
autonomy, 31–32, 135–42

balance, 177–204, 248–49
beliefs, 25, 35, 180–82, 196–204, 206–15, 237–39
benevolence, 68–72, 215–25
Berger, 205
Berlin, 9, 14, 144, 225–26
Blum, 9
boredom, 239–44
Butler, 217–18

Capek, 240–44
Casey, 107
character, 25, 35, 72–83, 142–57
civic friendship, 63–67
Clark, 225
Collins, 113
commitments, 19, 21–25, 35
conflicts, 132–35, 140–42, 143–44, 149–57, 196–204, 205–33
Confucius, 46–48, 58, 59
consequentialism, 121–22, 206–15
contingency, 85–106
custom, 67–72

Darwin, 91
decency, 10, 61–84, 200
denial, 103–4

deontology, 121–22, 206–15
depth, 10, 85–106, 201
Diamond, 113
disengagement, 99–103
dishonor, 120–21

egalitarianism, 122–23
Einstein, 91
Elfstrom, 107
emotions, 25, 35, 171, 182–85, 196–204, 215–25, 237–39

Fotion, 107
Frankfurt, 9, 177, 227–32
fragmentation, 196–204
freedom, 135–38
French, 9
Freud, 91
Friedrich, 44

Gide, 198–99

Hadot, 9
Hampshire, 177
Hegel, 8, 88–89
Hill, 131
honor, 10, 107–25, 201–2
hope, 85–90, 105–6
Hume, 9, 13, 24, 67–72, 85, 91, 217–18, 220, 248–49

ideals, 6, 124–25, 153–57, 158–76, 186–88, 189–96, 234–39, 242–44
impartiality, 135–42, 206–15
impersonality, 135–42, 206–15
individual, requirements, 4–5, 133–34, 151–52, 154–55, 249–50
individuality, 25–31, 190, 246–48
integration, 177–80, 196–204

Janacek, 240–44
Jesus, 198

Kant, 8, 85–90, 135–42, 143, 144–45, 147, 149–50, 157, 245, 248–49
Kierkegaard, 217
Knox, 225
Kosman, 183–84
Kupperman, 9

Lovejoy, 129, 225
Lukes, 44

MacIntyre, 177
Makropulos, 204–44
Malesherbes, 113–16, 119, 23, 159, 161–62, 165, 167, 171, 172, 178, 186, 190, 194, 207, 210, 212–13, 219, 221, 235, 243
Mann, 33–35
Marx, 91
Mill, 8, 9, 132–34, 137, 143, 155, 197–98, 199, 217–18, 245
Montaigne, 9, 15–19, 25, 26, 27–30, 123, 124, 160–62, 165, 167, 168, 172, 178, 186, 190, 194, 212–13, 219, 235, 243
moral approach, 129–32, 135–42, 157
moral authority, 10, 37–60, 200
moral education, 173–76
moralism, 206–15
morality, 4–5, 19, 124–25, 129–34, 135–42, 149–57, 249–50
More, 19–25, 26, 123, 124, 158, 160–61, 165, 167, 168, 171, 172, 178, 186, 190, 194, 207, 210, 219, 235, 243
motives, 25, 35, 185–88, 196–204, 225–32, 237–39
Murdoch, 1, 9, 165–66, 195, 234

Nagel, 100–103
Nehamas, 9
Nietzsche, 9, 31, 91, 144–50, 157, 181, 239–45
Norton, 33

Oakeshott, 9
Oedipus, 86–87, 92–99, 103–04, 123, 158, 161, 165, 171, 172, 178, 186, 190, 194, 207–08, 210, 212–13, 219, 235, 243
Olenska, 72–83, 123, 158, 160–62, 165, 167, 168, 171, 172, 178, 186, 190, 194, 210, 219, 221, 235, 243

particularity, 149–57, 249–52
personal, excellence, 3–4, 9–10, 36, 61–63, 124–25, 142–49, 149–57, 158–76, 234–39
Plato, 8, 13, 37, 53–54, 85–86, 91, 144, 245, 248–49
pluralism, 5–6, 49, 59–60, 244–46
Plutarch, 9
projects, 4, 158–76, 186–88, 234–39, 242–44

Rawls, 118
reasons, 7–9, 19, 29–30, 44–45, 56–59, 68–72, 131–32, 135–42, 152–57, 206–15, 230–32
reflectiveness, 51–53
resignation, 104–5
romanticism, 30–31, 142–49, 225–32
rules, 6–9, 72–83, 152–57
Russell, 106

Schopenhauer, 218
self-creation, 129–49, 142–49
self-direction, 10, 13–36, 199–200
self-esteem, 116–21
self-realization, 32–35
sentimentalism, 215–25
Shakespeare, 107
Shusterman, 9
Sidgwick, 100, 217
Smart, 217
social, requirements, 4–5, 150–51, 153–54, 249–50
Socrates, 32, 85–86, 181
Sophocles, 86–87, 92–99
Sophron, 37–39, 58, 59, 60, 123, 160–62, 165, 167, 168, 172, 178, 186, 190, 194, 207–8, 219, 235, 243
Spinoza, 8, 91
Stewart, 107, 113
Stoics, 8
Strawson, 52, 158
style, 24, 169–73, 191–96
sympathy, 67–72

Taylor, 107, 178
Tolstoy, 103–4
tradition, 25–30, 48–59

universal, requirements, 4–5, 132–33, 135–42, 150, 153, 206–15, 249–50

virtues, 164–73
Vlastos, 118

Warnock, 217
Watson, 107
Wharton, 72–83
will, 131–32, 135–49, 225–32
Williams, 240–44

Wolf, 9
Wolff, 40
Wollheim, 177
Wordsworth, 88

Yeats, 26